Ziegfeld

Ziegfeld

Charles Higham

HENRY REGNERY COMPANY · CHICAGO

One day Ziegfeld received news that his great friend and backer, wealthy Jim Donohue, had been ruined by the stock market crash and had thrown himself out of a window. Immediately after he heard the news he wrote the following words to Donohue's widow: "Your late husband promised me $20,000 just before he fell."

The money arrived two days later.

Contents

Acknowledgments

I am deeply grateful to Goldie Clough, Ziegfeld's secretary, and to his daughter Patricia Ziegfeld Stephenson for their help in preparing this volume. The following were also of the greatest assistance: the late Ann Pennington, Gordon Wedertz, Dr. Felix Ganz, Mlle. Dazie, Ruth Waterbury, the late Sophie Tucker, Mecca Graham, Mae West, the late Billie Burke, Cherrie Watson Offerman, Ina Claire, Hazel Dawn, Mary Pickford, Vivienne Segal, Captain Herman Gray, Rudolph Friml, Ethel Shutta, Peggy Fears, Charles Rogers, Alan Dwan, Adele and Fred Astaire, George Cukor, Lillian Ziegfeld, Izzy Cohn, the late Oscar Hammerstein II, Mrs. William Anthony McGuire, Reginald Owen, Ruby Keeler, Bessie Lasky, Jeanette Ziegfeld, and Robert Baral.

I am also deeply grateful to Paul Myers, of the New York Public Library Theatre Collection, the staff of the Museum of the City of New York, the Academy of Motion Picture Arts and Sciences, and the Los Angeles Public Library, Literature Division, for their unfailing help and kindness at all times, and to Colin Baskerville, Jac McAnelly, and Don Madison for their help in copying.

Ziegfeld

1

The Beginning

Ziegfeld's father was the cause of everything that his dazzling son became. Smooth, austere, and dignified, "Dr." Ziegfeld (there is no evidence that this title had any basis in truth) arrived in America in 1862, at the age of 21. His own version of his youth was that he had been a close friend of the greatest musical figures of his age and before that a child prodigy, capable of composing for the piano at the age of six.

While Dr. Ziegfeld's story is doubtless exaggerated, it seems to be true that he studied under Carl Stiehl at the age of six, that he was a moderately good student at Leipzig Conservatory, and that he had a genuine degree in music. He was born to Lutheran parents Florenz and Louise Kirschoff Ziegfeld in Jenvier in the Duchy of Oldenbourg, Germany, on June 10, 1841; with those facts all resemblance to the truth in his various statements ceases entirely. His motive in building a structure of fantasy is clear: he was fully aware of the ignorance of the

New World and of the need of its social leaders to acquire intellectual respectability, the one thing left that they could not buy.

The stiff-backed young man's bristling moustache, German accent, peremptory manner, flashes of charm, and imposing physique—combined with his smoothly constructed account of a career—were enough to secure him a ready ear in the salons of Chicago and New York. A shameless social climber, he acquired the friendship of a long list of celebrities. He did not have the sophistication necessary to stay the distance in New York, so he settled on Chicago, to which he had paid a visit in 1858, as the scene of his career, settling there early in 1863.

In 1865 he married Rosalie deGez, an attractive French woman with a little money, a descendant of one of Napoleon's marshals. Using their combined savings he set up a small office on the North Side of Chicago, joining forces with piano maker W. W. Kimball, who later founded the most successful piano manufacturing company in the Midwest. He also became friendly with composer George Root, author of those popular Union Army songs "Tramp, Tramp, Tramp" and "Marching Through Georgia." The three men became close friends, and they spent long evenings drinking steins of beer in the German restaurants of what was then a largely German city. Their joint funds were plunged into a modest music publishing business, with piano lessons given on the side.

In 1865, when Ziegfeld was 23, he bought a small house at 298 Superior Street. He established offices in the Chicago Conservatorium of Music in Reed's Temple of Music, at Dearborn and Randolph Streets. A year later he and his partners moved into the top floor of the Crosby Opera House. A landmark of Chicago, this handsome new building had been the dream-child of distiller Uranus H. Crosby, a man with a passion for Grand Opera who poured $600,000 into its construction. Unfortunately, his policy of bringing fine music to rough-and-ready Chicago was a financial disaster, and he died bankrupt.

In 1867 Ziegfeld, the brothers George and Frederick Root, Dudley Buck, Alfred Pease, Albert Ruff, and Louis Falk began to advertise what they called the "Academy of Music." They published songs and piano *soirée* pieces composed by Ziegfeld himself—pretty, tinkling trifles that still have a mild-mannered charm. The daughters of the better Chicago families learned to play the songs at evening musicales, earning for their composer a substantial local reputation and increasing the number of his pupils. Ziegfeld made a sensible business arrangement with Kimball, whose music store was housed on the lower floors of the Opera House. When somebody bought a Kimball piano, they also bought a pound of music published and often written by Ziegfeld.

A review of the college's first recital, on December 26, 1867, appeared in the *Chicago Republican* the following day:

> An interesting entertainment was given at Kimball's Music Store by Mr. Ziegfeld and his pupils, assisted by Miss Heinrichs and Mrs. Bischoff, Allen and Schroeder. The programme indicated the excellence of Mr. Ziegfeld's taste, and the creditable performances by his pupils prove him to be a careful and successful teacher. . . . Mr. Ziegfeld's own compositions . . . were very pretty, and show that he is a fine composer as well as a teacher, fully deserving of the encouragement of the public.

Among the attractions of the recital was Miss Nettie Roberts, who played Mendelssohn's Capriccio Brillante Opus 22 with a small ensemble of musicians conducted by Ziegfeld himself.

In 1869 the College of Music was advertising instruction in "piano, organ, theory, singing, violin, flute, and all

other orchestral instruments." Tuition for a term of ten
weeks was $15.00.

Ziegfeld's home was at 298 East Chicago Street when
Florenz, Jr., was born, on March 15, 1867. Unlike their
other children, who were christened Lutherans, he was
christened in his mother's Catholic faith. Flo began his
life in a city that had boomed astonishingly since his
father's arrival, some ten years earlier. The home in which
he spent his first two years was a small but charmingly
elegant residence, furnished in a Germanic mode. The
street and its adjoining thoroughfares were lined with
gracious shade trees, the front yards beautifully kept and
attractively uniform. Sidewalks rose and fell with the un-
even level of the lots: the streets were made of large wood
blocks because Chicago was built on a swamp.

The wooden city's chief business section, known as The
Loop, was just beginning to emerge from the sleepy provincial business area that it had been during the Civil
War. Department stores had begun to rise and flaunt all
their vulgar magnificence. As described by a contemporary resident, Francesca Falk Miller, "Over the block or
asphalt pavements of the main residential streets, pha-
etons, dignified surreys, or rakish teetering cabs passed in
endless procession, drawn by horses of every rank and
condition from smart, shining 'spans' to a single plodding
old family nag."

A few months after young Ziegfeld's birth the family
moved to a more elaborate home on Wabash Avenue, and
the Musical College and the private residence of the
family were combined under one roof. Young Ziegfeld's
first memories were of the meetings of the musical figures
of the city in the rooms below his nursery, the sounds of
solemn Germanic discussions floating up through the floor,
and rehearsals for recitals at the Kimball shop. Sometimes
the adoring French mother would carry her baby into

the back parlor to be admired by distinguished visitors from overseas, and the child would look wonderingly up at the rich crimson curtains of heavy plush and the looming bookcases of somber mahogany. In the middle of the green-clothed parlor table a magnificent gas-lamp hung with glittering purple-painted crystals the size of pine cones, quietly illuminating the clusters of family portraits crowded up the plum-colored paper of the walls.

From the first conscious moments of his life Florenz Ziegfeld, Jr., was surrounded by the contrast between an austere family discipline and the warmth and luxury of his environment. Almost at the outset he was to become aware not only of rich comforts but also of the threat of death and destruction that was to haunt and obsess him in later years.

When he was only four years old, the great Chicago fire swept through the city. On the morning of the conflagration a strange murmuring filled the air like a restless sea, and everyone in the Wabash Avenue college except Mrs. Ziegfeld, who stayed with the children in the back parlor, went out in the street to look. The air was hot and stifling, and the wind carried burning ashes toward the little group. A moment later flames began to rush toward the building, and Mrs. Ziegfeld emerged with the children. A great crowd engulfed the family, the teachers, and the pupils as the cry came to head to Lake Park, at the edge of Lake Michigan. For 28 hours Flo and his family found shelter under a bridge in Lake Park with thousands of refugees, who watched the clouds of smoke tinged with an unearthly crimson light drift across the city and choked at the smell of burning cinders.

The intrepid father stayed behind with Kimball to rescue the pianos from the burning college. Two days later he hung up a sign on an unburned building farther down Wabash Avenue announcing "Ziegfeld and Kimball Piano

Lessons." After a week of living with his family in a tent he moved them to the new address (493 Wabash) and started the college again.

With meticulous care the father set out to copy every detail of his previous establishment. Bit by bit the red plush curtains, the tall bookcases, and even something resembling the famous old gas chandelier returned. Two sons and a daughter, Carl, William, and Louise, were by then added to the family.

Life in the Ziegfeld family was not easy in the years after the fire. None of the children was musically minded. When musicales were held on Sunday afternoons, the children sat at the back of the parlor shuffling nervously and wishing they were out playing in the yard. They were permitted to play only classical music with their own small piano; if they were caught playing popular songs, they were locked in without supper. At such times the cook, who adored them, would put some favorite food in a basket, and the children would pull it up through the window on a rope.

Often when the Ziegfeld parents were out, Carl, Will, and Flo would aim rifles at pigeons on the roof, leaving a litter of dead birds, which they threw into the garden. On other occasions they would stage little plays; Louise would often play a queen, and the boys would be rivals for her hand in marriage.

It is not known for certain where young Flo went to school. It is almost completely established that he attended famous Ogden High School, where a few years earlier the brilliant composer and lyricist Harry B. Smith had been a pupil. Fashionable and expensive, Ogden had the admirable George Heath as a head teacher.

Though Ziegfeld left no record of his time there, Harry B. Smith's memoirs (*First Nights and First Editions*, published in 1931) gave a clear account of the life at Ogden: the genial pedagogy of George Heath, the terrorizing of the Market Street bums (a rough gang of louts still active in Ziegfeld's time), and the activities of the famous Ogden baseball club, the Modocs, who in their white flannel and blue braided uniforms used to play vigorous matches against the South and West Sides.

In his early teens Ziegfeld was lanky, already saturnine in features, impatient at the constant sound of classical music, and maddened by his father's austerities. He would slip away at night to gaze in wonder at the brightly lit doorways of the local music halls, then in their first flush of success.

In 1882 the family moved twice: first to 44 Loomis Street, and next to a splendid home on West Adams Street (renumbered twice, it was finally changed from 501 to 1448). It was a narrow residence, in the style of the early 1860s, with a carved walnut banister leading up a beautifully elegant staircase. The lower rooms were divided by heavy mahogany sliding panels, reminiscent of the Slopers' house in Henry James's *Washington Square*.

The shape of the back parlor was still fairly evident as late as 1971, and time had not touched the beautiful curve of the facade, the stained glass windows that cast a pale red glow on the floors. Age had not tarnished the exquisite design of the family rooms, each with a view of the city and allowing for a free passage of air. Yet despite the house's beauty, it carried with it, 100 years after it was built, an aura of cold asperity.

During young Flo's upbringing the Chicago Musical College was a school of transients. Most of the employees left as soon as their contracts expired because they became exasperated by Ziegfeld's highhandedness and disrespect for their great talent. There was also a continual struggle between the administration and other college administrations for supremacy in the field of music in

Chicago. There was even a running squabble about which college had been founded the earliest. Talk of a merger that could give Chicago one single music school of world stature never came to fruition because of the large number of dissenters. Ultimately only the Chicago Musical College and the Chicago Conservatory were left as warring establishments, with virtually the whole field between them.

Flo's greatest experience as a boy was seeing Buffalo Bill and the great Wild West Show. The great frontiersman and showman was then past his great career as a scout for the 9th Kansas Cavalry in the campaign against the Indians during the Civil War and as a champion buffalo hunter, killing scores of buffalo to feed the stomachs of crews building the Kansas Pacific Railroad. His exploits while in Custer's service against the Sioux and Cheyennes, especially his famous scalping of Chief Yellow Hand, were already legend.

In 1883 Buffalo Bill embarked on his magnificent nationwide tour with Annie Oakley. In May of that year the show arrived in Chicago and set up tents in the teeth of heavy rain in the West Side Driving Park. Forty thousand people jammed the park on the show's first Sunday, and by May 28 half a million had witnessed the brilliant recreations of Bill Cody's career. They marveled at Buck Taylor, King of the Cowboys, Captain David C. Payne, the Oklahoma Raider, Johnnie Baker, the Cowboy Kid, and, of course, Annie Oakley, the Marvel of the West.

Flo went to the show several times, frequently playing hooky from school, exhausting the entire contents of his piggy bank. When Buffalo Bill offered members of the audience a free pass if they could defeat Annie Oakley in a display of marksmanship, he jumped into the arena, picked up a gun, and beat her hollow. Cody was enormously impressed, and he asked Flo to join the show.

Without saying a word to his parents the boy shook Cody's hand in agreement and left on tour a few weeks later. But much to his boyish chagrin a combination of the child labor laws and pressure from Dr. Ziegfeld brought him back almost at once. For some time after that father and son were not on speaking terms.

At the age of 18 Flo graduated from Ogden High and took a post as secretary-treasurer of the Musical College. Extravagant and reckless with money, he was definitely ill-suited to the post. Though he would clearly have preferred to have gone to New York to seek his fortune, he was intensely loyal to his father. However, he did indicate his preferences by running shows for a yacht club and for various other organizations, mainly of a raucous vaudeville kind.

When he was 22, he briefly staged a show called "The Dancing Ducks of Denmark." He claimed that he had imported the act, but in fact the ducks had been bought from a local farm. Visitors paid 15 cents a head to see the ducks "dancing"—lifting their feet with loud squawks to the tune of a gavotte composed by Ziegfeld, Sr.—in a tent set up in one of the city's parks. One or two diligent older women noticed something peculiar about the exhibition and reported it to the SPCA. When officials descended on the tent, they were shocked to find that Ziegfeld had placed the ducks on an iron grid, which was lit from underneath by specially graduated gas flames. When his assistant, who would lie under the tent, turned up the jets, the unhappy ducks had no alternative but to dance. We may well imagine Dr. Ziegfeld's thunderous fury when he learned of this disgrace to the family name.

In a later attempt Ziegfeld exhibited a large, beautifully illuminated bowl containing nothing but water. The show was "The Invisible Brazilian Fish." This, not surprisingly, was also a disaster.

In 1882, after continuous lobbying in Washington, Chicago won the right to be the stage of the great Columbian Exposition, a World's Fair planned to celebrate the 400th anniversary of the arrival of Columbus.

At the time of the fair Chicago was far different from the comfortable wooden city into which Ziegfeld had been born. Flo's early adulthood was spent in an atmosphere in which he was painfully aware of the contrast between wealth and poverty: with his father he was a frequent visitor to the homes of the wealthy—the sumptuous Tudor mansion of Mrs. Potter Palmer, queen of society in the Middle West, where Dr. Ziegfeld frequently arranged private recitals; the bizarre Romanesque domicile of Franklin MacVeagh, head of the Board of Trade; and the rambling home of Mrs. George Pullman.

But at night when he was alone, Flo would escape from his stifling home and wander off to gaze gloomily at the city's murky slums or to visit the levee on the South Side, with its sordid gambling halls, in which chuck-a-luck, roulette, and baccarat were played feverishly until the small hours. And then there were the bordellos, heavy with scarlet hangings and nude portraits in gold frames, where famous madams such as Carrie Watson and Vina Fields ruled over small empires amid the downing of champagne and the constant sounds of the brothel pianos.

The Columbian Exposition gave birth to a new Chicago, more resplendent than ever before. Because so many sparkling white buildings went up, it became known as the White City. Millions of people poured in, braving the severe Depression to see the vulgar magnificence of the fair. They could gaze upon immense collections of china, tapestries, and glass, a giant telescope, a 130-ton Krupp cannon, and a map of the United States composed entirely of pickles.

Appointed director of musical events, Dr. Ziegfeld's plans for the Columbian Exposition were elaborate and carefully considered. He wanted to have a handsome music hall in which the many visitors to the fair would be able to enjoy the best of food and wines and hear the world's finest musicians. With the aid of some of the best designers in the city he created a lovely setting in the converted First Regiment Armory Building, at Michigan Avenue and 16th Street. He tore out the building's interior and installed a magnificent kitchen and bar. But a fire—that curse of Chicago—destroyed his dreams, and he had to start again. He arranged for the conversion of the Illinois National Guard Armory Building in Lake Park, where the Ziegfeld family had taken refuge during the great fire, retitling it the Trocadero.

Bogged down with work at home, Dr. Ziegfeld was forced to send his son to Europe in his stead to engage various performers. Flo sailed in the winter of 1892. Instead of hiring the classical musicians his father wanted, Flo simply began snapping up various music hall acts in London, Paris, and Berlin. In place of the great Von Bülow, whom his father wanted, he engaged the second-rate "Von Bülow Military Band," of Hamburg, under the direction of a mediocre conductor, Fritz Scheel. He hired the Mühlemann Swiss Mountaineer Trio of Interlaken, "The Great Zanzic," who produced "startling unaccountable phenomena by invisible agencies," and many run-of-the-mill acrobats, trapeze artists, and jugglers.

Ziegfeld, Sr., was astounded to find he had on his hands not fine musical attractions but a miniature circus. He insisted on keeping the various acts in abeyance while using the Von Bülow group (which he despised) and some other musicians obtained by cable from contacts in Europe. This second wave of musical figures completely exhausted his budget. Worse, the debut of this cheaply-obtained and motley assemblage was a disaster. Despite the immense influx of thousands of visitors to the fair in the early part of 1893, few even bothered to visit Lake

Park and the Trocadero. Finally, when he was $30,000 in debt, Ziegfeld, Sr., was forced to capitulate and admit some of the impatiently waiting vaudeville and circus acts his son had engaged. Business picked up a little, but it was clear that the Trocadero needed one single major attraction to pack people in. Ziegfeld immediately set out for New York to obtain a new act.

Of the variety shows that most interested him the best was at the Casino Theater, at Broadway and 39th Street, a picturesque building in the Moorish style, topped by an onion dome. Inside it was a riot of Oriental color. Quite apart from the vaudeville show itself, Ziegfeld was fascinated by the New York Concert Company's brilliant use of design: in addition to the balcony and the boxes there was a buffet floor, a huge room in which people enjoyed the show over food, drinks, and clouds of cigarette fumes. More interesting still was the Casino Roof Garden, a charming café in which bands played and stars of the time sang. The owner of this magnificent home of pleasures was the expansive Rudolph Aronson, whom Ziegfeld immediately liked.

The most important act on the show was The Great Sandow. The 23-year-old athlete's fame was already considerable in Europe; German by birth, he had built his superb physique in early youth after long sieges of illness. The painter Aubrey Hunt had seen him emerge from the Adriatic at the Lido and engaged him to pose as a gladiator in a painting of the Roman games. At the London Aquarium, Sandow had successfully challenged Samson, "the most powerful man on earth," for a prize of one thousand pounds. As a result of Sandow's reputation, Henry Abbey had engaged him for the Casino, but when Ziegfeld saw his act the audience applause was only lukewarm. When Ziegfeld decided to take Sandow off Abbey's and Aronson's hands, they were greatly relieved. Sandow accepted Ziegfeld's offer of 10 percent of the box office take, which, as it happened, was far in excess of the $1000 a week Abbey had been paying him. The two men struck up a congenial relationship and took the train to Chicago together a week later.

The Sandow show opened at the Trocadero early in August, 1893, showing at 8 o'clock each night, with meals and drink served at the tables during the performance. The beautifully designed hall was packed for the first night despite the oppressive late summer heat. Ziegfeld's brilliant publicity campaign worked well—Sandow's likeness had been papered over every inch of the city—and there was a feeling of excitement in the air as the Bülow Military Band struck up Scheel's own "Trocadero March," followed by Verdi's overture from *Nabucco,* and Strauss's lovely *Kaiser Waltz.*

Astarte performed "Aerial Evolutions." Gustav Marschner, "Champion Trick Bicyclist of the World," gave a fine performance, and Iwanoff's Imperial Troupe from St. Petersburg did rousing Russian dances. During the gymnastic feat of Marko and Dunham, Frank Marko performed a feat never before done by anyone: he somersaulted over the middle to the third bar, then double-somersaulted to the stage. All this was amusing, enthralling fare, but nothing matched the appearance, in the second part, of *Sandow, the Perfect Man.*

With special music by his great friend and traveling companion Martinus Sieveking, Sandow held a man in the palm of his hand, bent a poker, opened a safe with his teeth, and balanced weights up to 300 pounds. His flawless physique caused an excitement among the great women Ziegfeld had invited, and at the end of the performance Flo walked to the footlights and said that any woman willing to contribute $300 to a charity fund could come backstage to feel the Apollo's biceps. Mrs. Potter

Palmer and Mrs. George Pullman immediately stood up.
Once they had felt the muscles backstage and reported on
them to their friends, Sandow was "made" in Chicago.

Flo's promotion was inspired. He walked Sandow
through the woods with influential Chicago theatre critic
Amy Leslie to show that the gentle strong man really
loved spring flowers. He told the press a story—a fair ap-
proximation of the truth—that at the age of 10 Sandow
had been to a museum in Naples and had seen the statue
of Hercules. His father had told him that diligence and
exercise would earn him a similar physique, so he began
to build up his body. Ziegfeld challenged Chicago doctors
to find one single flaw in Sandow's physique, but they
were unable to do so.

Flo decided to change Sandow's act. Strong men of the
time usually appeared in discreet leopard skins, with most
of their chests covered and their legs encased in thick
white tights. In the revised performance Flo showed his
Apollo completely stripped except for a pair of tight silk
shorts and a set of bay leaves classically ornamenting his
brow. In the first scene, accompanied by an exquisite com-
position by Sieveking and a brilliantly effective roll of
drums, Sandow appeared in a single spotlight. Flo made
sure that the entire theater was completely dark so that
the magnificent body would be disclosed gradually. When
he appeared, covered in bronze makeup, a spotlight catching the gleam of his golden hair, the women in the audience gasped. Following Ziegfeld's strict instructions, Sandow struck a series of classical poses—the runner, the
discus thrower, the wrestler, Rodin's *The Thinker*.

Then came the master stroke of showmanship. Flo's
assistants wheeled in the fragile Sieveking at the piano.
First Sandow lifted Sieveking aloft in one hand; then he
lifted the piano! The applause was tremendous, and as he
juggled with a man in one hand or lifted a horse, it in-

creased enormously. As a grand finale Flo had Sandow raise a mighty dumbbell that, when lowered, showed a man climbing out of each ball. Then his assistants drove three horses over a plank that covered Apollo's reclining body.

In six weeks Flo made $30,000, and he gave his father half. Despite his basic disappointment with his son the father was forced to admit a triumph, and at the end of the run, when the final receipts came in, this cold man flung his arms around his son and wept in gratitude.

On weekends young Ziegfeld and Sandow hugely enjoyed Chicago. The reconstructed city was bright and sparkling, the new exhibition buildings gleamed white in the brilliant Illinois sunshine, the wind swept bracingly through the city, and the social life was boisterous and warm. On the North Side new Beer Gardens had sprung up, where concerts filled the warm summer evenings with the latest music hall songs, and there was a plethora of fine restaurants in which long, leisurely meals could be enjoyed together with foaming steins of beer: The Union, where regular meetings of the Ziegfeld Club met every month for dinner and a good time, the Kaiserhof, famous for steaks, and the bizarre Relic House, in Lincoln Park, which was made up of debris from the fire and had pieces of cups or plates sticking out of the walls.

Ziegfeld and Sandow enjoyed the food, the beer, the pretty girls, and the endless evenings in an atmosphere utterly and completely German. It was in such places too that young Flo could at last feel close to his father; the old and the young man were drawn together by common traditions, common enjoyments.

When Ziegfeld and Sandow left for a nationwide tour in the winter of 1893, father and son were closer than they had ever been. Despite reports to the contrary, they remained close until the father's death, in 1923. Their joint success notwithstanding, there was a cooling off be-

tween Flo and Sandow during the course of the tour;
exactly why is not known. Sandow and Sieveking huddled
in conversations on trains and backstage while Flo was
left to his own devices or to the charms of an available
chorus girl. Evenings often were spent with Sandow training the frail Sieveking in body-building while Flo spent
solitary hours in his room puffing a cigar. Both found the
tour something of a strain, and it continued for two tedi-
ous years both at home and in Europe.

One moment in the long trail of hotel rooms and one-
night or one-week stopovers stood out in both their
memories later on: the episode of the fight with the San
Francisco lion. It was reported nationally and was a considerable boost to Sandow's growing fame. Sandow and
Sieveking were appearing in the city as part of its 1893
Mid-Winter Fair. A local promoter, Colonel Bone, was ex-
hibiting a recently acquired zoo, and he advertised a battle
to the death between a lion and a bear. He set up a tent
that could house 20,000 spectators. The ever-vigilant
SPCA stepped in and complained, however, and police
forced the cancellation of the performance.

It was Ziegfeld's inspiration that Sandow should fight
the lion instead, though Sandow later claimed—incorrectly
—that it was his own idea. Colonel Bone insisted that if
the fight took place, the lion's paws would have to be
covered in mittens and a muzzle would be put over his
head. Sandow wrote in *Strand* magazine (April, 1903),
"The lion, I must tell you, was a particularly fierce animal,
and only a week before had enjoyed a dish that was not
on the menu—his keeper."

Ziegfeld promoted the Sandow *vs* lion encounter with
great success, and on the first night of the great battle the
tent was packed. First, however, Sandow had a rehearsal.
Six strong men muzzled and mittened the lion. As soon as
Sandow entered the cage, the beast flung itself upon him.

Sandow stepped aside and caught him around the throat with his left arm and around the midsection with his right. He lifted all 530 pounds of animal over one shoulder, hugged him tight, and dropped him to the floor. Once again the lion rushed forward. This time Sandow gripped the lion's body; the chests of the combatants were touching, and the lion's paws were over Sandow's shoulders. The strong man jumped away and deliberately turned his back on the beast, at which point it leaped on his back. Sandow threw up his arms, gripped the great head as firmly as possible, caught him by the neck, and sent him flying across the stage in a complete somersault. Colonel Bone and Ziegfeld were watching with loaded revolvers in case the worst happened. When the amazing feat of strength was over, they applauded loudly and fired two barrels into the cage to see if the lion wanted any further fight. He did not. Sandow walked shakily out of the cage, bleeding from a few scratches caused by the mittened claws, and the two men embraced him proudly.

The actual performance was scheduled for that same night. The immense tent was overflowing, and there was a ripple of excitement as the lion was unveiled. It ran into the arena only to be lassoed around the neck and legs by six men and hauled up a pole to be muzzled. Infuriated, the lion snapped the pole and started to bound into the audience. Immediately Sandow struck the creature across the nose with sufficient force to stun him and shouted to the assistants to bring up a smaller cage, into which Sandow thrust him. This time the beast was thoroughly defeated and ready to accept the strong man as his master. An assistant prodded the beast with a stick, which made him give one quick short leap in Sandow's direction. But it was a half-hearted sally; Sandow picked him up easily and carried him around the arena. The audience was greatly disappointed in the brevity of the battle, and many thought that the show had been faked. Sandow and Ziegfeld were lucky to escape in safety.

After the fiasco in San Francisco another noteworthy incident took place. The train taking Ziegfeld and his partners to Oakland was held up for hours by a wreck on the track. Ziegfeld suggested that Sandow collect one of the smashed engine's enormous wheels as a souvenir. When they arrived at Oakland, the reporters were pleased to see Sandow rolling the wheel as easily as though it were a child's hoop. The couple left in triumph for Los Angeles.

Occurrences of this kind continued to earn Ziegfeld and Sandow notoriety during their tour and their later successful collaboration at the Brooklyn Academy. Ziegfeld made about a quarter of a million dollars out of the tour, but he lost most of it at the gaming tables of New York. By early 1896 he was becoming short of money. He had been bailed out of gambling sessions by a new friend, Diamond Jim Brady, and by Charles Dillingham, a young ex-reporter for the *Chicago Daily News*, who had become interested in various theatrical enterprises and had saved his earnings to invest in them.

Instead of staying in an average hotel in New York, in those years Ziegfeld usually stopped at the Netherland, then in its finest fern-and-gilt glory. He used his impressive name to obtain a remarkable amount of credit. He spent many evenings at Rector's, on Broadway, with its white and gold decor redolent of the Second Empire, its crystal chandeliers and ocean of white tablecloths covered in the finest silver and flanked by giant plants in gleaming bronze pots. Dressed in suits flawlessly handmade by London tailors, he would cut an exceptionally elegant figure as he arrived night after night, with a beautiful woman on his arm, twirling a cane and doffing a hat to some influential society woman as he passed by. It was at Rector's in 1895 that he first met the gifted and charming Charles Evan Evans, the tall and dashing young vaudeville comedian who at just over 30 years of age was already a millionaire.

Evans, the angular swell, and Bill Hoey, his shorter, more vulgar partner, had become the most popular comedy team in the country. For years they had been overpowering successes in the music halls from coast to coast, most notably in the act called *The Book Agent*, written by the celebrated comedy playwright Charles Hoyt. In *The Book Agent* Evans appeared as I. McCorker—a kind of traveling bookseller involved in every kind of amusing and bizarre crime, and Hoey played Old Hoss, an ingenious tramp either assisting I. McCorker or—more often —outfoxing him. In 1884 Evans and Hoey were touring with the act in Brooklyn when Evans hit on the idea of expanding the act to a full-length play. He cabled Hoyt, who was living in Boston at the time, and Hoyt immediately cabled back that he would love to do it. Working at a feverish pace, Hoyt came up with the play, entitled *A Parlor Match, or Turning a Crank*, and the team opened in it on September 5, 1884, at Asbury Park.

The play was a witty trifle that effectively parodied both American acquisitiveness and the contemporary popularity of spiritualism. The hero, Captain Kidd, is the descendant of the famous pirate, an irascible old gentleman obsessed with the need to find a map that will disclose the whereabouts of his ancestor's fortune. His daughter, Lucille, falls in love with Ralph, the descendant of Governor Bellmont, who brought about pirate Kidd's destruction. The captain's younger daughter, Miss Innocent, is anxious to see her sister married, much to her father's annoyance.

McCorker arrives at the house selling books, and he manages to insinuate himself into the family. He tells Kidd that at a "mediumistic seance" Kidd will learn the location of the treasure. At the seance various bizarre spirits emerge, impersonated by Lucille and the Innocent Kidd, who have made several quick changes in the cabinet. They tell Kidd where to dig. When he does so, he comes up with only some old IOUs. After a series of very complicated events the ending is a happy one, however, and McCorker and Old Hoss preside over the wedding of Lucille and Ralph.

Light-hearted and expertly geared to the tastes of the time, *A Parlor Match* became the longest running play in American theatrical history until that time. Theodore Dreiser called Evans and Hoey "the epitome of the comedy of the era." The comedy ran for 2,550 performances without a break, and it made Hoyt, Evans and Hoey, who shared the proceeds, enormous fortunes. It would tour the country like a vaudeville show; then it would return periodically for brief runs in New York. After several years the partnership broke up, and Evans retired.

It was Ziegfeld's masterstroke of showmanship to reunite these two men for a full-scale revival of the play with the addition of lively musical numbers. At first Evans was unwilling. He had everything he wanted in the world: he was a luminary at every theatrical party and fashionable restaurant, a continually bubbling personality, described by Ziegfeld as "a mass of laughter-provoking angular humanity." Every time he walked into a restaurant the band would strike up his famous song, "The Man Who Broke the Bank in Monte Carlo," first introduced in *A Parlor Match*. But Evans was no less susceptible to flattery than any other star. Across the table at Rector's, among the pretty girls, the dazzle of chandeliers, and the rich scent of expensive cigars, he was carried away by Ziegfeld's scheme. Moreover, Ziegfeld had a wonderful sheaf of new music, including one song that exactly embodied the latest craze—for bicycles. It was entitled "Daisy Bell," with the swinging refrain "Daisy, Daisy, Give Me Your Answer Do." In his rather high-pitched, acid voice Ziegfeld sang the song, and Evans was delighted with it.

Almost at once the two men sailed for Europe to find a new actress—naughty and French if possible—who could play Lucille. A new star would further enliven the play and justify its revival at the Herald Square Theater, on which Evans had a lease. The trip to Europe was to alter the whole tenor of Ziegfeld's young life.

2

Anna

Arriving in London, Ziegfeld and Charles Evan Evans spent more time seeking pleasure in the luxurious brothels than in looking for star players. The intoxicating city— even in the depths of winter—offered an infinity of pleasure, and their visits to the theater were infrequent. When they did finally start inquiring about available acts, they discovered that every one had been secured by Oscar Hammerstein and other leading New York impressarios. One night they were dining at the Café Royal when Teddy Marks, a London theatrical manager, strolled over, splendid in cutaway and red carnation, and told them that he had a client at the Palace they simply had to see: Anna Held.

She was a new girl from Paris. Toulouse-Lautrec had sketched her, and she had been a great hit at La Scala and El Dorado music halls. Marks explained that Anna Held had had equally great triumphs throughout the Con-

tinent, but that she had retired after a Dutch tour to marry
and have a child. Now she had made a comeback, and she
was available but at a very modest price. He neglected to
mention that she already had a contract with Edouard
Marchand, of the Folies Bergère. Ziegfeld and Evans
shrugged the whole thing off and went to Paris. There
they found that, in fact, Anna Held was the only star not
currently booked by an American theater. They returned
to London, and Marks handed them two tickets to the
Palace, which was staging a predominantly French show
that winter.

They sat in the front row of the orchestra, concentrat-
ing grimly on every detail of Anna Held's performance.
Certainly she was pretty—with ravishing, opalescent eyes,
a perfect hour-glass figure (her waist was 18 inches), and
an exquisite style, which consisted of perfectly timed
shrugs, wriggles, and a tiny erotic laugh at the end of the
stanzas of a song. One of her numbers, an adaptation of
a German song called "Come and Play With Me," had a
naughty, provoking charm, and the star banged it across
with a sexuality and vigor reminiscent of the great stars
of Offenbach's era. The two men were excited, and they
repaired to the Café Royal for conversation over brandy
and cigars.

They decided to introduce Anna Held in the cabinet
scene, having her emerge as a particularly glamorous
ghost of A Parlor Match. She would sing her popular songs
to the audience. It would make an amusing if improbable
interlude, and she could also join in the last act tableau,
when the dead and the living joined for a splendid musical
finale. Moreover, she would be an amusing parody of
"phantoms" such as Katie King, materialized by the
medium Florrie Cook as the daughter of Sir Henry Morgan some 20 years earlier in London. The parallel between
Kidd and Morgan could be amusingly drawn in additional

dialogue to be written by the author. By the early morning hours a decision had been reached: she would be offered a run-of-the-play contract for $1,500 a week.

Ziegfeld and Evans spent the next 24 hours finding out everything they could about Anna Held from the Palace manager, Alfred Butt. It seemed she had been born in Warsaw in 1873 but always maintained—for professional reasons—that she was born in Paris. She was the only one of 12 children to survive. Her father, a glove-maker, was Jewish-French, and her mother was Polish (most journalists reversed those facts). The family, neither rich nor poor, lived in a pleasant small house near a schoolhouse in the Fourth Arrondissement.

When Anna was nine, the father fell ill, and his glove business collapsed. Some attempt was made by her mother to start a small restaurant, but this project collapsed. Anna Held began to work at the age of 11, cleaning and curling plumes for feathered hats for a firm in the Latin Quarter. Later she made boutonnières and fur caps in a basement workshop. When her father died, in the alcoholic ward of the Hotel Dien, a Paris hospital, she and her mother went to stay with relatives in London. Their Zolaesque career continued, with mother and daughter starving as they worked on benches in East End clothing factories. They lived in a small lodging next to the Princess Theater. Eventually spotted by a stage-door Johnny, Anna Held was promoted to a job in the chorus, for which she earned five shillings a week. When the company at the Princess went to Amsterdam, she left the chorus and began to sing in the local music halls.

Anna's legitimate debut was in *Shulamith*, by Abraham Goldfaden. She joined Jacob Adler's Jewish troupe in Whitechapel and appeared in the chorus, where she made so vivid an impression that she was given the job of understudying the leading lady. When that starring player eloped, Anna assumed her role. Later she played Dina in *Bar Chovcha* and the title role in *The Spanish Queen*, a Yiddish version of *The Ticket-of-Brave Man*.

Later she went to Rotterdam, Christiania, and The Hague. Her reputation was growing steadily. She progressed to having songs written for her, and finally she managed to get a job at La Scala in Paris and El Dorado.

Her cafe-concert act was "Le Colignon"—she was dressed as a driver with a small coat and hat and a whip. Another act had her dressed in a white ballet dress with a white hat and large green postage stamps all over her. Her act was a success in Paris, and she had ambitions to be a dramatic actress like her idol, Sarah Bernhardt. While playing at the Wintergarden in Berlin in the winter of 1895, she adapted a popular German song, *Die Kleine Schrecke* (The Little Teaser), which eventually became "Won't You Come and Play With Me." George Plumpton, who was representing the Palace, saw her there and engaged her for the Palace on the spot.

In 1894 Anna had fallen in love with and married Maximo Carrera, a Spanish emigré recently returned from the Argentine. Carrera's family had settled in Uruguay; a colonel at the age of 25, Carrera had served under the Uruguayan General Flores in the war against Brazil and the Argentine. He had later changed his allegiance and settled in Buenos Aires. At the time Anna encountered him he was just over 50 years old and very wealthy. They had a child, Liane, and they lived part of the time in Paris and part of the time in Trouville. Opposition from Carrera's relatives was so severe that, even after Anna was converted from Judaism to Catholicism, they made her position intolerable. After a series of quarrels the couple was separated by consent, although the Roman Catholic church ruled out the possibility of divorce. The father retained custody of the child, a matter that was settled to Anna's acute distress. It was, in fact, several years before the child was allowed to join her mother.

Flo was immensely pleased by what he heard about Anna's history. This colorful life story read like a popular novel and would be enormously exploitable in publicity. Moreover, Anna Held was clearly appropriate for import to New York in the wake of Yvette Guilbert's recent successful appearance for Oscar Hammerstein.

Failing to reach Anna Held through the usual channels, Ziegfeld borrowed some money from Evans and sent her a magnificent basket of orchids and a diamond bracelet, which he attached to the handle in an envelope. He received no reply. He begged Beatrice, Anna Held's Italian maid, to arrange his admittance to the dressing room, but Beatrice closed the door in his face. He asked Evans to advance some more cash. Evans reluctantly agreed. The following night he sent a still more magnificent basket and an even finer diamond bracelet. Anna Held asked her maid to return them at once. Beatrice begged Anna to reconsider. While they were hesitating, with the door half open, Ziegfeld thrust his way in and kissed Anna's hand. She was about to have him thrown out when something about his manner made her stop. He had an air of enormous self-possession and elegance. Moreover, he was not bad looking, and he was only 29. She decided, rather against her better judgment, to grant him an audience.

Anna was quite impressed by her visitor's smartness, boldness, and charm—she even found his high pitched tenor voice oddly attractive—and Ziegfeld was completely and hopelessly infatuated from the outset. He looked steadily into the star's eyes as she reminded him coldly that she had returned his flowers the day before and wondered whether he was suffering from amnesia. Disregarding her question, Ziegfeld sank uninvited onto a chaise lounge and snapped brightly: "Would you like to work for me?"

Without waiting for a reply he launched into a description of his father's life and his own, talking nonstop for an hour, until Anna was completely exhausted. At the end he said: "I am the man who will help you conquer America!" He was startled by Anna's reply: she told him she had been in America the year before and hated it; she had had a few disastrous appearances in the East Side music halls, had canceled her last engagements, and had sailed home. Ziegfeld explained that if she would return, she would be properly promoted, that she had had an unsuccessful tour because nobody had heard of her. He pointed out that in New York only great publicity could launch any star, that stars were not sought out by the discriminating as they were in Europe. She seemed mollified by this announcement, but when he mentioned Evans and Hoey, she was adamant. She positively would not appear with "two old men" who were known for their raucous and dirty humor.

Once again Ziegfeld ignored her complaint. He took out an envelope and started making notes. "You'll sail in September. New York will open its arms to you. I'll pay you $1,500 a week. That's far more than Edouard Marchand gave you in Paris or the Palace management can come up with."

It was at that moment that Anna delivered a stunning blow. "I regret to inform you that I have signed a contract with Marchand of the Folies Bergère for the winter season." Just for a moment Ziegfeld looked crestfallen. And according to Anna's diaries, at that precise moment Anna Held fell in love with him. "Although we argued," she wrote in her memoirs, "there was already something between us. . . . Without one tender word between us we were already bound by a thread." Within an hour she had accepted the terms: $1,500 a week for five months in New York and on tour in *A Parlor Match* and $1,000 to bring her to America. She said, with crumbling caution: "I'll consider your offer . . ." and he replied, "Splendid! We'll draw up the contract."

Anna Held wrote: "I fell down on my chaise lounge as he left, outraged with horror and delight at this incredible man who without a centime had managed to do all this. . . ." But she was somewhat less delighted, if rather more outraged, when he arrived at her dressing room the next day and said he would not be able to give an advance on the contract until he was back in New York. She told him to forget the whole arrangement, but he held the contract under her nose. Reluctantly she signed it; then she burst into laughter as he vanished into the winter fog.

Each night after the show for several days until his ship sailed for New York, Ziegfeld arrived at the stage door with his arms full of flowers. He took Anna Held to midnight suppers and ravished her with accounts of his dreams for the Broadway stage. Even at that early stage he was determined to reject the coarse, vulgar, ugly atmosphere of vaudeville and replace it with glamour, taste, and charm. Doubtless she was fascinated by him and intrigued by the romantic character of his career to date, including the fact that he had lost a fortune to her own husband at the Monte Carlo gambling tables. A cynic might insist that Ziegfeld, vibrating with ambition, reckless and ruthless, simply set out to seduce Anna Held in order to secure her complete cooperation in his most ambitious theatrical venture so far. It is more likely that, with all the intensity of a 29-year-old, he was totally and passionately in love with this tiny, enchanting, and ravishingly pretty woman.

During the nights that followed their somewhat uneasy first encounter developed into a full-scale love affair. They traveled to Paris together at the end of the London run. Ziegfeld was a frequent visitor at Anna's exquisite house in the Faubourg St. Honoré, and Sundays were spent sitting at the tall windows looking at the scarlet uniformed guard outside the Elysée Palace or observing visitors to the home of the president rolling through the ornamental gates.

Ziegfeld and Evans returned to America on the SS *Havel* with a galaxy of clothes and sets for the show that was to introduce Anna to American audiences.

Meanwhile, when Anna returned to London she found a number of problems to dampen her enthusiasm. Her estranged husband, Maximo Carrera, had lost every franc he owned at the early morning gambling tables in Paris and had begun to sell his paintings, his statues, and even the furnishings of his suite at the Hotel Paiva to pay his debts. In view of the French laws, in which a wife is responsible for her husband's debts, Anna's apartment in the Faubourg St. Honoré was stripped of almost everything. When she told Marchand of her American contract, he was furious. Her contract with him was binding, and he would legally prevent her from sailing. Only the immediate payment of a $1,500 fine would force him to tear up the agreement he had with her. Anna did not have the money to pay Marchand.

Anna cabled Ziegfeld immediately after she left Marchand's office: "SEND $1,500 OR CONTRACT CANCELED." Back in New York Ziegfeld took out his handkerchief, spread his jewelry on it, and sent an assistant to a pawnbroker. The jewels fetched $500, and Charles Evans, ever loyal, came up with $1,000.

He cabled Anna: "$1,500 SENT VIA GARFIELD BANK STOP EXPERTS ADVISE MARCHAND CANNOT PREVENT YOUR DEPARTURE STOP A MUSI-

CAL DELEGATION AWAITS YOU AT THE QUAR-
ANTINE STOP."

Anna booked passage on the SS *New York*, which sailed
from Le Havre in early September. She fulfilled her engagement at La Scala and played a two-week season in
Lucerne before boarding the ship with Beatrice, her
mother, her pug dog, Dizi, and Teddy Marks. Just before
boarding she got word from a friend that Marchand's men
were waiting at the dock to prevent her departure. She
implored Maximo Carrera to come to her rescue. Carrying her baby in one arm, he made his way up the gangplank with her luggage, deposited it, and came back to
her and hurried her past Marchand's men to the safety of
her luxury suite. There she broke into tears, agonized by
her separation from her child and—for the first time in a
year—overcome by feelings for her husband.

By the time the ship sailed, Anna was virtually pros-
trate. Her terror of the sea and of testing her slender talents in America combined to produce an overpowering
anxiety. She was also nervous about her limited command
of the English language, believing that Americans, unlike
the kinder British, would scourge her for her insufficient
knowledge. Once on board she was delighted with her
large and comfortable suite, and she relaxed for a few
hours until the ship was at sea. Southampton provided a
pleasant interlude. When she was only two days out into
the Atlantic, however, she became dreadfully unsettled by
some events on board.

Her bedroom steward, William Hyde, was a pleasant
man in his mid-twenties, fresh-faced, open, and seemingly
normal. He had risen from pantry boy and was, it seemed,
happy with his humble calling. But when Anna called for
him on the second morning he did not answer her. Despite diligent searching he could not be found.

It was assumed he had jumped overboard during the

night. Though Anna scarcely knew the young man, she cried disconsolately. She was delighted when a fellow passenger told her that in its search the crew had overlooked the baggage room. Two officers went ahead of a small group of interested passengers, including Anna, to inspect the area. When the door was opened, they were horrified to see a person standing in the middle of the baggage, his eyes blazing and a cutthroat razor in each hand.

Master-At-Arms Dickson, Storekeeper Collins, and Boatswain's Mate Crockett overpowered a man named Moran and placed him in irons. Anna was appalled to notice that among several boxes he had broken open was her own large one. He had stuffed some inexpensive bangles and a necklace into his pockets from the jewel compartment. The man had also stolen a case of surgical instruments, three brooches, two rings, and a diamond pin given by the Prince of Wales to the Australian cricketer, Jack Darling, whom Anna had met the day before in the saloon.

A worse shock was to come. Under cross-examination in Captain Passow's cabin Moran revealed that Hyde, Anna's steward, had put him up to the job. Hyde was found, and both men were placed in the brig.

After this disquieting incident heavy seas made the vessel pitch and roll unbearably. Anna was in an agony of seasickness in her cabin. No sooner had the weather cleared up than she was distressed to learn of another disturbing event: a deck steward, George Candy, had gone overboard during the last day of the storm. Since he was an experienced salt, it was assumed that he had committed suicide. Anna immediately spoke to two senators on board—J. B. Foraker, of Ohio, and James Smith, Jr., of New Jersey. She made arrangements for a concert in

which she would star, the proceeds of which would go to
Candy's widow and children. She captivated the audience
in the saloon with her version of "Come and Play With
Me," passing round a feathered hat, in which was col-
lected $517. She also sold $300 worth of programs.

At the end of the performance the audience rose to its
feet and cheered her for several minutes. Thanking her,
Senator Foraker said: "I—and I hope I speak for every
man aboard this vessel—will come and play with you,
Miss Held, when you open at the Herald Square Theater
next week. And I'll bring an umbrella with me and pound
the floor when my hands become too tired to go on
applauding." Anna laughed and flung her arms around
him, earning more cheers.

Anna spent hours preparing for her return to American
soil. Dressed magnificently in her favorite dress, with a
small fur muff, her hair tumbling down her back, and her
pallor disguised by a skillful application of rouge, she
stepped off the ship looking as exquisite as a Sevres figu-
rine. Ziegfeld sailed out to the quarantine island to greet
her in a yacht crowded with theatrical figures, including
Diamond Jim Brady and Lillian Russell, a 30-piece band,
and the crack reporters of the New York press. Fireworks
snaked through the gray New York sky as she gave her
interview in prettily fractured English, captivating the
press, which devoted immense space to her arrival. Then,
hand in hand with Ziegfeld, she stepped into a fast carriage and rode happily off to the Hotel Savoy.

Anna was delighted with the Savoy: the rich Italian
Renaissance façades, the Indiana limestone walls, and the
exquisite dining room, a riot of Siena marble and rouge
jasper, green and white Killarney marbles, satinwood and
white holly, sculptures and frescos. The breakfast room
was reminiscent of a room in an English manor house; the

billiard room was a copy of a palace chamber in Pompeii; and the drawing rooms were in the style of Louis XIV, XV, and XVI.

Most splendid of all was the suite that Ziegfeld had arranged for Anna's arrival: the state suite on the second floor overlooking Central Park, a perfect replica of the boudoir of Marie Antoinette at the Petit Trianon Palace at Versailles, decorated for the visit in 1893 of the Infanta Eulalia of Spain.

Late in the golden afternoon Anna and Flo took a long and leisurely drive through Central Park to see the flowers and the beautiful, melancholy sight of the first leaves turning gold. They returned to the Savoy at 5:30 P.M. to meet the press.

Thoroughly recovered from the ocean voyage, Anna looked ravishing. The reporters capitulated before her charm and her brilliantly conceived opening line: "What exactly *eez* a *cocktail?*" Ziegfeld had crowded every inch of her suite with roses and orchids, and Anna had changed —at his advice—into a semitransparent negligee for the reception. A buffet was crowded with truffles, pate de fois gras, and magnums of champagne in silver buckets. With her adoring friends nearby, Anna spoke of the silver-plated bicycle given her by the Trafalgar Square Cycling Club, of the nickel-plated bicycle that Ziegfeld had ready for her to ride in Central Park, and of the two spanking bays she had imported on the *New York* (she would dress them in winter coats and leggings when the snow began). Sighing about her mistake in leaving the bicycle at home, she went into the bedroom and brought out an elegant cycling outfit with a skirt cut just below the knee. "I tried knickerbockers once, and they were, oh, so shocking!" she told a *Times* reporter. He asked her if she intended to go to Flo's home town.

"Cheecago? *Cheecago?* Oh yes; I heard of Cheecago. I

heard of my geography. They had an exposition in Chicago." And she and Flo winked at each other. She sang her most famous songs in a clear, fresh voice that seemed, if anything, to have been improved by the Atlantic crossing.

Only a month remained till the opening of the play, and Anna, with her usual energy, plunged into rehearsals the next morning. While doing so, she was visited by the widow of the deck steward who had jumped off the *New York*. Flo drove Anna very hard, complaining constantly about her accent yet keeping her spirits up by sending a dozen orchids around to the Savoy every day.

They dined out constantly, and during that beautiful fall of 1896 their affair developed into sexual expression. Anna was unable to resist so passionate a man as Ziegfeld, and indeed she was already in love with him. His uncanny intuition with women did not desert him in his pursuit of this ravishing prize. Their weekends were always kept free of work, and they cycled together happily around Coney Island, enjoying its distractions like a pair of children.

Charles Evans and Bill (Old Hoss) Hoey kept Anna happy with their endless pranks during the strain of rehearsals. She and Flo sang "A Bicycle Built For Two" as they rode their separate bicycles around New York. On a rare free evening they would meet Diamond Jim Brady for leisurely meals that ended after midnight, Anna taking risks with her figure since she had a penchant for rich pastries.

Anna was enchanted with New York: Luchow's, with its dark interior and steak-with-ale, Tony Pastor's, Prospect Garden Music Hall, the hansom cabs in the park, where Anna liked to ride horses in the early morning. Waltzes and ragtime were the rage. Anna was intensely excited by everything that was happening in music, and when she was out dancing with Flo, she often would break into a current song. The crowd would part and applaud her loudly. Flo's press agents kept her constantly in the public eye until the first night of *A Parlor Match*, on October 21.

The crowd at the Herald Square Theater on the opening night was gratifyingly large. Flo had achieved miracles of advance publicity for Anna, and there was the added attraction of the fact that Evans and Hoey were reunited for the first time in several seasons. Although the farce had been revived several times during the previous decade, the hardened first-nighters—led by representatives of the greatest families in New York—laughed as though every hoary joke were new.

Flo saved Anna's appearance until toward the end, and when the curtains parted on the cabinet scene, she presented an exquisite sight. The audience uttered what the *New York Times* described as a: "prolonged and utterly sincere *oh*! from every moderately young person in the theater, and from more than two or three who [were] approaching middle age. As a spectacle Mlle. Held is a success, absolute and complete."

Dressed in pale blue and pink embroidered silk, she sang "Come and Play With Me." The *Times* remarked: "Her eyes are long, narrow, and heavily circled; her nose is straight; her mouth, perfect; and as for her chin, people might go some ways to see it without regretting the experience."

The *New York Times* and other papers were less enthusiastic about her talents as a singer and actress than about her appearance, and the *Times* indeed became rather cruel on the following Sunday: "Miss Held has created no furor in Paris. Her abilities are of the most ordinary kind. Her voice is not sweet or very strong, and she uses it with no remarkable skill. . . . She would not be a 'sensation' at all if the idea had not been ingeniously forced upon the public mind that she is . . . naughty."

The public, by contrast, adored her. The moment at which she conquered New York at the end of the second act is legend. Applause was only polite as she stepped out of the cabinet in her ghostly dress lit by a pale green spotlight. Provincial New York was baffled by the fact that her voice had an acid sophistication far removed from the warm-hearted warbling of so many contemporary American singers and that she sang uncompromisingly in French. Sensing the lukewarm reaction, she cut one song and raced forward to "Come and Play With Me," with its English lyrics. She was a triumph. As she took her third curtain, Ziegfeld, who had been pacing about backstage and then running through the lobby to the back orchestra to see that his (planted) employees were clapping and cheering, had a sudden inspiration. He told Bill Hoey to go onto the stage and sit in a chair with his back to Anna while the curtain was down. When the curtain went up, the audience saw him there and laughed automatically as they always did at his battered top hat, checked waistcoat, and baggy pants. Anna was completely cowed by his sudden appearance, but when she saw Ziegfeld winking in the wings, she sang an encore of the song. In reply to the repeated "Come and Play With Me," Hoey got up, said, "You won't have to wait long! I'm coming," and waltzed her around the stage. The entire audience stood up and cheered. At that precise moment Anna Held was launched.

Anna's most exciting moment came during the weekend, when a special exhibition of prize-winning bicycles was held at the theater. The boxes were decorated with silver-plated wheels. Anna presented the prizes in royal blue silk amid an ocean of New York bicycling club officials. As she left the theater she was astonished and a little frightened to see an immense crowd of young men sweeping down on her, howling with pleasure. They carried her by force into her hansom cab and uncoupled the horses. Anna screamed with terror; Ziegfeld yelled out from the mass of people that there was nothing to be afraid of. He was laughing with pleasure at his success. Then dozens of young men began to draw the cab along Herald Square and up the avenues to the Netherland Hotel. It was a tremendous moment, repeated often when Anna played after a football game on tour.

Flo and Anna could afford to smile over the reviews as they read them together at the Netherland. The bookings were excellent, and the envisioned three-month run seemed a sure thing. Flo felt that the flow of publicity about his beautiful star must not be allowed to slacken. He and his press agent, Leon Blum, put their heads together and devised an ingenious scheme, to which Anna was a willing party.

Anna loved to bathe in a starch solution, a milky fluid that she believed did wonders for her skin. Between two and four every afternoon at the Savoy she immersed herself and sang prettily to her devoted Beatrice. One day Ziegfeld arrived unexpectedly and saw her in the bath. He was astounded, and he asked her what on earth she was doing. Even as he did so, he realized the potential of her ritual in terms of publicity, and he ran out of the room to write an urgent message to Blum to come to the hotel.

A quick inquiry to the manager produced the information that the hotel milk supply came from a dairyman named H. R. Wallace, of Brooklyn. Flo took a carriage to Brooklyn at once and shook the surprised milkman's hand. The visit of a celebrated theatrical manager and a well-known agent overwhelmed Wallace, and he eagerly accepted their idea. He was to supply Anna with a personal delivery of 400 gallons of milk over the next three weeks for her to bathe in. Before that period elapsed, Anna would cancel the order, and the milkman would sue her for nonpayment. Flo would release the story to the press, and New York—and all of America—would learn that Anna Held took milk baths.

Everything went smoothly at first. The pageboys at the Savoy arrived at the suite laden with the cans marked "For Miss Anna Held." Flo and Anna enjoyed pouring the liquid down the bathroom basin. After several days of masquerade Flo announced to the press that "Miss Anna Held's milk was not fresh" and sent a message to Wallace telling him to call the newspapers and say he was suing.

Every paper in New York, including the usually cautious *Times*, fell for the hoax. It reported solemnly that John Anderson, a lawyer of the Eagle Building in Brooklyn, had been engaged to sue Flo and Anna for $64 in unpaid milk bills and that Anna had engaged a "Colonel Talafierro" to act in her defense. Teddy Marks said, "The matter will be settled out of court, as milk baths were too peculiar to be discussed in public." In a press conference held while she was in a bath of real—and discreetly opaque —milk, Anna enchanted the newspapers by saying, "The milk Mr. Wallace sent was not fresh. This milk is much better."

Flo added, straightfaced: "I don't believe the cows were milked at 1:00 P.M. Miss Held took her baths between 3:00 and 5:00 in the afternoon. The cows were milked days before, and by the time she got it, the milk was sour."

Flo arranged for Wallace's writ to be handed to Anna on stage at an actors' benefit at the Brooklyn Academy of Music. Besieged once again by reporters, she said to them: "The milk was oh—*horrible!* A milk bath should be very grateful and refreshing. It is for the skin, to benefit the skin. Wasn't it Marie Antoinette who used to bathe in milk? But this milk was *cream!*"

Unfortunately Anna's charge that the milk was sour—not in the original verbal agreement—infuriated Wallace, who found that his business was falling off. He called a press conference in his dairy and announced that the entire event was a hoax. "Sour milk, eh?" he raged. "I sell sour milk, do I? That's more than an insult. It's calculated to injure me. I'll tell you the truth—I never heard of Anna Held, or whatever her name is, until this deal was made."

A few weeks later Anna was back in the headlines. On November 28 Ziegfeld was dining in the private room at the Hotel Martin with Anna and a group of friends. As always for her parties, the room resembled a bower of American Beauty roses; at least 1,000 had been bought for the occasion. Coffee was being served, the tables were crowded with half-filled glasses of Chartreuse and Benedictine. From the main restaurant, beyond the walnut doors, came the strains of a violin playing "Drink To Me Only." One of the guests, the magnificent Julius Steger, handsome star of *His Excellency*, in which he played the Prince Regent, began to hum the song. A Dr. Frank Müller interrupted, remarking that a man in Berlin had just won a bet by kissing his girlfriend 1,000 times. Ziegfeld immediately got up and fetched over a *Telegraph* reporter from the bar, inviting him to join the party. Then he challenged Steger, who was more than a little drunk, to kiss Anna Held: "The bet is my horse—my new horse, the one you admired so extravagantly in Paris last summer." Steger accepted. News got about, and every inch of the restaurant was filled. Up to the 114th kiss, all seemed well, but after that Anna began to sag.

The *New York Journal* reported Steger's reaction to the

115th kiss: "[The actor] seemed to perceive that his vis-a-vis was giving out. It nerved him to fresh action. He clinched with vigor and recovered in good shape. Anna Held looked as if she was almost crying. The pupils of her eyes were dilated, her lips seemed uncontrolled. Suddenly her head fell forward, and she sank back in her chair. Steger turned about smiling and faced the crowd. He protested that he was ready to go on indefinitely, but his looks belied him. He was breathing hard, and the perspiration was pouring from his forehead in beads, as though he had been through great muscular exertion."

Frank Müller, M.D., reported to the paper that, "The ordeal . . . left Miss Held bordering on a state of nervous collapse, as was indicated by a high, rapid pulse, which registered 152. Mr. Steger's pulse was at 144, and he signified his willingness to proceed at the same rate. But there is every reason to believe that he could not have repeated the performance. I am more thoroughly convinced than ever that the German record of something over 3,000 kisses is a fiction."

Anna recorded her impressions later: "After the hundred mark . . . I experienced a most unpleasant tingling. . . . This increased so much that I wanted to scream. . . . Perhaps it was the 130th kiss—I felt a muscular contraction, a twitching. . . . At the 150th I was muscularly exhausted, overwhelmed with such nausea that I could not stir."

Anna also became headline news thanks to the famous Brooklyn incident. One Sunday she and Ziegfeld were out in the sunshine riding their bicycles on the Boulevard in Brooklyn near the Manhattan Beach Railroad tracks when a buggy drove past driven by elderly Judge E. Clarence Murphy. Suddenly one of Murphy's trotter's reins snapped, and the carriage swerved violently, its shaft catching the wheel of Anna's cycle. It threw her off her high perch to the ground. The judge rode off with a wave and an apology, not stopping to pick her up. Back at the Savoy, Ziegfeld decided to embroider the incident. They called à press conference and told the reporters that Miss Held, after being upset from her bicycle, had risen to her feet, noticed that the judge's trotter was rearing and about to charge off toward the railroad tracks, and flung herself forward, seizing the broken reins and—at imminent risk to life and limb—preventing the horse from running away. Most newspapers eagerly ran the story. Only the *Times* was cautious, ruling out the story as an absurdity and printing instead an editorial criticizing the activities of press agents.

By mid-November, Anna Held was a household word in America. Her kissing contest, her progress up Broadway drawn by 300 young men, her milk baths, and her rescue of a runaway judge had been printed in every part of the nation. Manufacturers of cosmetics, corsets, and every conceivable article of clothing rushed to seek her endorsement, and Ziegfeld made them pay through the nose, seeking a share of any proceeds for the star and even arranging for brand goods to be created in her name. Soon women were wearing Anna Held foundation garments, Anna Held stockings, and Anna Held makeup. Not even Lillian Russell had reached this degree of fame, and Ziegfeld had good reason to be proud of himself. Everywhere she went, bicycling or riding her coated and breeched horses in Central Park, shopping on Fifth Avenue, visiting the cathedral, Anna was relentlessly followed.

In short, she had arrived.

3

A Kind of Marriage

AFTER they closed *A Parlor Match*, Ziegfeld and Anna left for a long cross-country tour with the play. They spent Christmas in Pittsburgh, where Anna sang carols in the snowy streets for the benefit of the orphan children. In Philadelphia she told friends that she and Ziegfeld would be married shortly. Back in New York in the spring of 1897, they gave a joint champagne supper party at the Netherland and announced to their friends that they would simply sign papers to the effect that they were married, since Held's Roman Catholic husband could not secure a dissolution. Anna herself had been converted at the time of her marriage. Apparently this curious arrangement satisfied their friends, and everyone agreed to say that a real marriage had been performed (it was not recognized in common law until 1904). The press made no announcement of any kind, and Ziegfeld told inquiring reporters that the marriage had taken place in Chicago in March. Surprisingly not a single columnist felt sufficiently confident to utter a word about the fact that the most famous "marriage" of show business was, in fact, not a marriage at all.

In the summer of 1897 Anna was besieged by offers from the managements of New York. The most handsome sum—$2,500 a week—was suggested by Oscar Hammerstein, then in severe financial difficulties. Hammerstein needed a new attraction for his Lyric Theater, which was part of his immense Olympia complex of showcases on Broadway. Overextended at the banks because of the expense of this venture, he had recouped a great deal with the importing of Yvette Guilbert, who conquered New York in 1895 in Jules Jouy's musical play *La Pierreuse*. He hoped that Anna would repeat Guilbert's success.

Hammerstein selected *La Poupée* (*The Puppet*) as her vehicle, an operetta scored by the brilliant Edmond Audran and written by Maurice Ordonneau. An obscure writer, Arthur Sturges, was given the job of translating the libretto; his hurried work annoyed Hammerstein, but the impresario was committed to an opening date of October 21, 1897. Rehearsals were tense because Hammerstein resented Ziegfeld's close watch over Anna; Hammerstein was under constant pressure from a number of his mistresses to have her replaced. Faced with the challenge of a major role, Anna was even more nervous and temperamental than usual, and she frequently burst into tears at moments of stress.

The role in *La Poupée* was an extremely challenging one. A young novice in a monastery that had fallen on hard times discovers that he can inherit 100,000 francs from an uncle if he will marry. The prior finds a way out of the problem: he makes a doll so lifelike that it cannot be distinguished from a real woman. At the last minute the doll breaks, and a beautiful girl takes its place. Risqué, Coppélia-like comedy events occur when the monk finds that he is married not to a lifelike puppet but to a woman of flesh and blood.

Anna found it extremely difficult to imitate the stiff, lifeless movements of the puppet. But in later scenes when she came to life, she played with effortless sparkle and charm. There was no mistaking the fact that she had been miscast.

The bad notices of *La Poupée* severely affected business. After the initial excitement attendance fell off, and Hammerstein fired Anna from the cast. He began trying to borrow money, but by November 5 his property had been assigned. Auctioneer Louis Phillips was the assignee, and the employees of the Olympia Music Hall and the Lyric Theater were preferred creditors. Hammerstein rushed another actress into the leading role, followed by his mistress, Alice Rose, whose plump charms were futile in attracting audiences. The Olympia and the Lyric closed down in mid-November, and only a month after she had opened in *La Poupée*, Anna went to appear at Koster and Bial's Music Hall.

Anna had played in *La Poupée* for only one week. Hammerstein claimed that she had walked out of the production because she had overheard him say he was going to replace her, and his attorney, ex-Judge Dittenhofer, sent a writ to Ziegfeld for $7,500 for breach of contract. Hammerstein sued for an additional $10,000 in damages. Ziegfeld countersued for $2,500, due to Anna for one week's work, and for $10,000 for "uncalled for humiliation" caused by the hiring of Alice Rose. Both sides ultimately abandoned the battle; neither could afford to fight it.

The whole event caused a very severe setback for Anna. She and Ziegfeld scarcely knew what to do next. They did not dare to abandon their luxurious way of life, and Anna had to appear dressed in the height of fashion in her every public appearance. Ziegfeld decided to tour her again; managements had been clamoring to see her, and he could hold out no longer.

Before leaving for her tour Anna played for a limited season at the Harlem Opera House in February, 1898. She appeared in *A Gay Deceiver*, a farce written by Paul Wilstach and Joseph Grismer. It did not run long. The leading player was the veteran farceur M. A. Kennedy, who specialized in the role of a fat, bald old man given to pinching women's bottoms; the plot concerned his attempt to pass himself off as his twin to deceive his own wife with another woman. There were a number of familiar characters in the farce: a saucy prima donna given to smashing ashtrays in fits of high-powered temperament, a pert maid, and a knowing bellboy. The audience roared obediently, but Anna was the real show-stopper. In the last act, in a specially interpolated scene, she was introduced as a celebrity visiting the house in which the farce was set. The curtain was pulled wide, and Anna stepped out of a giant replica of herself, tickled M. A. Kennedy's bald pate, and sang "I Don't Want Dem Presents Back"—referring to the gifts with which the infatuated ancient had showered her.

Ziegfeld had a brilliant idea, years ahead of its time, for a background for Anna during the number. A huge sheet of music from the song was set up behind her, filling the proscenium. As she sang, the heads of black singers emerged individually from the black notes in the score, and at each chorus they pushed out simultaneously to accompany her. It was a masterstroke of showmanship. One critic wrote: "The $1.50 table d'hote dinner at the Harlem Opera House rests absolutely on its dessert. . . . Miss Held is a dainty delight. She is the great bewildering climax." Other reviews were equally enthusiastic.

In March, 1898, the production opened in San Francisco. The *Examiner* wrote: "When someone said, 'I will now introduce you to the Parisian Celebrity, Mlle. Anna Held,' the green curtains swung apart, and the little creature stepped forward in the toppling hat, as cumbrous as an umbrella stand, my eyes felt as big as hers." Anna added some new touches to her performance: she addressed the bass fiddle amorously and embraced it passionately, and sang with artless charm:

> *For I have such a way with me*
> *A way with me, a way with me,*
> *I have such a nice little way with me,*
> *Oh, do not think it wrong.*

She delighted the audience with her curtain speech: "Ladies and gentlemen, I thank you very much for your kind reception. I like California very much, and I hope to stay with you a very long time." After these words Ziegfeld had a stagehand carry a milk can across the stage. The *Chronicle* deplored the stunt, and in fact was less than kind about Anna's performance as a whole: "Miss Held was as pretty as was expected, which is saying a great deal, and it may be she sang—if it can be called singing—and acted—or behaved—is a better description."

At Christmas, 1898, Anna and her "animated magic score" were back in New York playing with a mixed group of acts at Koster and Bial's Music Hall: Adelman and Lowe, xylophonists, Leveria Charmon, trapeze dancer, contortionist Pablo Diaz, and Caicedo the wire king. She loved the circus people, and she elected one Sunday to visit the circus itself. She and Ziegfeld walked happily hand in hand to their seats at Ringling Brothers Circus, with John Ringling in person to show them to their places. Scores of people turned from their cups of pink lemonade

and bags of peanuts to see them as they arrived. It was
after the show that both Anna and Ziegfeld first fell in
love with elephants. Ringling showed them around after
the performance and proudly introduced them to Lockhart, the famous elephant trainer.

Ringling gave Lockhart a wink, and at Lockhart's instructions one of the biggest creatures seized Anna about
the waist and hoisted her onto its back. At first Anna
screamed with terror, but soon she called down to Ziegfeld: "It is great fun! I am the Queen of India!" Then the
great pachyderm knelt, and Anna slid down its nose to
the sawdust floor. As she left, Anna said, "I should so love
to have a menagerie of my own."

Ziegfeld sighed. He had recently given her a present
of a bear cub from the New York Zoo, and there was always her tiny pug dog, Dizi. But the next day he gave
her a tiger cub, its claws carefully shaved, and two more
pug puppies.

Early in 1898 he gave her a still more splendid present:
the Anna Held Railroad Car. The possession of a private car had been a mark of prestige in theatrical cir-
cles ever since manager Harry J. Sargent hired one for
Modjeska on her first American tour. Sarah Bernhardt had
traveled in a magnificent car, and Sam T. Jack's famous
troupe of girls had used one on their successful travels
from New York to the Pacific Coast.

The car Ziegfeld settled upon had once been the property of Lily Langtry, "The Jersey Lily," who had left it
idle when her fortunes ebbed in later years. Finally it had
been bought by magician Alexander Herrmann, whose
death left the car in a tangle of posthumous lawsuits.
After the season at Koster and Bial's, Ziegfeld hired the
car with an option to buy; Anna saw it and traveled in it
to the first out-of-town engagement at Philadelphia. Zieg-

feld immediately took up the option, at a cost of some $22,000.

With his already emerging taste and flair, Ziegfeld personally supervised the refurbishing of the car. It included an observation saloon with three large plate windows, a splendid state room, a boudoir that was a miniature copy of Anna's own in the Faubourg St. Honoré, a powder room with pink walls, and a rear platform (the car was hooked on the end of the train) fixed up like a piazza, where Anna and her guests could sit and enjoy the passing scenery. There was also a small compartment for her animals. "The fortunate possessor," wrote Arthur Brooks in *Metropolitan* magazine, "may enjoy the comforts of the Waldorf Astoria."

The walls were of dark mahogany, copied under Ziegfeld's instructions from his Chicago home at West Adams Street. The windows were of stained glass—as in Chicago—and the sitting room contained richly upholstered sofas, potted ferns, sumptuous carpets, and decorations in the French Oriental style. A piano, phonograph, music boxes, and even a five-piece band accompanied her wherever she went so that the drab atmosphere of remote towns at night would be lit up by the strains of her favorite composers.

Anna left for Europe in June, 1898, on board the *Kaiser Wilhelm der Grosse* with Ziegfeld and her entourage. She slipped away virtually unobserved because she was terrified that Hammerstein would attempt to prevent her departure by serving her with a new writ for breach of contract. Reporters at the wharf noticed that she looked a little pale alongside the flushed and vigorous Ziegfeld, but they attributed her pallor to her recent bout with influenza. Color certainly came to her cheeks as she entered her state room on A deck and found all of her friends

headed by Diamond Jim Brady and Lillian Russell ready
to bid her farewell. Every inch of space was crowded with
flowers, and downstairs there were still more flowers, spill-
ing out of the grand saloon. Passengers wandered about,
examining with pleasure each gift: 300 Jack roses woven
into a miniature bower, a present of the Martin brothers,
restaurateurs, a French flag made up of tulips from Koster
and Bial's Music Hall, and gigantic horseshoes among
the bouquets.

The voyage, unlike Anna's last one, was pleasant and
uneventful, and by the time she arrived at Le Havre, her
health was fully restored. The first thing to be settled on
arrival in Paris was Anna's debt to Marchand of the Folies
Bergère, to whom she had already lost 30,000 francs in
the courts for breach of contract. Marchand agreed to
wipe off future debts if she would appear for him without
salary for one month. She agreed.

The agreement infuriated Ziegfeld, but there was nothing he could do about it. Besides, there was Paris to be
enjoyed in high summer: the Bois, the great restaurants,
the wonderful nights out to the Opera, and the *Comédie
française*. Anna's apartment was again a delight; fastid-
ious though he was, Ziegfeld could still not fault it: the
pale green wallpaper, the rich carvings and clocks, the
busts, the perfectly placed palms, and the gold mirrors.
Piece by piece, Anna's agents had been buying back everything she had lost to the debt collectors when her husband was ruined, and the apartment had almost been restored to its former grandeur. Moreover, Ziegfeld once
more could look out of the tall windows and see the endless spectacle of the Elyseé Palace, the changing of the
guard, the scarlet uniforms and gold buttons shining in
the sun, the tall gates gleaming, the endless stream of
visitors to the head of state. Those were halcyon days. The

couple was blissfully happy, Paris was at its loveliest, and plans piled on plans over leisurely breakfasts for new plays to excite the American public.

The play they finally settled on was a Parisian farce translated as *The French Maid*, in which Anna would play Suzette, a quintessential cocotte. Before she began her American tour that fall, Anna bought the small Prey Farm, near Belgrade Lakes, Maine. Ziegfeld announced the purchase in an amusingly worded press release: "Miss Anna Held has purchased the farm of Prey, and guests are invited to come and inspect her calves."

Another diversion that summer was the fashioning of a sculpture of Anna by Barconi, whose busts of Pope Leo XIII and President McKinley had been much admired. The sculpture was designed to be shown at the Paris Exhibition of 1900. There were endless fittings for the magnificent $30,000 Pascaud dress covered in real diamonds that she was to wear in the third act of the play: slit to the waist, it showed a pair of blue silk tights calculated to excite the most tired of businessmen. Even though the provinces found the dress and its owner outrageous and shocking (the *Detroit Journal* said, "Miss Held, her private car, her promoters and her jeweled skirts [should be sent] back to la Belle France"), New York, which saw her only briefly in the touring play, once again capitulated to her charms.

By 1900 the pattern of Ziegfeld's and Anna's life was comfortably set. Each fall they would open a new production, more elegant and accomplished than the last, run it for a carefully limited season to insure a pressure of public attention, and leave in the palace car for a long and beautifully planned season, which always included Chicago and a visit to the Ziegfeld family home. When

the run was over, they would leave for Europe, stop over
for a time at the Faubourg St. Honoré apartment, resist
Marchand's demands for a return season at the Folies
Bergère, visit Pascaud, and shop for new plays. Anna
would finally settle on a play she liked and arrange for
some new songs. Many of her songs were written by
Harry B. Smith, whose wife, Irene, was an adored companion of Anna's.

Then the couple would set out on marvelous long va-
cations in their favorite cities—Brussels, Berlin, Vienna,
Moscow, St. Petersburg—looking for additional material
and seeing all of the shows. Back by early September, they
would be greeted by friends and musicians in a specially
hired boat in New York Harbor, surrounded by thousands of roses and orchids. The lovely 13-room suite at
the Hotel Ansonia would be waiting. Then would come
the opening in a number of different theaters, the applause, the success, and again the tours.

Anna spent a fortune on the Ansonia Apartments over
the years. They were furnished in blue and gold, with
exquisite antiques, paintings, sculptures, busts, and lavish
sofas. The boudoir was based on the style of Louis XIV,
the bed of heavily carved ivory laden with Irish point
lace and blue satin, its canopy made of satin and lace. The
bath and dressing room were done in Dresden brocade
and ivory, the screens covered in exquisite eighteenth-
century woodland designs. The drawing room was of yellow moire antique—walls, divans, chairs and sofas. The
piano was stained a rich red-gold and embossed with
solid gold; its keyboard was made of pure mother-of-pearl.

In all of those years the most exciting moment of all for
Ziegfeld and Anna occurred in June, 1899: the triumphant experience of the Festival of the Flowers in Paris.
It would remain for both of them until the end of their
lives a memory of heart-stopping romantic glamour. On a

day of golden sunshine the fashionable society of Paris poured into the Bois de Boulogne to compete for the prize awarded to the most magnificent carriage. It was a sunset occasion, for the automobile, shining and snarling, was ready to crush that age of elegance forever. Of the thousands of vehicles that arrived that summer day 80 percent were Victorias, drawn by a single horse. Only a small minority could afford the splendors of four horses and special carriages. Ziegfeld and Anna spent weeks working on their own conveyance.

Drawn by four spanking chestnuts, it was covered in a white canopy of pure Indian silk, decorated from one end to the other with 3,000 orchids. Even the wheels had delicate sprays of purple blooms, and the coachman's whip was entwined with fragrant creeping plants. Anna Held was in white to match the carriage, and Ziegfeld wore a white suit specially made for him in London. Anna's corsage was composed of a series of enormous white hothouse orchids in a spray of 18 carat diamonds, and as she traveled toward the scene of the contest, she strewed orchids out of the windows. The great Avenue de Longchamps, with its interlacing foliage, formed a tunnel of green above them. The sightseers along the way numbered in the thousands. The tricolors fluttered at every 100 yards of the journey, and the mounted Cuirassiers, vivid in blue and scarlet and gold, rode past on their bays and saluted the young people in their glory. At noon Anna wept when she learned that she had won the Grand Prix de Fleurs, and the crowd shouted "Viva la Held" as Ziegfeld held her in his arms.

In January, 1900, sculptor W.H. Millins cast Anna in solid gold. The statue cost $35,000 to make. It was agonizing to pose for: twice a day she had to stand on a pedestal two feet high with one arm raised without moving. But the results were dazzling, and the statue's showing at the

Paris Exposition of 1900 was a rousing success. By 1901 Anna was rich enough to buy a Welsh castle for $500,000—and never set foot in it. More and more luxurious objects were added to her farm in Maine, and her homes at the Ansonia and the Faubourg. They were wonderful, crazy years, and the Ziegfelds—as they chose to be known—lived them to the hilt.

In 1905 a sudden setback disturbed their happiness. The couple had taken a year off to travel and enjoy each other in areas where publicity was pointless, and privacy was assured.

Their nemesis almost came in Biarritz in June, 1906. In a single afternoon at the Casino Ziegfeld won and lost 2,500,000 francs at baccarat. Unable to pay, he was forced to hand over most of the titles to his property and a sheaf of promissory notes to the casino's proprietor, Alfred Baulant. Five years later Baulant was still seeking restitution in the American courts. Anna was furious, and she narrowly escaped paying off her husband's debts for a second time in her career due to the fact that her marriage had never been official.

After this debacle Ziegfeld was desperate for cash. On March 7, 1907, he received a cable from promoter Lee Shubert in Paris: "HAVE GREAT PLAY SUIT HELD CAN PUT YOU IN REHEARSAL IMMEDIATELY ARE YOU INTERESTED."

Ziegfeld cabled back: "IF FOR CASINO INTERESTED SHOW YOUR CONFIDENCE CABLE ME MUNRO TODAY THOUSAND DOLLARS WILL SAIL SATURDAY IF WE FAIL TO DO BUSINESS YOU PAY TRIP IF WE CONTRACT WE SHARE EXPENSES ANSWER TODAY."

Shubert replied: "WILL CABLE YOU ONE HUNDRED POUNDS FOR SAILING PURPOSES ANSWER."

Ziegfeld's next cable ran: "PERSONAL INTERVIEW

IMPERATIVE MY CABLE STATED ONLY TERMS ON WHICH I WOULD SAIL AT ONCE ANSWER TODAY OR TOO LATE."

Shubert sent the following message: "CASINO OPENS SPRING PLAY MOTOR GIRL GREAT STAR PART SALARY HELD ONE THOUSAND DOLLARS 50 PERCENT PROFIT I MAKE PRODUCTION IF TERMS SATISFACTORY I WILL CABLE MONEY." He sent another cable: "WILL SEND YOU THOUSAND ON CONDITION THAT MADAME HELD SEND CABLE ORIGINAL OF WHICH SHE MUST SIGN STATING THAT IF WE SHOULD BE UNABLE TO AGREE ON A COPARTNERSHIP THAT SHE WILL AGREE THAT HER FIRST TOUR OF THIS COUNTRY IMMEDIATELY AFTER HER RETURN MUST BE IN THEATERS OR OPERA HOUSES BOOKED OR CONTROLLED BY MYSELF."

Ziegfeld sent the necessary agreement, and Anna complied. When they reached New York, having spent most of the money, Ziegfeld's backer, Abe Erlanger, flew into a rage and told Ziegfeld that he had no business to deal with the Shuberts at all, that they were in defiance of Erlanger's theatrical syndicate. Aware of the fact that if he crossed the powerful Erlanger interests, he might jeopardize his career, Ziegfeld renèged on his arrangement with the Shuberts. They never forgave him.

Ziegfeld cast Anna in Harry B. Smith's *The Parisian Model*, in every way a revolutionary show. It was in this production that Ziegfeld for the first time displayed his brilliance in presenting beautiful women in exciting and daring dance routines, and the production shocked many bluenoses of the time. Ziegfeld's regular team worked on it with transcendent skill; Smith's book and lyrics, Max Hoffman's music, and Julian Mitchell's staging were very fine.

Director Julian Mitchell was an interesting personality. He began his theatrical career with Weber and Fields after the onset of deafness ruined his acting career. He had a major success directing Victor Herbert's *The Idol's Eye*, an opera starring Frank Daniels. His *Babes in Toyland* was a masterpiece of vivid ensemble dancing and staging. He never regained his hearing, but by putting his forehead or ear to the piano he was able to measure every dancer's steps to perfection, to calculate precisely the rhythm of a scene.

Everyone who worked with him adored the small, dapper man and his lovely wife, Bessie Clayton. And everyone had stories to tell about his deafness: Hazel Dawn recalled that when a great thunderstorm broke outside a theater where he was working, he said irritably: "Why are you girls shuffling your feet?"

Ziegfeld was fascinated by Mitchell's genius, and he had the wit to give him a free hand. Anna trusted and worshipped him, as did every one of the "Anna Held Girls." The Mitchell/Smith/Held combination was a formidable one, and Ziegfeld brilliantly manipulated and promoted it at all times.

Anna had begun to mature as an artist, and she looked superb in *The Parisian Model*. She changed costumes in every scene and sang two particularly notable songs: a number in which she embraced two human-sized teddy bears and a witty Smith/Hoffman item called "I Can't Make My Eyes Behave," in which her eyes spelled an erotic promise while her body was held in a rigidly resistant stance. The costumes, by Pascaud and other Parisian designers, were ravishing. Anna had a brilliant co-star in young Gertrude Hoffman, who did imitations of Eddie Foy and Anna Held herself; Ziegfeld featured her in an extraordinarily daring dance routine, in which she and 16 other girls lay down and kicked their legs in the air. On their ankles were tied large bells, which chimed with the orchestra, and the girls revolved on a special turntable in a manner that anticipated Busby Berkeley's presentations on the screen. In one "shocking" number Gertrude Hoffman, dressed as a boy with cropped hair, danced the then enormously popular *maxixe* with Anna; in another the stage was converted into a roller skating rink, with the members of the cast whirling on skates and embracing one another in a fashion unusually direct for the time. Most notorious of all, however, was the *Parisian Model* title number itself. The curtain rose on an artist's studio. One by one, walking very slowly, six stately and beautiful girls walked onto the stage wearing cloaks that completely covered them from their necks to the floor. They stood for a moment behind some discreetly placed easels that hid them from the shoulders to the thighs. Suddenly they flung off their cloaks and showed—to the audience's shocked amazement—naked shoulders and legs.

Anna appeared in the simple black gown of a modiste's model; then she stepped behind a screen of chorus girls and slipped off all her clothing except a diaphanous ribbon-trimmed nightgown that revealed a corset and flesh-colored stockings. She sang the first verse of a song, and for each succeeding verse she assumed a different costume. The *New York Telegraph* remarked: "The intermissions, as it were, between the gowns attracted far more attention than did those magnificent creations when they were displayed." In the grand finale the curtain rose on a large salon, with 150 guests superbly dressed against a background of chorus girls arranged in the shape of a silver fan. At the end of the scene golden curtains parted at the back of the stage to reveal Anna in a frame like a living portrait. She stepped out of the frame and sang

"I Can't Make My Eyes Behave" in a reprise. The show was
a triumph, and it ran for 33 weeks in New York.

While *The Parisian Model* was on tour in the fall of
1906, the extraordinary episode of the Anna Held jewelry
theft took place. On this particular tour the famous palace
car was out of commission, being redecorated in a style
appropriate to a new period. Ziegfeld, Anna, and the
entourage rode instead in a lavish Pullman car, and on
the night of Sunday, October 20, they left Baltimore for
Cleveland for the next stage of the tour. They spent most
of Sunday night playing cards, and they retired at about
10:00 P.M.

When the train went into the station at Harrisburg,
Pennsylvania, Anna's satchel, containing jewelry, money,
and other valuables worth $280,000, was placed in an
open compartment. (Anna had copied the habit of traveling with her possessions from her idol, Sarah Bernhardt.
But the "Divine Sarah" had the sense to keep her riches
in a locked iron box; the satchel had only one flimsy lock
that a child could pick.) When the couple awoke the next
morning, the satchel was still there. After dressing they
went out into the corridor to talk to members of the company. They closed the door of the state room when they
went into the sitting room. Just after passing Euclid Station, Cleveland, Anna was horrified to find her satchel
missing. She burst into tears and flung herself on Ziegfeld's shoulder. He was sympathetic but calm. The moment the train entered Cleveland, the station guards con-
tacted the local police. Chief of Police Kohler and representatives of the Pinkerton Detective Bureau came aboard.

Kohler's thought at first was that the theft was a press
agent ruse on Ziegfeld's part. If so, Anna was evidently
not a party to the arrangement; not even a peerless mistress of acting could have matched her red-nosed grief.

She sobbed brokenly to Kohler that her entire earnings of a career were in that satchel—not quite true, since she had substantial bonds and shares in France and an account amounting to well over half a million francs in the Credit Lyonnaise in Paris and the Garfield Bank in New York. Kohler was touched by her distress, but he was not convinced of the authenticity of the theft. In addition to hiring Special Detectives Inspector Rowe and Sergeant Doran to apprehend the thieves, he put on a somewhat stronger squad to uncover possible evidence of fake. He told reporters, "I really am at sea on this proposition. It is no more than natural that we should be suspicious of press agents' diamond robbery tales. This little woman, however, appears to be sincere."

Anna cried uncontrollably at the hotel in Cleveland, and Ziegfeld, who detested displays of feminine emotion, grew increasingly short-tempered with her. Anna said that she would not go on the stage that night at the Opera House, but he pushed her into the spotlight with the back of his hand when she faltered in the wings. She broke down twice in the middle of her songs, but she pulled through. At the first curtain the audience gave her a standing ovation. She appeared on stage without a single jewel, and in a little speech she begged the audience to assist in recovering the gems. The most valuable items, she told them, were a 15-inch corsage piece made of diamonds and emeralds, valued at $25,000, and a string of 63 pearls valued at $35,000. She also lost her $5,000 diamond, sapphire, ruby, and pearl chain, a present from Ziegfeld, with "Forever" inscribed in turquoises.

Acting on behalf of Anna, the Philadelphia lawyer A.S.L. Shields offered a reward for the return of the jewels.

Meanwhile, under further questioning, Ziegfeld and

Anna remembered that just before the train reached
Woodland Station, Cleveland, Ziegfeld was sitting in the
corner of a berth, and the state room door was open. A
large gray-haired man had leaned across Ziegfeld, block-
ing his view of the doorway. A moment later the man got
off with "a small, ferret-looking sort of an individual."
Ziegfeld said he believed that the two men had followed
Anna from Baltimore. He claimed that two of the chorus
girls had noticed the men following Anna.

Throughout Monday night, after the performance, and
all through Tuesday, Anna was in a constant fit of hys-
terics. Ziegfeld dismissed reporters who charged into their
suite asking him point blank if it was all a major stunt.
"It is nonsense," he told the man from the *Cleveland
News*. "We don't have to stoop to such things. Our houses
are full, anyway. Look at Miss Held—that ought to tell
whether it is true or not."

After a brief run the company proceeded to Detroit.
There on October 30 newspapers printed word that after
trailing the thieves over several states the police had
finally run them to earth in Toledo. Anna received the
news as she left the Hotel Cadillac one afternoon. She
ran back into the lobby to tell her friends, one of whom
was sent to Toledo at once to check the news. On October
31 another version of the story appeared in the press: two
men stepped from a Lake Shore train in Painesville, Ohio,
were seen by detectives, and ran—with a black satchel.
They were caught, and the bag was examined. Detective
Hennessey of Detroit was informed of the capture. However, a quick check of Painesville and Toledo resulted in
the discovery that both stories were hoaxes.

On instructions from the Detroit police, Detective Sergeant O'Connor, then on leave in Mount Clemens, Michigan, was recalled to investigate the case. He was chosen
for a very special reason. O'Connor had been detailed six

months before to investigate the robbery of $5,000 worth of jewels from a Mrs. Halsey Corwin, who was now a member of Anna Held's company. There had been some suspicion that Mrs. Corwin had arranged for the theft of the jewels from herself to obtain insurance money.

Anna Held remembered that she had seen the two mysterious men she had seen on the train—the tall gray one and the short foxy one—talking with Mrs. Corwin on the platform before the train left Baltimore. At the Rogues Gallery in Detroit, Anna unhesitatingly picked out pictures of the two men. Meanwhile, Mrs. Corwin vanished and was later arrested in New York. The two men were traced to Chicago and were likewise arrested.

Mrs. Corwin insisted that she knew nothing about the theft except what she had read in the newspapers and that she had yet to act on the stage. When the detectives pressed her further, she changed her version of the story somewhat.

The two men and the extremely nervous actress were questioned constantly. The rest of the story is told in Anna Held's memoirs. One night, she recorded, Ziegfeld came to her and told her that he had received an extraordinary message. He must go to a certain hotel—he promised not to divulge its name—and engage two adjoining rooms. He must wait in one room, placing the reward money on a table in its neighbor. Obeying these instructions to the letter, he placed the reward money in a bag on the table and sat waiting, with a gun on his lap. Suddenly he heard a door open and close. When he got up, some of the less expensive jewels had been returned—but not the money and papers—and the reward was gone.

To the end of her life Anna refused to believe this story. She was convinced that Ziegfeld had engineered the theft himself in order to prop up his failing fortunes. Whether or not the story is true, it marked the beginning of the deterioration of their relationship. Anna never trusted Ziegfeld again. She told her friend Irene Smith that she thought Flo wanted the money to start a new show. Perhaps aware of the problems involved, the press dropped the story with mysterious suddenness early in December; and no one ever went to trial for the crime.

4
The "Follies" and a New Romance

THE *Parisian Model* returned to New York late in 1906 and continued for 179 further performances at the Broadway Theater. All the gay blades in New York whistled Anna's new hit song, "It's Delightful to be Married." Newspapers ran pictures of her eyes trying their best to behave—without success. Behind the scenes Anna was moody and tense, and there were times when she and Ziegfeld barely spoke. The tension was broken slightly in the spring of 1907 when Klaw and Erlanger engaged Ziegfeld—at a meager $200 a week—to stage an experimental show, *Follies of 1907*. The title was suggested by Harry B. Smith, who had run a column in Chicago called "Follies of the Day." The title was contracted from *Ziegfeld Follies of 1907* because Ziegfeld wanted no more than 13 letters in the title: 13 was his lucky number.

As it happened, the idea of a Follies had already occurred to Ziegfeld, in Paris in 1906. At Anna's suggestion he had decided to adopt the current vogue in that city for contemporary skits, dances, songs, and vaudeville turns, all presented in rapid succession with many changes of scene. He remembered the casino in which he first saw Sandow the Great. He knew that the ideal place for such a show was the roof garden of the New York Theater, used chiefly for burlesque shows.

With the aid of several expert designers Ziegfeld converted the roof into a virtual replica of a Parisian café, with large plants and bright awnings. Customers arrived through a vividly striped pavilion and went to their seats between attractive circus-colored canvas screens. Ziegfeld decided to bring the acts on and send them off again at bewildering speed, amid a constant riot of colors. At the climax 64 Anna Held Girls dressed as drummer-boys lined up on the stage, beating snare drums, and marching down a flight of steps into the audience, up the aisle, around the back, and then up on to the stage once more. The cost was $13,000, with $4,000 a week estimated weekly costs, including half that sum to the star, Grace LaRue.

Opening night was extremely hot and uncomfortable, but that scarcely bothered the hardy and enthusiastic audience. Although there was much talk of the *Follies* being a revolutionary production, it was little more than a pleasantly staged vaudeville show with a number of tried-and-true actors and acts and a topical slant. Skillfully but not originally Ziegfeld presented popular figures of the time on the stage in caricature, including composer John Philip Sousa (who attended the opening night and applauded his own image), Theodore Roosevelt (who came later and was equally pleased), and Ziegfeld's former rival, Oscar Hammerstein, then in the first flush of his glory as an opera producer.

The Anna Held Girls splashed in a bathing pool number. The comedy was raucous and broad, and Julian

Mitchell's staging was gaudier and more vulgar than his productions for Anna Held had been. Harry B. Smith's score was as effervescent as always. Yet in every way the show was inferior to the stunning Held creations. It was simply not promising as a new venture, and at first it was not successful. It was only when it went on tour to Washington that it picked up business; when it returned to New York, with the popular harsh-voiced and big-bosomed Nora Bayes as a cast member, it finally achieved some degree of success. Only one single item in its crowded program can be said to have matched the imagination of *The Parisian Model:* Mlle. Dazie's witty and expertly staged parody of *Salome,* Richard Strauss's opera based on the play of Oscar Wilde (the play had created a sensation when it had its American première at the Metropolitan Opera House on January 22, with Olive Fremstad as the star).

Biancha Froelich's "Dance of the Seven Veils" had been an astonishment, and every vaudeville show worth its salt featured a parody of the dance. Ziegfeld's and Julian Mitchell's version was the cleverest of all, based on Aubrey Beardsley's illustrations to Wilde's pages.

During the bathing number on the closing night, when the heat was unusually oppressive, Ziegfeld arrived in the wings dressed in a new broadstripe, a pink shirt, and diamond cufflinks and studs. He was watching the performance with a benevolent smile when comedian Billy Reeves, standing next to him, said, "Come on in to the tank; it might cool you off."

"Not for me," Ziegfeld said. "I had a bath—well, yesterday, anyway." A trio of bathers nearby urged him to plunge in. Before Ziegfeld could protest, Reeves—whose cue to take a high dive into the tank had just been heard—dragged Ziegfeld onto the stage and threw him into the tank. The audience became hysterical with laughter as, in the words of the *New York Telegraph*, "The sorriest spectacle that has ever been permitted on the New York roof" dragged himself from the water.

Julian Mitchell, also on stage, said to the audience, "When he's all wetted up like that, he doesn't look like a human being at all but more like a pickled string bean." Bedraggled, dripping, and miserable, Ziegfeld sat among the chorus girls until the end of the scene. He was the victim of loud wisecracks from the front rows of the audience.

A Ziegfeld show of 1908 was Harry B. Smith's and Maurice Levi's *The Soul Kiss*, presented at the converted New York Theater, retitled *Moulin Rouge*. For this magnificent production Ziegfeld imported Danish ballerina Adeline Genée, who enjoyed immense success in this, her first American role. The story was a characteristic Harry B. Smith confection: Maurice, a young sculptor (W. H. Weldon) is in love with his model, the pretty Suzette (Florence Holbrook), who refuses to kiss him unless he will guarantee to marry her. J. Lucifer Mephisto (R. C. Herz), looking down on New York cynically from a skyscraper, wagers a million dollars against the possession of their souls that Suzette cannot hold on to Maurice without permitting him the kiss. In order to tempt him Mephisto summons up such beauties as Carmen, Marguerite (from Faust), Cleopatra, and a Gibson bathing girl, but Maurice resists them all. Finally, Adeline Genée appears, and her soul kiss makes him her abject slave. Suzette later falls in love with another man, Maurice and the dancer marry, and Mephisto abandons his claim on the couple.

Adeline Genée had four great scenes, received with rapture by the first-night audience: a Parisian New Year's Eve revel, in which she wins the "soul kiss" competition and enchantingly seduces Maurice; a Monte Carlo gambling scene, drawn from Ziegfeld's own memories of the

Monte Carlo casinos; a *pas de deux*, witty and graceful, with comic Sol Skevinsky; and the final hunting ballet, which caused a furor in New York. "Hunt Meadowbrooke" was set in an autumn forest glade; it was so authentically reproduced that, in the rapturous account of one critic, "You can almost scent the red fox streaking by."

Ziegfeld, who loved to have animals on the stage, showed a hunter blowing his horn and a pack of hounds hurtling across the stage followed by red-coated riders on horseback. Suddenly Genée appeared, also on horseback, at a wild gallop; then she dismounted to execute a highly erotic dance in riding boots.

Like the films included in Ziegfeld *Follies* shows just a few years after movies were invented, this incredible spectacle, challenging the screen on its own terms, was years ahead of its time.

Ziegfeld's most important production of 1908 was not the *Follies*—staged on the New York Theater Roof and featuring Nora Bayes and Jack Norworth singing "Shine on Harvest Moon." It was the dazzling *Miss Innocence*, designed as the most splendid showcase for Anna Held to date. Ziegfeld worked constantly to excite advance interest in the show: Miss Held would wear a $25,000 sable coat and a new $30,000 dress on stage. It was to her great advantage that police in several towns insisted on removing from the theater lobbies a six-foot-square photograph of Anna in the studio scene in the second act, showing her partly unclothed and surrounded by a bare-shouldered chorus of girls.

Ziegfeld arranged for the largest electric light sign in American history to be put up in front of the New York Theater: it was 80 feet long and 45 feet high, and it contained 32,000 square feet of glass. The glass and metal weighed 8 tons and required 11 miles of wire; around the huge letters there was a zigzag design representing twin bolts of lightning. Light seemed to explode around the title into cascades of leaping flame. Framing Anna's name, which was twice as big as the title, were 2,300 gas globes. The current employed was more powerful than that used to illuminate the Brooklyn Bridge; it could heat 150 rooms. The concentrated light of the sign could cast a searchlight beam 30 miles.

These statistics, released to the press by Ziegfeld, were widely reprinted. He made sure that in small towns specially hired old men got up in mid-performance and denounced the show as disgusting. The book and lyrics by Harry Smith and the music by Ludwig Englander were charming trifles: a young girl, brought up as a complete innocent, goes to Paris and Vienna and is astounded by the wonders of the world before her. A Montmartre café scene outdid in glamour even the famous evocation of Maxim's in *The Merry Widow*, and the ballet school in Vienna was brilliantly evoked.

Ziegfeld made sure that Anna's dressing room for *Miss Innocence* was the most lavish ever seen in New York. The two rooms, situated on a corner of the Green Room at the theater, were made over into one large boudoir, lined on four walls with red plush and mirrors originally owned by Marie Antoinette. The sofa had once belonged to Mme. de Pompadour. The publicity attendant on Anna's *rentrée* was so overwhelming that the *Philadelphia Telegraph* printed a satirical article:

"Confidential to dramatic editors: Miss Anna Jeld desires the press to know that this year she will do none of the following things:

Lose her diamonds or find anybody else's.
Refuse to live at the Chicago hotel which declines to admit her nine pet hippopotami.
Wear a hooded cobra as a corsage ornament.

Minister nobly unto the dead and dying when she gets into
a train wreck.
Discover that she is descended from Godfrey de Bouillon,
the Crusader.
Drop through a coal hole the nine million dollar emerald
containing on its surface forty engraved verses from the
Koran, given to her by the Buff-Bhaff of Bheet-Itt.
Almost fall from the rear platform of her private car into a
Rocky Mountain gorge 7,000 feet deep."

During first rehearsals for *Miss Innocence* Anna began
to feel unwell. Impatient as ever with weakness, Ziegfeld
had several doctors checking every part of her anatomy
to seek out the cause of her trouble. They did not take
too long to determine that she was pregnant. Ziegfeld was
horrified. This meant that the show on which he had
lavished such immense promotion would not be produced.
He tried out a newcomer, Lillian Lorraine, whom he had
seen in the chorus of a show called *The Tourists*, in the
second lead as a possible replacement, but she was quite
unsuitable to play an innocent abroad. Despite immense
pressure from her, he refused her the role. Unable to
sleep, furious, and desperate, he finally returned to the
Ansonia after walking all night and told Anna point blank
she would have to have an abortion, that nothing must
interfere with the show. She refused to comply and expressed horror that Ziegfeld would destroy the life of his
own child. He told her that *Miss Innocence* was more important than anything else, including their happiness.
They quarreled for hours, and the battle ended with
Ziegfeld finally walking out slamming the door. He returned a few hours later with a seedy-looking doctor who
smelled of alcohol. Anna was disgusted by the man. A new
and more serious argument erupted between all three. At
its height Anna suddenly collapsed. She was vaguely

aware that Ziegfeld and the doctor were carrying her to
the table of the private dining room. Chloroform fumes
enveloped her. When she came to, she was told that her
infant son had "left the world." She became hysterical.
Ziegfeld kissed her, but she thrust him furiously from her.
She recorded in her memoirs that if she had had any re-
spect or love left for him, it deserted her at that moment.

But she did not desert Ziegfeld. She willed herself into
fittings and the two grueling weeks of rehearsals. The
opening was a sensation, unquestionably her greatest triumph to that time. But backstage the tension—with Lillian Lorraine in the adjoining dressing room and Ziegfeld
ignoring Anna in favor of Miss Lorraine—was lethal.

One afternoon during the run Anna and Lillian were
rehearsing a new song when the bunting above the huge
electric sign on the theater's facade caught fire. Faulty in-
sulation caused a blaze among the decorations, and the
flames mounted past the windows of the roof garden.
Noticing smoke come up from the Broadway side of the
theater, Anna leaned out of the window, snatched a section of bunting, tore it from the wall, and pulled it in so
that the flames would not mount any higher. Then she
waited calmly with the rest of the cast until the fire
wagons arrived. Ziegfeld made the most of the incident,
of course, and further excitements were caused during
the run of the play. A plant—a handsome young man—
flung his coat at Anna's feet during a second-act reprise;
this won some headlines, as did the appearance of Anna
at Morris Park to break a bottle of Le Comte Vernon over
the bow of a brand new airship—which refused to leave
the ground. The following night her own airship, the one
she rode on the stage with Leo Mars, ran into problems.
It jammed and hung over the Paris rooftops, threatening
to throw her out at any moment.

In the scene Anna and Mars took their seats in the model, especially built by the stage carpenter. The propellors whirled, and the contraption slowly took to the air. Suddenly the airship stalled and hung from its wires, and the propellors slowed to a halt. Anna became hysterical, and the curtain was rung down to applause and laughter. Under the zealous command of Ziegfeld and Julian Mitchell Anna was gradually led to safety on the stage by a series of ladders.

At the conclusion of the run Abe Erlanger and his partner, Marc Klaw, presented Anna with a magnificent gold cup to commemorate the record season of the play. Whitney Warren threw a huge party to celebrate the occasion. A few days later Anna Held presided over the official opening of the City Theater, turned down an offer of $5,000 to make her eyes behave for the motion picture cameras of the Arnold Film Company, and sailed for Europe on the *Kronprinzessen Cecile*, leaving Ziegfeld, as she bitterly told Irene Smith, "to heaven and Lillian Lorraine."

5

Lillian

LILLIAN Lorraine was in every way an extraordinary personality. Dark and extremely beautiful, she had been born Eulallean de Jacques, of French and Irish parentage, in San Francisco in 1890. She frequently used her mother's maiden name, Mary Ann Brennan. Her first performance was in *Uncle Tom's Cabin* at the age of four. At thirteen she had her first affair with a man, who had paid her father for the privilege of sleeping with her. She grew up to be a willful, sad, beautiful, promiscuous, and extremely voluptuous young woman with a heart-stopping smile, large eyes, and a figure that until the late 1920s was flawless.

Ziegfeld was fascinated by Lillian. The strange girl's lack of breeding intoxicated him. Their affair, conducted openly, was passionate and desperate. Ziegfeld installed her in a suite on the thirteenth floor of the Ansonia in an exact copy of his and Anna Held's suite on the tenth, and he appeared with her publicly at Rector's, Louis Martin's, and Luchow's almost constantly.

Anna returned from Europe in August, 1908. Her
friends, led by Irene Smith, told her that the affair between Flo and Lillian had intensified. She was desolate.
As if the situation were not bad enough, it was worsened
by the fact that Lillian Lorraine was constantly in the
headlines. In 1909 it was discovered, to Anna's horror and
Ziegfeld's fury, that Lillian was involved in an unsavory
affair with her chauffeur, Charles Brockway. One night
in mid-August, she was dancing with Ziegfeld at Rector's
when Boots Durrell, a well-known man-about-town, cut
in and offered to teach her some new steps. He danced her
away and told her that she must return home at once or
Brockway might go to jail. She picked up her wrap, and
Durrell's chauffeur drove her back to her apartment.
There she was met by three men, one of them a private
detective, who told her that unless she could raise $3,000,
her lover would be jailed immediately over a bad debt.

After a policeman arrived and showed her a warrant,
she handed over a $3,000 diamond necklace. The men
pawned it and disappeared. She never saw Brockway
again. She ultimately decided that the entire episode had
been a masquerade to force her to dispose of her jewelry.
The policeman and the warrant turned out to be fakes.
She charged Brockway with theft, and the police finally
traced him to a West 45th Street rooming house, where
he was practicing as a clairvoyant. He was arrested, and
he served a term in the Tombs Prison.

Ziegfeld was so infatuated that he forgave Lillian this
awkward episode. In fact, his forgiveness was so complete
that he presented her in the *Follies of 1909*. Lillian continued to infuriate Ziegfeld with her lack of punctuality at
rehearsals, her stupidity, and her heavy drinking, but an
hour in the boudoir dispelled his anger. He spent a fortune on her, receiving in return not the blind and naive
devotion of Anna but a ruthless temper, constant an-

nouncements of other liaisons, and demands for jewelry and money.

The presentation of the 1909 *Follies* caused Ziegfeld other heartaches. He was faced with the collision of two great stars: Sophie Tucker and Nora Bayes.

Sophie Tucker had appeared in the traveling *Gay Masqueraders* show. Marc Klaw had seen her in Holyoke, Massachusetts, and had hired her on the strength of a brilliant blackface number. Ziegfeld was annoyed that Klaw had hired her without consulting him, and when Sophie Tucker appeared, big, ungainly, and awkward at the age of 24, at rehearsals in the New York Theater, he snubbed her. He greeted her with cool politeness and left her to sit in the wings for eight weeks to watch the rehearsals. Just before the June 17 opening in Atlantic City Ziegfeld walked past her onto the stage with a pile of clippings dealing with Teddy Roosevelt's recent return from an African hunting expedition, including a cartoon of the animals climbing up a tree because they knew Roosevelt was coming. He demanded, over the protests of Harry B. Smith, that a new song cashing in on the current news should be added. When Smith insisted that there was no one to sing it, Ziegfeld pointed to Sophie Tucker. "Here's a singer," he said to Smith and his partner Maurice Levi. "Go on, boys, get busy. Write the song. Teach it to her. Mitchell will stage it."

The next day Smith and Levi—who had been working all night—came up with "It's Moving Day Down in Jungle Town," a witty number in which animals climbed up trees in terror, and natives fled as the intrepid Teddy arrived. Sophie had to be a leopard, and even Ziegfeld broke up when he saw her in the costume, flouncing miserably out of her dressing room to rehearse the movements with Julian Mitchell.

Sophie Tucker was the smash hit of the *Follies* when it

opened in Atlantic City. She received a standing ovation and had to repeat every one of her songs three times. Diamond Jim Brady, Lillian Russell, Charles Dillingham, and Irving Berlin led the applause.

Ziegfeld was delighted. He was on his way to Sophie's dressing room to congratulate her when a furious Nora Bayes intercepted him and told him that he must remove the newcomer from the show at once. "Either she's out, or I go!" she said as she slammed her dressing room door. Ziegfeld immediately called Abe Erlanger and Julian Mitchell, and the men held an urgent consultation outside Nora Bayes's door. They decided they dared not lose their star, their major drawcard. At rehearsal the next morning Ziegfeld announced from the stage that Sophie would do only the jungle song. Sophie burst into tears. Later Nora Bayes had her removed from the show entirely.

Opening night of the *Follies of 1909*, on the New York Theater roof, was one of the hottest in living memory. After almost 16 hours of nonstop rehearsal (those were preunion days) the cast was exhausted, but Ziegfeld and Mitchell drove them on. First night boasted not only Ziegfeld's galaxy of famous friends but also Teddy Roosevelt, who came to applaud his own image on the stage.

One evening after the show, at the Apollo Theater, Charles Alexander, a Pittsburgh millionaire, turned up at a party with various chorus girls at Young's Hotel. Showing them a scar on his left wrist, he said that Ziegfeld had fired at him with a revolver and that the scar was the trophy. "He was jealous of my love for Anna Held," Alexander said. Ziegfeld heard about the incident and flew into a terrible rage. Unable to find Alexander at the Hotel Shelbourne or at any of his other haunts, he finally ran him to earth after a matinee of the *Follies* at the Apollo Theater. In front of the audience, which was filing out, he struck Alexander in both eyes and on the chin, threw him to the ground, and kicked him. Bystanders had to drag Ziegfeld away from the bleeding man.

The newly reconstructed show opened on the Court of Venus with Annabelle Whitford as the goddess, Edna Chase as Psyche, and beautiful Mae Murray as Cupid. Marlon Whitney, possessor of the most flawless physique on Broadway, played Apollo. The scene changed to the Manhattan Opera House, where Oscar Hammerstein was shown involved in a quarrel with his associates. Nora Bayes emerged from the wings as La Tosca, the very picture of a high-powered prima donna, and sang "Mad House Opera" with hysterical emphasis. Dragging an immense gold chatelaine and dressed in a billowing dress, which got stuck in the door, she was a triumph. Lillian Lorraine was at her most beautiful, though even the most scrupulous instruction had failed to do anything with her voice. Supremely attractive as an exact replica of Maxfield Parrish's famous *Life* magazine cover girl, she sang "Nothing But a Bubble" in a whirling dance of soap. Forty-eight girls wearing battleship headdresses appeared as the states of the union. In an effect brilliantly achieved by Julian Mitchell and Herbert Gresham the girls pressed lights attached to their costumes, bobbed behind a screen, and suddenly a cheering audience saw 48 illuminated battleships riding on the blue waves of New York Harbor. As a group of Anna Held Girls dressed as planes sang "Up, Up, Up, in My Aeroplane," Lillian emerged from the ceiling of the theater in a Wright Brothers model and circled as she scattered American Beauty roses to the audience below. In the final scenes the Polo Grounds were on display, with Lillian on an actual prize pony; at the end of the show the cast played ball with the audience, tossing into its midst 500 multicolored balls.

In 1910 Ziegfeld busied himself with a new and more

elaborate *Follies* than ever before. Aware that public taste was growing more sophisticated and that there was a growing need for strong comedy, he began looking for stars to back up Lillian, of whose limitations, despite the extreme intensity of their romance, he was becoming more and more painfully aware.

In the spring of 1910 Ziegfeld discovered two of his greatest stars, Fanny Brice and Bert Williams. Fanny was an obscure Jewish comedian, appearing in a burlesque show called *The College Girls*, in which she sang "Sadie Salome," a number composed for her by Irving Berlin. The song crystalized the essence of her early New York days. She wrote in *Colliers* (February, 1936), "[The song summed up] Loscha of the Coney Island popcorn counter, and Marta of the cheeses at Brodsky's Delicatessen and the Sadies and the Rachels and the Birdies with the turn-over heels at the Second Avenue dance halls."

Despite her awkward program position, between the famous Lew Fields and Raymond Hitchcock, she created an immediate sensation in the song, and the audience began applauding the moment she started to roll her eyes. As she sang, she stood like a slender, grotesque crane. Later, when she played the scene with an additional range of crazy, funny gestures, Klaw, Erlanger, and Ziegfeld decided that she must be engaged at once. Ziegfeld saw her at his office and said: "There may be a spot for you in the Follies. How much do you want?"

She gulped and replied, "Forty dollars."

Ziegfeld walked to the window, frowning. "Forty dollars?" "Well, maybe less if you—" He stopped her with a raised hand. "We'll make it seventy-five, and you'll get a year's work."

Grabbing the contract from his hand, Fanny signed it. Without waiting to thank him she ran out into the street. He heard later from Irving Berlin that she flourished it in the face of everyone she met on the way up Broadway, whirled it around Times Square, and thrust it into Berlin's astonished face.

Ziegfeld handed her a new song—"Lovie Joe." Ziegfeld was fascinated by her dedication as she rehearsed it over and over again in the corner of the stage. But one important person did not like the song, and as a result it was nearly dropped from the show. Abe Erlanger considered the song ridiculous and Fanny's interpretation and phrasing, atrocious. At the first Atlantic City rehearsal he told her so. According to her memoirs in *Colliers*, she walked, fighting mad, to the footlights and shouted at the little man, "I live on 128th Street. It's on the edge of Harlem. They all talk that way!"

Erlanger screamed out of the darkness: "Replace it! You're out! No one says 'no' to me on stage!" She returned to her boarding house in a fury. Ziegfeld sent a message that he wanted to see her, and she returned to the theater. He said that he had persuaded Erlanger to admit the song for Atlantic City but that it would be dropped for New York. She was desperate, and she decided to perpetrate a ruse. Instead of the dress Ziegfeld had had designed for her, with the aid of Lillian Lorraine's maid she managed to acquire one several sizes too small. While she sang the song, she wriggled to and fro in blackface, trying to make the clinging sheath accommodate her ungainly figure. At the end she drew the skirt up and struck a knock-kneed pose. She gazed, horrified, at her legs and stalked off the stage with one hand shielding her eyes from the horrible sight. The applause was overwhelming, and she took eight encores. When she finally walked off the stage, Erlanger was in the wings, his straw hat clenched in his hand. As he handed it to her, she saw the rim was broken. "See, I broke this applauding you," he said. She always kept that hat.

The other great star whom Ziegfeld developed in the *Follies of 1910* was Bert Williams, a black comedian. Tall, handsome, and well built, he was a courtly gentleman. Ina Claire, who appeared with him in the Follies five years later, still remembers his enchanting behavior, how he bowed to kiss her hand whenever he greeted her and talked with great warmth and kindness of his good friends in the South when she asked him if he was afraid to tour there.

Williams was, according to his extant recordings, a genius of comedy and popular song, with a lowdown, mournful voice, which expressed all the suffering of his race. He was far and away the greatest black comedian of his generation. He specialized in lazy, slovenly, tired talk, playing the kind of people who, in his own words, "If they get served soup, always have a fork and not a spoon in sight."

He learned his material by eavesdropping on conversation all over the country, incorporating scenes from real life in his sketches. Ann Charters described him to perfection in *Nobody*, her biography of him:

> Usually his appearance onstage was announced by a spotlight that caught the tentative wiggling of gloved hands against the closed plush curtains. Hesitantly the hand followed the fingers, then an arm, a shoulder, and finally, with awkward reluctance, a tall man in a shabby dress suit pushed through the curtains and walked slowly to the front of the stage. The applause started before he reached the footlights, but the face behind the mask of blackface remained constant. As if resigned to some inevitable and unending stroke of bad fortune, he shrugged his shoulders. . . . He began to sing. . . .

Williams's origins are obscure. He was born in either Riverside, California, or Nassau, in the Bahamas, on either

March 11, 1875, or November 12, 1874. He had years of struggle, with a comedy partner, George Walker. It is possible that Ziegfeld saw them when they were playing on the Chicago Midway in 1893. They built up a steady reputation in the music halls, and they often ran into Ziegfeld and his set at Marshall's Restaurant or at Rector's at the turn of the century. Walker died of paresis, the last stage of syphilis, in 1908. After the death of his partner Williams appeared in a show called *Banana Land* on his own, and he was a great success. Later he played *Mr. Load of Koal*, with equal triumph.

In the spring of 1910 Ziegfeld learned that David Belasco was negotiating for Williams's services in order to break theatrical tradition (Williams would star in an otherwise all-white show). Not to be outdone, Ziegfeld outbid Belasco and signed Williams to a long-term contract. The comedian's style appealed to him enormously, and when members of the company threatened to go on strike in Atlantic City because a black man had joined the cast, Ziegfeld browbeat them into submission or fired them from the show.

In addition to the introduction of Fanny Brice and Bert Williams, Ziegfeld also saw to it that the *Follies of 1910* created a sensation by including both Anna Held and Lillian Lorraine in the cast. Back from Europe, Anna went into a second tour of *Miss Innocence* with Lillian repeating her original role; then they proceeded to rehearse the *Follies*. By then Anna was resigned to having "lost" Ziegfeld, but somewhat masochistically she insisted on working for him, even with her chief rival.

Follies of 1910 was probably the most extraordinary variety show seen up to that time in America. It began with a view of the Manhattan skyline and a replica of the New York Theater itself. A rehearsal was shown in progress, with Harry Watson playing Julian Mitchell and

George Bickel portraying the temperamental composer Maurice Levi. Harry B. Smith made much playful fun of the techniques of presenting the *Follies*. In a later scene Anna was seen (an effect 25 years ahead of its time) in a film as a comet, with her smiling face emerging from a backdrop of stars. Suddenly she burst through the screen, mounted on a silver rocket, flew earthward, kissed Earth (Harry Edwards), and sailed back again.

Against a backdrop of the Killarney Lakes, Lillian Lorraine rode into the audience and back onto the stage mounted on an Irish pony, singing "Sweet Kitty Bellair" in shamrock green. The song was a parody of Henrietta Crossman's appearance in the Belasco production of the same name.

In the second act Julian Mitchell himself made a surprise appearance. While the show was in Atlantic City, Ziegfeld had decided to improvise a parody of Theda Bara's "vamp" picture, *A Fool There Was*, for Louise Alexander. He disliked the vampire dance that Mitchell created, and during the subsequent row Louise Alexander's dancing partner walked out of the show. Unable to find a replacement at the last minute in New York, Mitchell simply went on the stage in street clothes himself and danced with Louise, who was dressed in a spider costume. It created an immense sensation. Lillian and the Anna Held Girls, with bells attached to their toes, swung over the audience on swings, and the final scene was a rousing recreation of a West Point parade with all of the girls in uniform.

Throughout the run of the *Follies of 1910*, Lillian Lorraine was a constant worry to Ziegfeld. He never knew whom she would be sleeping with next. Her drunken scenes, tantrums, demands for money, and sudden nervous collapses were constant. On May 26, 1911, only a few weeks before the 1911 *Follies*, something happened that aggravated him beyond endurance. He picked up the morning papers at the Ansonia, dropped them on the floor, and took the next train to Denver, Colorado. There Tony van Pühl, the well-known St. Louis aeronaut, had fought in a bar of the Brown Palace Hotel with Frank Harwood, of the New York Harwoods. Harwood shot van Pühl dead. The subject of the quarrel was Lillian, whom Harwood had been visiting in New York. It seemed that both men had been enjoying Lillian's favors for several weeks.

In Denver, Ziegfeld constantly badgered Lillian with demands for the particulars of what had been going on, but she refused to reply. He was still sufficiently in love with her to forgive her, and he summoned her to Atlantic City to rehearse her scenes with the new Australian discovery, rubber-legged comedian Leon Errol.

While the 1911 *Follies* were being tried out in Atlantic City, Lillian became attracted to Fred Gresheimer, the wastrel son of a rich family. Tall, handsome, and built like Apollo, he captivated her completely, and she fled the *Follies* the day after she met him. Ziegfeld was beside himself. It was obvious that the girl was worthless, but he was insane about her. When she told him by telephone from New York that she had left the show, he told her that if she did not return at once, he would ruin her career, blackball her with every management in the country. She replied that she would join the Shuberts, his archrivals. He slammed the phone receiver down. Disillusioned by her first night with Gresheimer, and terrified of losing her career, Lillian returned to the company the next day.

Only one day later she married Gresheimer and eloped to New York. Ziegfeld heard the news in Atlantic City.

Fanny Brice was standing beside him in the wings when the call came through, and she knew what was being said. She did not dare mention that she had met Gresheimer herself in Chicago and succumbed to his charm, that she had shown Lillian love letters from Gresheimer and his picture in a swimming costume. Ziegfeld burst into tears. "She married someone!" he said. He walked away without another word.

As Flo was writing Lillian out of the show, she arrived one afternoon, dressed superbly and looking her best, and told him that she was ready to resume her work. "Are you divorced?" he asked her. "No," she told him. "But you and I are through."

Ziegfeld was in agony when the show opened, at the New York Theater. He refused to laugh at anyone's jokes, and he brooded alone for hours. He snapped at everyone except Fanny, who was constantly accused by Lillian of continuing to see Gresheimer. Matters reached a head one night when Fanny was preparing for a scene entitled "The Texas Tommy Swing," in which she alternated the lyrics with Vera Maxwell. She was dressed in a billowing hooped skirt, which caught in a chair, knocking the chair over and wrecking Lillian's entrance. Backstage Lillian screamed at her and began pulling her hair. The two women beat each other with their fists, fell on the ground, and stripped off each other's clothes. The company gathered to watch, and the audience, hearing the screams, tried to peer into the wings. Meanwhile, the actors waiting for Lillian's appearance on stage froze in embarrassment. Finally Fanny marched onto the stage, cave-woman style, dragging Lillian behind her by the hair. It brought the house down.

Even after her marriage Ziegfeld was prepared to endure Lillian's behavior in order to keep her in the *Follies*.

Florenz Ziegfeld, Jr., master showman. *Collection of the Public Library of the City of New York.*

Austere and dignified "Dr." Ziegfeld, Flo's father, in 1882.

Ziegfeld's paternal grandfather. This photograph was taken in Oldenbourg, Germany, in 1921.

The Ziegfeld siblings in Chicago in 1881: Flo (standing), Carl, William, and Louise (seated left to right).

The Ziegfeld family home, 1448 West Adams Street, Chicago. Photo was taken in 1971, just before the building was torn down.

Sandow, acclaimed as "The Perfect Man" and "The Modern Hercules," received star billing at the Trocadero in 1893. *Chicago Historical Society.*

Ziegfeld with The Great Sandow and company, 1892. *Hoblitzelle Theatre Arts Library, University of Texas.*

PROGRAMME

TROCADERO . .

MICHIGAN AVENUE AND MONROE STREET.

COMING AUGUST 1ST, — SANDOW

Unprecedented Sensation of this Century.

The Modern Hercules. —

LOOK FOR SPECIAL NOTICE.

Anna Held at her piano in the Hotel Ansonia. A native of France, the Polish-French actress was an amazing popular success in New York. *Collection of the Public Library of the City of New York.*

Anna in *The Parisian Model.* During the 1906 tour of the play the famous jewelry theft, considered a publicity hoax by many, took place.

Anna Held's name was rarely out of the papers. One of the most newsworthy items was her habit of taking milk baths.

Collection of the Public Library of the City of New York.

Robert Baral Collection, property of Charles Higham.

In 1908 Lillian Lorraine replaced Anna Held in Flo Ziegfeld's affections. Flo presented Lillian to the public in the *Follies of 1909*. The photograph at right is taken from a miniature painting. *Goldie Clough Collection.*

Flo and Lillian Lorraine. *Hoblitzelle Theatre Arts Library, University of Texas.*

A typically daring publicity photo. Pictured here is Hazel Forbes. *Alfred Cheney Johnston.*

The Dolly Twins, later known as the Dolly Sisters, captivated the theatergoing public with their dance duets. *Alfred Cheney Johnston.*

The *Follies of 1908* featured Nora Baye pictured below, and Jack Norworth singin "Shine On, Harvest Moon."

Stage director Ned Wayburn and the *Follies* girls. *Hoblitzelle Theatre Arts Library, University of Texas.*

Follies girls in front of the Hotel Astor in 1907. *Hoblitzelle Theatre Arts Library, University of Texas.*

Ziegfeld insisted that neither money nor effort would be spared in designing costumes for his showgirls. Top left is Gertrude Selden, and top right is Evelyn Law. Bottom left to right: Jessie Reed, Marie Shelton, and glowworm Marjorie Chapin. *Robert Baral Collection, property of Charles Higham.*

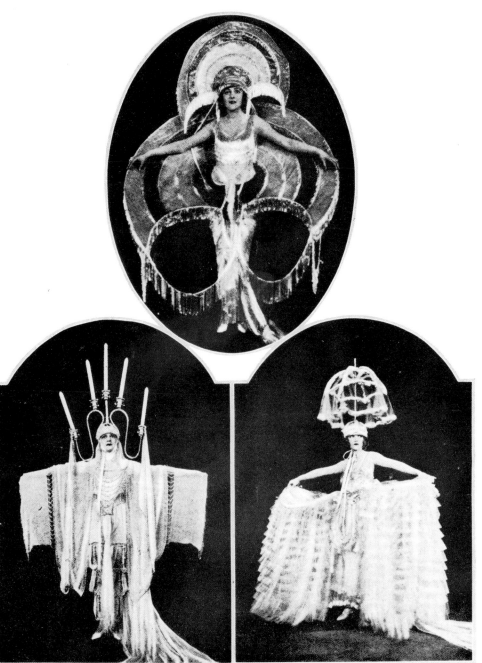

Ziegfeld's *Midnight Frolics*, no less elaborate than the *Follies*, presented such stars as Billie Dane (top, as the Northern Lights), Martha Pierre (left, as Candlelight), and Avonne Taylor (as Twilight).

Timely cheesecake photo of Drucilla Strain. *Alfred Cheney Johnston.*

Katherine Burke, wearing a skimpy but elaborate *Follies* costume. *Alfred Cheney Johnston.*

Flo Ziegfeld (in fur coat) flanked by performers in his 1928 company.

Showgirl Imogene Wilson. Imogene's affair with Frank Tinney made show business headlines. *Hoblitzelle Theatre Arts Library, University of Texas.*

The Ziegfeld girls did not always wear feathers and jewels. Avonne Taylor appears in conservative attire. *Edward Thayer-Monroe.*

The flamboyant and dramatic Dolores, dressed in her celebrated peacock costume. *Alfred Cheney Johnston.*

Actress Billie Burke, Ziegfeld's wife, in 1918. *Robert Baral Collection, property of Charles Higham.*

Beautiful Marilyn Miller in *Rosalie.*

Kay Laurell as La Patrie in the *Midnight Frolics.*

In the *Midnight Frolics* the showgirls (left) masqueraded as movie idols of the day: Charlie Chaplin, John Barrymore, Harold Lloyd, William S. Hart, Douglas Fairbanks, and Larry Semon. Unmasked (above) the girls are: Nina Whitmore, Edna Wheaton, Marjorie Chapin, Betty Williams, Helen Worthing, and Irene Marcellus.

The ballet scene from Anna Held's extravaganza, *Miss Innocence*, at the New York Theater.

Sybil Carmen in the *Midnight Frolics*.

Joseph Urban's genius for design combined perfectly with Ziegfeld's taste and superb color sense. At left are pictured some of the striking stage sets designed by Urban for the *Follies of 1915. Robert Baral Collection, property of Charles Higham.*

A portrayal of "an old-time showgirl."

The song-writing team of Gene Buck and Dave Stamper began collaborating on the *Follies* in 1913 and wrote for all editions through 1931.

Bert Williams, a popular comedian, was introduced in the *Follies of 1910*.

Jack Donahue (left), Marilyn Miller, and Florenz Ziegfeld. *Hoblitzelle Theatre Arts Library, University of Texas.*

He continued to spend nearly every night with her. But Abe Erlanger, who had always hated her, was adamant: unless she behaved perfectly, she would be dismissed from the *Follies*. Ziegfeld had no alternative but to concur.

The crisis came during a run-through of some new songs late one afternoon. Erlanger was sitting in the second row, dressed in his traditional straw hat. Behind him were a 26-year-old composer, Gene Buck, who had started the vogue for illustrated song covers with his brilliant art nouveau designs, and Dave Stamper, his collaborator. They had written a new song for Lillian, "Daddy Has a Sweetheart" ("and mother is her name"). When the time came for her to go on stage to try it out, she did not appear. "Where's Lorraine?" Erlanger snapped at Julian Mitchell. "She's in her dressing room, I think," Mitchell replied. "Tell her she's through. And the song as well," Erlanger shouted. And he walked out.

It was just the excuse that Erlanger had been waiting for. Ziegfeld begged him to reconsider, but it was futile. Buck took the song to Oscar Hammerstein, who had an immediate hit with it—and Lillian. Soon after that Ziegfeld hired Buck as his chief composer for the *Follies*, a decision that he did not regret.

In the winter of 1911–1912 Ziegfeld and Anna Held visited a Sunday night concert at the Columbia Theater, where they saw a marvelous singer and comedian, 17-year-old Mae West. He and Anna went out during the intermission and bought armfuls of roses and orchids, which they flung onto the stage at Mae West's feet when she made her *rentrée*. To this day Mae remembers her intense pleasure at their homage. Ziegfeld called Mae to his office at the theater and asked her if she would like to appear in the *Follies*; she astonished him, she recalls, by saying that the theater was not "intimate" enough for her. After appearing in several Shubert shows she relented, however, and she appeared as La Petite Daffy, a baby vamp, in *A Winsome Widow*.

A Winsome Widow, based on *A Trip to Chinatown*, by Charles Hoyt, with music by Raymond Hubbell, was produced by Ziegfeld at the New York Theater on April 11, 1912. Julian Mitchell's staging was magical, with the ice skating scene a special highlight: under a hundred multicolored globes and against huge black and lavender windows the show girls spun around the stage, revolving slowly on ice skates until day changed to night and the entire theater, not just the proscenium, was bathed in artificial moonlight from a dozen spots. The skaters finally came spinning out into the audience.

The Dolly Twins (later known as the Dolly Sisters) were marvelous in dance duets, while Mlle. Nana and M. Alexis, in silver and metal clothes, spun like human pinwheels. It was in every way a marvelous show, and Mae West was its most tremendous attraction. "She assaults the welkin vigorously," wrote the critic from the New York *Dramatic Mirror*.

Anna sued Ziegfeld for divorce in 1912 at the end of a long, almost two-year return tour of *Miss Innocence*. At first she denied the reports of the divorce. She sent a wire from Seattle to the *New York Morning Telegram* denying the rumors. Finally Ziegfeld's attorney, Leon Laski, made the necessary arrangements. It was officially given out to the press that the couple had been married in "1897 in Paris."

Announcing yet another retirement, Anna sailed for Paris on the French steamship *La Savoie* in the summer. She returned in August, and on August 28 she appeared with Ziegfeld before a special referee, Edward G. Whittaker, to testify that they had agreed to live together as husband and wife. The referee found that the marriage was legal in common law. Misconduct required to be proven between two women was defined at the Ansonia Hotel on April 1, 1910, with "Mary Ann Brennan" and on April 2, 1909, on a railroad train in Nevada with a woman identified as "D. E. Jacques." Both women were, of course, Lillian Lorraine. Anna made no application for alimony.

During the next few months there was constant talk of a reconciliation, but it never materialized. Ziegfeld told the *New York Journal* on December 27, 1912: "Our remarriage is not improbable. I received an affectionate Christmas greeting from Anna, as did my father. I have learned to appreciate her now; there is no one like her. I am going abroad in a few weeks; chiefly to see Miss Held about our remarriage, which I trust will take place in the spring."

Anna replied by cable to the newspaper's request for a comment: "IF HE DOES NOT WISH TO MAKE ME HIS WIFE FOR LOVE PERHAPS HE IS ACTIVATED BY BUSINESS MOTIVES."

Meanwhile, Lillian's marriage to Frederick Gresheimer had proved to be a disaster. During a quarrel early in 1912 he wrenched the rings from her hands, seized her boxes of jewels, and disappeared. For some months he had been utterly dependent on her, and he confessed that he had lost every cent of the Pittsburgh fortune he had inherited. Ziegfeld immediately summoned the police. Frederick Gresheimer fled to Atlantic City, where he pawned some of the jewels, for $2,200; then he left for Montreal. He returned to America, turning up at various times in Detroit, Chicago, and Boston. Lillian moved back into her old suite on the thirteenth floor of the Ansonia, which Ziegfeld had never relinquished. He also saw Anna constantly, though she told him quite firmly that their marriage was over.

One summer evening in 1912, when Ziegfeld was dining with Lillian in the white and gold dining room at Louis Martin's, an argument was heard at the door. Disheveled, wearing a battered tophat and carrying a silver-topped cane, Gresheimer strode in and threw several waiters outside. Several diners abandoned all delicacy and stood up to have a look. White with anger, Ziegfeld half rose to his feet. Gresheimer struck him across the side of the head with the cane and sent him crashing across the table.

"Oh, Freddie, don't, *don't!*" Lillian screamed. Louis Martin came to the table, and Gresheimer knocked him to the floor with a single blow of his fist. Before anybody could stop him, Gresheimer dragged Ziegfeld into the back alley and began to beat him to death.

Gresheimer would have killed him if police had not arrived in time. Gresheimer ran back into the restaurant, seized Lillian, and escaped in a Rolls Royce to a small house on Long Island, where he kept her prisoner for several days. Ziegfeld, bleeding and covered with bruises, crawled into Martin's and feebly sipped brandy. When he got back to the Ansonia, he called William Pinkerton and had a private meeting with several senior police officials. After a week's search the police found Gresheimer. He was arrested and, after a brief trial, sentenced to five years' imprisonment.

Anna's divorce decree was declared absolute in January, 1913. Shortly after that she was almost killed in a car accident in the south of France. On February 27, 1913, she was driving with a friend, H. Keene Hargreaves, along the French Riviera on her way to Cape Martin. The brakes failed, and the emergency brake snapped. The car crashed down a long slope toward the sea.

The chauffeur managed to swerve into a tree, which blocked the fall, but the car was almost overturned in the process. Anna, Hargreaves, and the chauffeur managed to crawl back to the road. Anna had to throw off her $20,000 sable coat to make the ascent, and it fell into the sea. She hailed a passing car, which turned out to be driven by the Chief of Police of Monte Carlo. He told her jokingly, "I thought you were stopping me for furious driving." Laughing uproariously at the mishap, they all drove back into Monte Carlo.

6
Billie

Jack Rumsey's Sixty Club, downstairs from the Ballroom of the Astor, was restricted to theater people. During big parties there it was customary for stars to make a grand entrance down the staircase on the arm of somebody equally famous. New Year's Eve, 1913–1914, was, as usual, a gala fancy dress occasion, and Ziegfeld arrived wearing a clown's outfit with a bulbous nose and baggy pants kept up by a pair of suspenders. Lillian, dressed as a shepherdess, went with him. Anna was also at the party, accompanied by Harry and Irene Smith, Diamond Jim Brady, and Lillian Russell. Anna was dressed as the Empress Josephine, with an attentive French count as Napoleon. Among the Shuberts' large party was Marilyn Miller, young, blonde, and exquisite. Ethel Barrymore and Laurette Taylor also were there.

Just before midnight Ziegfeld and Lillian had a violent quarrel in front of the guests, and she stormed out. A moment after he spoke harshly to her, he regretted it. He changed into the evening suit laid out for him by his valet, who had accompanied him to the ball. The costume had begun to vex him, and all he could think about was telephoning Lillian and asking her to see reason.

He was unable to reach her. Since several of her friends were having big parties, he knew it would be impossible to get her for the rest of the night. At the suggestion of Jack Rumsey, he walked back onto the dance floor and halfheartedly joined in the Paul Jones. One girl who danced back to him again and again at the sound of the Paul Jones whistle was the lovely and celebrated Frohman star, Billie Burke, whom he had noticed on her arrival. He swept her out of the line, up the stairs, and onto the landing, where they talked until dawn.

Billie was the contrast to Lillian that Ziegfeld needed at that particular moment. She was not spoiled, anguished, and neurotic; she was bright, witty, charmingly and entertainingly talkative. Clearly she had good connections— after all, Somerset Maugham was her escort that night. She had made her reputation first in England, achieving a great triumph in *Mrs. Ponderberry's Past*. Charles Frohman had engaged her at $500 a week to play in *My Wife*, with John Drew. *My Wife* was a triumph, and under Frohman's careful guidance Billie Burke had gone on to great success in *Love Watches*, Maugham's *Mrs. Dot*, and Pinero's *The Mind-the-Paint Girl*, among other plays. Her sparkling comedy style was an expression of her brilliant, sunny personality. Ziegfeld had seen her on the stage, and she had not impressed him deeply (he thought her "piano" legs appalling), but at that black moment in his life she seemed to be just the tonic he needed.

He did not neglect to note that she had money, social position, and a splendid mansion, Burkely Crest, at Hastings-on-the-Hudson. From the outset he decided to marry her, if only to prove that he could. He was tired of tantrums and grand passions. He wanted to settle down. He set about conquering her with the determination with which he had captured Anna Held.

On the day after the ball he sent a superb bouquet to the theater in which Billie was playing, and he ordered the complete stock of a Fifth Avenue florist delivered to her home. When he heard that she had been unable to reach him because his line was busy, he installed a special telephone in his office and a direct line to Hastings-on-the-Hudson.

He had his chauffeur follow her car down Fifth Avenue, and when she alighted to buy some gloves at a store, he helped her out. Finally he managed to talk her into allowing him to call on her at Burkely Crest, where he met—and carefully flattered—Blanche, her mother.

By mid-February the romance was an open secret. Ziegfeld held dinner parties at the Ansonia—still crammed with Anna Held's possessions—for Blanche, Billie, and Billie's ward, Cherrie Watson, whom Billie had adopted after the death of Cherrie's mother. He showered gifts on the three and captivated them equally with his charm. If it was the last thing he did, he was going to make Billie Burke his wife.

Frohman was furious when he learned that one of his favorite stars was falling in love with Ziegfeld, of whom he had never approved. He feared—correctly—that Ziegfeld would not stop at marriage. He would want to take over as Billie's manager as well.

The couple had to take extraordinary precautions to avoid Frohman's spies, who followed them everywhere. They even had to meet at Grant's Tomb to avoid the slightly sinister figures who checked their every movement. Billie wrote in her memoirs that one snowy afternoon in February, 1914, Frohman and his partner, Alf Hayman, came to see her in the sun parlor of Burkely

Crest and told her, as they viciously spun billiard balls across the table among the ferns and tropical birds, that Ziegfeld must be dropped at once. She ignored every word they said.

When Lillian heard of the romance between Ziegfeld and Billie, she was as annoyed as Frohman. One night the recently engaged couple was sitting just before showtime at one of the tables on the New Amsterdam roof together with a large group of millionaires and their wives. Lillian Lorraine arrived drunk and walked shakily up to the table in a floor-length sable coat. "Flo, I want to talk to you a minute," she said, staring into his eyes. He flushed with embarrassment and told her it was impossible, that he would see her later. She demanded that he immediately leave the floor. Again he refused. Finally she said, "If you don't, I'm going to throw off this coat in front of your fiancee. I don't have a stitch on."

Ziegfeld grabbed her, literally ran out the door with her, and threw her in a taxi. As she got in, she tossed the sable out of the window, and the astonished driver took the stark naked woman home through the snowy streets.

During March, while Billie was enjoying a great deal of success at the Lyceum in Maugham's *The Land of Promise*, she and Ziegfeld were together constantly. Every day they had lunch at 1:00, tea at 4:00, dinner at 6:00, and supper at midnight. On April 11, 1914, they were married.

Ziegfeld's parents came up from Chicago, and together with Blanche Burke they waited in a limousine outside the Lyceum until the matinée was over. After the last curtain call Billie changed quickly, took the elevator down to the stage door, and stepped into the car. The chauffeur drove the little group down to Sherry's restaurant and picked up Ziegfeld. Then he crossed over to Hoboken, to a small Lutheran church.

Ziegfeld's parents were having their way: there would be nothing like the haphazard "wedding" that had taken place with Anna Held. Billie Burke wrote later that the back room in which the couple was married, by the Reverend Eberhardt, was cluttered "with baby carriages and cribs, old paint buckets, and step ladders."

The minister became very confused because the official names on the register were Ethelbert Burke and Florence Ziegfeld. "Will you, Ethelbert, take you, Florence, to be your wedded wife?" he started saying to Ziegfeld. The couple, helpless with laughter, stopped him. After the marriage they headed joyfully back to town on the ferry in time for the evening performance. They stood at the rail looking out at the Hudson at twilight like a young pair of newlyweds. The wedding party was at the Brevoort, and they spent the night at the Ansonia.

The next day they left for a two-day honeymoon at Long Beach, but they were not to enjoy their honeymoon undisturbed. On April 12 a process server arrived at Long Beach with a writ from Harry B. Smith for unpaid royalties of $4,330. Ziegfeld opened the door himself, and the document was thrust into his hand. He snatched it and slammed the door in the visitor's face. He had completely neglected to pay Smith any royalties for some time, and the serving of the writ terminated their relationship. Ziegfeld was far too involved in his new marriage and in the fitting out of a steam yacht to remember old friendships and obligations. It was only months later, when he was threatened with actual jail, that he instructed Leon Laski, his attorney, to have Smith's bill paid.

Two nights after returning from Long Beach the couple was given a magnificent party at Reisenweber's Salon de Danse. The post-theater crowd stopped dancing the tango and applauded as the pair arrived in each other's arms, and the orchestra struck up a vigorous version of the wedding march. Then Billie and her new husband danced until dawn.

The following weekend Ziegfeld and Billie moved to Burkely Crest. Ziegfeld fell in love with the house right away. A splendid drive swept up to the sandstone front, with gables and romantic eaves; flowering shrubs, great elms, maples, and oaks gave the whole place a fine "English" air on the edge of the great river.

The only things Ziegfeld did not like at Burkely Crest were Billie's literary dinner parties, at which people such as Somerset Maugham and Arthur Wing Pinero were present. He sat through many of these occasions in grim silence. Occasionally, however, he would come up with something that made the guests laugh uproariously. (One night he said suddenly, "All actresses are conceited." Cherrie Watson retorted, "But Uncle Flo, Auntie Billie isn't conceited." "Ah, yes, but Billie isn't an actress," Ziegfeld said.)

The next weeks were sublimely happy ones for Ziegfeld. He went down to Burkely Crest on weekends, between preparations for the 1914 *Follies*. He enjoyed gardening, and visitors to the house would see him mooning about in a straw hat, carrying pruning shears and insect powders, terrorizing the gardeners as he learned about chicken raising, rose grafting, and cross-pollinating. Billie often worked beside him, wearing pink or blue gingham and a white sunbonnet, trying to calm him as he subjected the staff to ruthless cross-examinations.

Diamond Jim Brady and Lillian Russell dropped by— they had not relinquished Ziegfeld even though they maintained a close friendship with Anna—and other friends visited, including Charles Dillingham. Almost as though he wanted to expunge the past, that spring and summer Ziegfeld eliminated many of his and Anna's mutual friends. He saw even Julian Mitchell less and less frequently away from the New Amsterdam.

When the Follies began, in June, the couple returned to live at the Ansonia for the rest of the summer. Billie immediately had all of Anna's furnishings sold, and she redecorated the suite in a cool eighteenth-century style, quite different from Anna's Second Empire lavishness.

The suite was a marvel of good taste, superbly maintained by a staff of servants. The walls of the eighteenth-century English drawing room were a pale Adam green. Heavy French taffeta curtains were of the same color, and there were large chairs covered in chintz, gay with pink and white water lilies, bright green leaves, and stalks. The carpet, hand-woven in France, was a soft sand color.

The blue dining room, decorated with sumptuous wall frescos dealing with various periods of history, was a masterpiece. The reception room was white, with paneled walls decorated with sprays and garlands of tiny French roses, an exact copy of a room in the Petit Trianon. The Ziegfelds' rooms were in red, gold, pink, and blue. Persian carpets and gilded mirrors, several of which had once belonged to Marie Antoinette, were abundant.

Ziegfeld immediately ordered improvements to make the place still more lavish: gold plate for the dining room, new handsome Persian and Indian rugs, gold leaf in the bathrooms.

After the first weeks the couple's happiness was never really complete. Despite all their efforts, Frohman refused to release Billie from her contract that summer. Instead, he rushed her out on a grueling tour of one-night stands in New Jersey and points west, which gradually wore down her constitution. Ziegfeld constantly visited her when she was within easy training distance of New York, frequently packing so hastily that he arrived with a few pieces of clothing wrapped loosely in newspapers.

He was in New York in February, 1915, when a terrifying incident took place. On the night of February 2, Billie was in Boston, playing at the Hollis Street Theater. Just before the first act she received a large bunch of roses from an admirer. She pricked her finger on a thorn, but she thought nothing of it and went on stage. Frohman was out front sitting in the fifth row of the orchestra to keep an eye on her. The show was fine for the first two acts, but in the third Frohman noticed that Billie kept going up on her lines and continually wiped her forehead with a handkerchief. Suddenly she collapsed. The audience, which adored her, cried out as the curtain was rung down. Billie was rushed to the hospital. As soon as he received the news from Frohman's secretary, Ziegfeld took the next train to Boston. Billie hovered between life and death for days. Ziegfeld was frantic, unable to sleep; the doctors said that the thorn had set up a poisoning of her bloodstream. But at last they said she was on the mend.

Even though Billie's recovery was slow and depressing during that February and March, Frohman never ceased to scold her about Ziegfeld. Back in New York that spring he was a constant worry to the couple. The brilliant little bulldog of a man was in agony with the effects of an injured right knee incurred as a result of a fall at his home at White Plains. His temper was not improved by the endless suffering, and he was constantly calling Billie into his gloomy offices at the Broadway Theater, reminding her of her debt to him, and insisting that she break her relationship with Ziegfeld. Sometimes he would lie down on a couch next to his grand piano and groan aloud as he spoke to her.

Ziegfeld dismissed Frohman's antics as "theatrics," but

Billie's heart went out to the man who had given her an American career. The tension was broken by Frohman's sudden announcement in the spring that he was leaving to attend to some business in London. Supporting himself with a cane, he hobbled aboard the SS *Lusitania* on May 1, 1915. Billie begged him not to go, as did all the major figures of the Broadway theater—except, of course, Ziegfeld himself. With war raging the Atlantic was full of U-boats. When Frohman's associate, Paul Potter, said to him as he settled into his suite, "Aren't you afraid of the U-Boats, C.F.?" He simply replied, "Only of the IOUs."

It was a dull, painful voyage to England—painful because Frohman had to walk extremely slowly, and the heavy swell of the ocean made movement still more difficult. At 2:33 P.M. on May 7 he had just finished a long, heavy luncheon, and he was taking an easy, slow hobble across the promenade deck. At that moment a U-boat torpedo hit the ship with a shuddering blow. Actress Rita Jolivet, who survived the disaster, remembered his saying, as the ship groaned and lurched and a wave came up to sweep him out to sea, a few words from his friend J.M. Barrie: "Why fear death? It is the most beautiful adventure in life."

The brave little man repeated the first three words before he was carried from the rail forever.

Ziegfeld heard the news by radio at the Ansonia and telephoned Billie in Stillwater, Michigan, where she was playing in *Jerry*. It was only a moment before she went on stage. She walked into the brilliant light of the first act, blinked for a moment, spoke a few lines, and broke into sobs. For a few moments the audience thought she was playing a scene, and she rallied sufficiently to give a little laugh when one of the cues called for it. But then she broke into tears again. She turned to the audience, spoke an apology, and screamed, pressing her hands to her face. She stumbled weakly toward the wings. The curtain was rung down, and she lay for ten minutes on the floor before the cast and manager could revive her.

7

Midnight "Frolics"

In the middle of rehearsals for the 1915 *Follies* Ziegfeld had the worry of Billie's distress over Frohman, her agonized guilt that she had not treated him properly. Her Frohman tour took her to the West Coast, where she discussed a number of film deals; these negotiations took her mind off the anguish she was suffering. Ziegfeld called her in San Francisco—a difficult matter in those early days of long-distance phoning. Trying to get through, he said, "Hello—'Frisco? Hello?" in his usual impatient voice. Gene Buck heard him through the half-open office door and immediately began work on a tune, "Hello, 'Frisco, Hello," which made history when it was sung by Ina Claire in the *Follies*.

Frohman's death and the increasingly bad news from the Western front cast a pall over Broadway in 1915. The previous year had been dismal, but this was worse. After the *Lusitania* incident it seemed inevitable that America would join in the war. Throughout that stifling summer play after play struggled along feebly and closed.

With his uncanny instinct Ziegfeld knew that what the
public needed in a dark hour was the most extraordinary
dazzlement ever seen on the Broadway stage. He also
knew that one era was ending for him, and another about
to begin. He had lost, at least for the time being, the
mainstays of his life and career: Harry B. Smith, dis-
affected and embittered over the debts owed him, had
drifted away; more seriously, the brilliant Julian Mitchell,
whom Ziegfeld had treated thoughtlessly during the difficult days of the previous year, had also abandoned him.

Gene Buck more than amply filled Harry's shoes, and
he was a far more genuinely twentieth-century composer,
destined to modernize the *Follies* in countless ways in the
years that followed. But who could replace Mitchell?
Above all, who could supply the breathtaking spectacle
that the public hungered for in those black days? Mitchell
was lured back briefly for some early work on the show's
direction, but he soon left, and Australian comedian Leon
Errol was induced to take over.

Then Gene Buck came up with a solution: Joseph
Urban. Although Urban was not a stage director, he was
such a brilliant set designer that his ability would cover
up the absence of Julian Mitchell. And Ned Wayburn,
next to Mitchell the most gifted director of musicals on
Broadway, would be available.

Urban was a fat, jolly, vastly amusing man, whose many
chins wobbled as he talked. Born in Vienna in 1872, he
had established a vivid reputation in Europe, designing
the new town hall in Vienna, the Czar's Bridge in St.
Petersburg, and the Austrian Building at the St. Louis
Fair of 1904, where he won the grand prize.

Ziegfeld met Urban in the following manner. One night
Ziegfeld and Gene Buck were walking past the Park
Theater, where Edward Sheldon's beautiful *Garden of
Paradise* was showing to poor houses. Buck suggested that

they go in, but Ziegfeld dismissed the idea at once. The show was a failure, so why should they waste their time? Buck said that he had heard the scenery was unusual and worth looking at.

There were only about 30 people in the audience, but as soon as the curtain rose, the two men were overwhelmed. At the end of the first act, with its vivid underwater scenes, they literally ran from the orchestra and demanded that the manager tell them how to find the designer, Joseph Urban. "He's in Pabst's, next door," the manager said.

The manager went into Pabst's Café with them and pointed out a man sitting in a corner drinking a stein of beer. They introduced themselves and asked Urban if he had any work on hand. "I have a few orders ahead," Urban said coolly. "How much will you make between now and June?" "About $10,000," Urban replied. Ziegfeld wrote out a check and handed it to him. "Here is $10,000," he said. "Consider yourself engaged by me to do the *Follies.*"

From the outset Urban learned that the failure of *The Garden of Paradise* was due to the long waits between scenes, necessitated by the heavy scenery. The essence of the *Follies*, Ziegfeld explained, was speed: something must be happening every minute, so there must be alternating "scenes in one" and heavier scenes. Urban nodded. As Ziegfeld's odd, whiny voice went on, he became more and more enthusiastic. When they parted, he shook Ziegfeld's hand. "It's done," he said.

Ziegfeld liked Urban instantly, and the feeling was mutual. Ziegfeld's perfect taste and superb color sense and Urban's genius for design married perfectly, and the sketches that poured onto Ziegfeld's desk at the New Amsterdam glowed with sumptuous colors. Blue was Urban's favorite shade, and by a miracle it was (together with pink) Ziegfeld's. The two men quite firmly decided

to make the 1915 *Follies* a "blue" *Follies,* with colors ranging from midnight blue to the pale turquoise of a South
Seas lagoon.

The opening sequence was to be underwater, and Urban
designed it in aquamarine. Kay Laurell appeared to be
swimming against a rippling background of blue light.
In a bold attempt to push America into the war Urban
and Ziegfeld created the dazzling "America" number, with
Mae Murray and Carl Randall emerging against a giant
flag. George White and Ann Pennington represented the
navy, and Murray and Randall, the army. Justine Johnston
posed as the spirit of Columbia. The Gates of Elysium sequence showed giant elephants with water sparkling in
multicolored lights from their trunks.

For his theatrical designs Urban began with an inten-
sive reading of a libretto and score. Next he did a series
of drawings, each one of which was meticulously drawn
in color. Later he made a ground plan and a full paste-
board model a foot high—a marvel of detail from the
windowed walls to the furnishings. Urban painted his can-
vases on the floor so as to give them a firmness of touch
not possible otherwise. He used *pointillage*—color applied
not in flat mixed washes but in pure colors laid side by
side. For a moonlit window casement he would have the
background flat but well rubbed in. Next he applied with
a finer brush a multitude of narrow green mottlings, like
irregular ribbons. Over this he splattered a stipple of brick
red. The casement turned gray-black under an amber
light. He believed that the artist of the theater must paint
with the glories of light itself. His light rehearsals were
immensely complex, developed in sophistication over 50
productions in Europe. With Ziegfeld's help he also re-
designed the New Amsterdam, taken over as the "Follies
Theater" in 1913.

The New Amsterdam was magnificent: pre-Raphaelite

in style and dazzlingly hand-carved. The wall panels were of dark mahogany, the side exit doors of polished bronze, and flanking the lobby high on the walls under the vaulted sumptuous ceilings were the figures of Shakespeare, Homer, and the heroes of the classical legends. Here Macbeth sees the three witches on the heath, there Ulysses sees the sirens arise from marble waves. The panels and the great curving green onyx staircase were carved with rich clusters of grapes, tropical monkeys, and the Barbary apes and elephants Ziegfeld adored; figures of Apollo, framed in a halo of golden light, and the Spirit of Progress shone down above classical groupings of clothed and unclothed figures.

In one exquisite carving at the foot of the banisters a benign ox-like head with curved horns glowed above a shield, flanked on either side by cherubs playing pipes as symbols of pagan gaiety. One odd feature of the theater was that the girls' dressing rooms were above the stage, reached by a series of elevators including one reserved for stars.

Ziegfeld, Urban, and Ned Wayburn worked together to perfect the Ziegfeld *Frolics*. With Wayburn, Ziegfeld began his policy of detailed auditions and rehearsals, as opposed to the casual method of hiring in the past.

Wayburn—slope-shouldered, fat, bespectacled, always wearing a beret and a large, floppy cardigan with his initials on the left lapel—was a brilliant successor to Julian Mitchell. When Ziegfeld and Gene Buck found him, he had been working for the Shuberts at the Winter Garden and had owned a large model school of his own. With the Shuberts he had raised the salaries of chorus girls in New York.

He altered Ziegfeld's schedules of rehearsal: in the first week he had musical rehearsals only, held from 10:25 A.M. to 12:25 P.M. and from 8:00 P.M. to 10:00 P.M. In the second week there were dance rehearsals twice a day. In the third week mechanical details were perfected while the principals and chorus, rehearsed separately, were brought together. The scenic effects were completed last, and the entire ensemble was brought together for a dress rehearsal, usually in Atlantic City.

Girls were divided into five groups: *A, B, C, D,* and *TW. A* were the tall girls, from five feet seven upward: *B* were the large medium girls, above five feet five; *C* were the ingenues, petite and from five feet up; the *D* girls were considered the ideal: from five feet to five feet five, they weighed from one hundred and ten to one hundred and thirty pounds, compact and athletic. *TW*s, "Train Wreckers," were girls who were absolutely out of the question from every point of view. They were quickly weeded out.

Preparations for the show were made very carefully. The floor of the roof was cleared, creating a space about 40 feet square. A row of chairs stood on each side, facing each other. On one side a pianist sat at an upright piano. On the opposite side Ziegfeld sat with Wayburn. Wayburn arranged the girls according to height. Patiently he explained to them that when the pianist started to play a march, they must walk in time to the music, occasionally giving a "hesitation step" in order to strike a pose.

All talking among the girls was forbidden, and there was to be no kidding around. Anyone who giggled or whispered was instantly silenced. Names and telephone numbers were taken as soon as the girls were seated in order. Wayburn wrote down against each name whether the girl should come again to have a voice test, whether she needed further training, whether she was hopeless, or whether she should be signed—at $50 a week and $60 weekly on tour. Wayburn's assistant told each girl—in a whisper so that the other girls could not hear—what the decision had been. During the rehearsals and the performance itself the same atmosphere of military discipline was retained.

From the outset of the *Frolics*, Ziegfeld laid new ground rules. As in the *Follies*, each girl must be made to feel that she was as perfectly dressed as the wealthiest woman in the orchestra. Her lace must be real, her silks and satins of the finest available quality, her hats made for her by the most expensive milliners in New York and Paris. A pair of stockings or shoes must be replaced the moment they showed the slightest damage. Every single item of clothing must be hand-cleaned as often as possible without injuring the fabric. Ziegfeld himself personally supervised the makeup (preferring to use none if possible) as well as selecting the wardrobe piece by piece. No one except the reigning stars must be permitted individual selection: Ziegfeld knew what was best for each of them.

Flo was likewise extremely strict about life backstage: there must be no drinking in the dressing rooms, and no beaux—not even members of the moneyed aristocracy— must be permitted in those sacred precincts. After the performance was over, a girl could do what she liked, although Ziegfeld preferred it if they would retire by 1:00 A.M. and keep their names out of the newspapers.

Ziegfeld detested scandals and spent half a lifetime trying to quell them. It was the irony of his life that the *Frolics* were constantly being mentioned in the most lurid and ugly terms and that murder, suicide, and drug-taking were constant blights on the image of noble dedication that he fought so hard to preserve.

The original concept of the *Frolics* was to have only eight girls and a comedian who would perform while people ate their supper. Urban was called in to make the roof beautiful, and almost from the first he clashed with Wayburn.

Wayburn's only concern was to flood the girls with brilliant light, which washed out Urban's sumptuous rainbow-
colored backgrounds. Ziegfeld had great difficulty sooth-
ing the two men. Finally he talked them into a compro-
mise: the girls would be lit by a series of spotlights from
the corners of the room, leaving some areas dark; the
settings would be illuminated in the darkness by variable
lights of different colors.

At the *Frolics* Wayburn introduced the famous "Ziegfeld Walk": that straight-backed strut with the breasts
jutting out sharply, designed to show off the brilliant
Ziegfeld costumes. The walk had another purpose: to prevent the customers from pawing the girls as they came
past the lighted tables. Girls ran about dressed as switch-
boards, and telephones on each table connected each cus-
tomer to the switchboard of his choice. Some girls dressed
as Zeppelins, with sweeping searchlights moving over
them against an Urban background of a burning city.
Dazzling arrangements of flowers were on every table, and
the stars and stripes, vividly used by Urban, blazed against
the dark star-spangled walls.

At that time Ziegfeld added two illustrious figures to
his group of associates: society painter Ben Ali Haggin
and Lady Duff-Gordon, the brilliant British society woman
whose fashion salon was the rage of New York. Flo wanted
the *Frolics* to be essentially a show created by, for, and
about the rich. Ben Ali Haggin's rich tableau effects, with
the girls posed like groupings in visual art, combined with
Lady Duff-Gordon's methods of parading her beauties,
were superb features of Ziegfeld's productions for many
years.

Entry to the roof cost $5. The customers could take an
elevator to the roof, where there was a restaurant surrounding a dance floor with a drop curtain on each side.
A balcony was suspended from the ceiling by chains. The

balcony floor was of plate glass; when the girls danced and the lights blazed, the people could look up between their legs. The stage was movable, thrusting out between the diners by means of special machinery.

A special attraction for the midnight show was Will Rogers, who stood among the girls laconically twirling a rope. Rogers had originally been part of a traveling Wild West Show, emerging successfully on Broadway in 1912 as one of six cowboys at the Victoria Theater. Attempting to lasso a pony in one routine, he delivered the famous remark, "Wal, if he'd a'stuck out his tongue, I'd sure enough caught him." The audience rolled in the aisles. At the Victoria he began his inimitable line of dryly humorous patter, parodying a mind-reading act and delivering gentle barbs at rich people in the audience.

Gene Buck liked Rogers's technique. Buck felt that Rogers would intrigue the wealthy customers for the roof show, but Ziegfeld would not hear of the idea. He wanted to create a European style, extremely sophisticated atmosphere with a strong erotic flavor, and Rogers would, he felt, be quite unsuitable.

Finally, Buck succeeded in persuading Ziegfeld to give the new comedian a trial run. Ziegfeld detested him from the outset and told Buck that he had three weeks to get rid of him. While Ziegfeld was away, however, Rogers devised the technique—suggested to him by his wife—of adding comments on the current news. The irreverent shrewdness of the barbs pleased the heavy-drinking midnight crowd. When Ziegfeld returned, he stood gloomily at the back of the room. Although he still found Rogers depressingly unfunny and even embarrassing, he was forced to admit that Rogers brought waves of laughter.

He allowed him to remain, and eventually the two men formed a lasting if somewhat uneasy friendship. Ziegfeld even added Rogers to the *Follies*, making him a national celebrity. He hired writers to build up his act, which Rogers "officially" created himself. Rogers became a hilarious, wickedly inspired commentator on anything and anybody in the news, sparking off Ziegfeld's desire (never properly consummated) to create a theatrical equivalent of the Berliner satirical revues, which he so admired.

One of the greatest highlights of the 1915 *Follies* and *Frolics* was Ina Claire. In the *Follies* she sang "Marie Odile," a devastating parody of that authoritative Belasco luminary, Frances Starr. The Belasco production of this name was the story of a convent girl so innocent that she mistakes a virile soldier for the patron saint of her order and is subsequently raped. With superb finesse and *eclat* Ina Claire proved herself the great comedian she was as she told the story of "poor Marie Odile," who didn't know the difference between a man and a saint in a stained glass window. Ziegfeld told her not to move during the song and to deliver the lines in an unchanging plaintive monotone. She won a standing ovation for her efforts.

The note of skeptical wit struck by this scene and its great star (she was destined to become the finest comedian of the 1920s and 1930s) was dear to Ziegfeld's heart, and like everything else in the 1915 *Follies*, it was a revolutionary break with crude burlesque. His ingrained sophistication was years ahead of the time; his barbs against religion and politics were ruthless and more typical of our own time than his. Because of the extraordinary packaging of his productions, he could get away with practically anything. He stood the whole of American puritanism firmly on its ear.

With the 1915 *Follies* and *Frolics* Ziegfeld's career as a great showman really began. With Frohman dead, he was the most celebrated figure on Broadway. He only wished Billie had been there to share his exaltation, but she was still on her interminable Frohman tour. She finally concluded it on July 9, 1915.

On July 13 she accepted an offer of $30,000 for five weeks' work with the New York Motion Picture Corporation. The film was to be shot by its associate, Triangle, in Hollywood. The same day she announced that she was severing her connection with the Charles Frohman Company and would be under Ziegfeld's management in the future.

Alf Hayman was furious. He called a press conference to announce that if Billie Burke went into pictures, she would be ruined and that hers was an act of gross ingratitude to the dead theatrical manager. She retorted by immediately booking a private car to Los Angeles in August. Hayman insisted that she had two years remaining on her contract; Ziegfeld said that Frohman's death automatically canceled the contract.

Ziegfeld took the train in August with Billie and Cherrie Watson. They arrived in Chicago on the Twentieth-Century Limited, where a foretaste of Hollywood excitements awaited Billie. The group was met at the station by Mason Peters, manager of the Studebaker Theater, which had an agreement to show Triangle Productions, and by George Bowles, manager of the Capitol Theater, which was currently showing *Birth of a Nation*. The photographers arrived *en masse* and asked Billie to get into a carriage and wave for an effect. She did so, and in midshot a switch engine hooked onto the empty train and began shunting it off to the yards. Billie screamed with fear and ran to the car platform. George Bowles proved to be the hero of the moment, running for 50 yards along the platform and pulling her to safety. Disheveled and shocked, Billie made her way into a waiting limousine. Ziegfeld was unable to console her. "I never want to ex-

perience anything like that again," she told him as they
drove off to the Blackstone Hotel.

Billie was cast in Thomas Ince's *Peggy*, in which she
played a vivacious American girl plunged into the life of
a grim Scottish family. Starting out as a tomboy, she
finally marries the local clergyman after straightening out
the life of a wronged girl and making sure that her se-
ducer made the relationship legal. The script was an expert blending of sentiment, fun, and romance, and—much
as he disliked motion pictures—Ziegfeld had to admit that
it was a charmer. Billie co-starred with William Desmond,
and the brilliant Victor Schertzinger composed a special
score.

Ziegfeld left the train in Chicago to stay with his parents, and Billie and Cherrie continued to California.

Greeting Cherrie and Billie at the train station, Ince
had a magnificent steam yacht ready to convey Billie
to the Catalina Islands when she felt inclined to go.
Schooner-rigged and measuring 123 feet, the yacht belonged to millionaire mining magnate Carlyle P. Anthony.
A superb bungalow was ready on the largest of the islands,
30 miles from the California coast, the home of wealthy
New Yorker Octavia Middleton. A special dressing room,
including a reception room, makeup parlor, and bathroom,
was prepared. A piano and victrola were there if Billie or
Cherrie felt the need for music. In addition, Ince built a
sumptuous bathhouse of solid marble on the beach, where
she could bathe in a landlocked ocean pool attended by
no fewer than 15 lifeguards.

He had also arranged for a lavish Santa Monica bunga-
low with a lovely Japanese garden. Ince fell in love with
Billie at first sight. Though she disliked him initially,
Billie gradually became seduced by his charm. She found
Inceville rough going, however.

Situated near the Pacific Ocean, it was simply a rambling ranch with a few "stages" open to the sun and air. Cast and crew were met at the streetcar and driven to the ranch by horse. Part of the ranch had been crudely converted into a Scottish village, with a Presbyterian church, a barn, a huddle of rough hewn cottages, and some rolling lowlands and cairns. The shooting of the picture was swift and sure, with no time wasted.

Oddly enough, Lillian Lorraine was also in Hollywood in those weeks, shooting a serial called *Neal of the Navy*. She played an intrepid heroine with so much vigor that in one scene she threw the leading villain off the bridge onto the foredeck, almost killing him. Her drinking constantly held up shooting, and her remarks about Hollywood made her very unpopular with the crew.

It was bizarre that both she and Billie were involved in near fatal accidents that fall, almost burning to death in fires engineered for their respective movies. Lillian had to be shown in a burning building from which a brave naval hero would rescue her. The building burned too fast, and the roof caved in on her, setting her hair and clothes on fire. She ran out screaming, and the director had her hosed down. Her arms were permanently scarred. She refused to be taken to the hospital and went back and replayed the entire scene that same afternoon.

Only a few days later Billie was shooting in Santa Ynéz Canyon. The scene was a glimpse the heroine has of the horrors of war, when the villagers attacked her with homemade bombs. They fell around her, hurling clouds of dirt and making her scream with genuine terror—exactly the effect Ince wanted. Suddenly one of the bombs settled on a thatched roof of a cottage just as she entered it for safety. The cottage burst into flames. As Billie emerged, her hair was still smoking. Ince found a hose and trained it on the house.

Meanwhile, Ziegfeld returned from Chicago to New

York—and an affair with a *Follies* girl, Olive Thomas. The romance was not an easy one. She was temperamental and not overendowed with intelligence, but the mixture of fiery emotion and mindlessness excited him. He spent weekends with Olive on his new steam yacht, cruising up and down Long Island Sound, enjoying lavish parties in which the guests carrying bottles of champagne frequently dove into the water, swam up to the homes of the rich, and invited the occupants to join them in a libation.

News of these orgiastic cruises reached Billie, who spent nights crying or screaming at friends. When *Peggy* was finished, she took the train to San Francisco and put up at the St. Francis, wiring Ziegfeld to join her to talk the whole thing over. After his arrival the quarrels went on for days. When he lied that it wasn't Olive Thomas but another girl he was having an affair with, Billie ripped the curtains from the windows, smashed the lamps and chinaware, and flung herself to the floor. Ziegfeld sat calmly in a tall chair, puffing at a cigar and watching her without much interest.

Further excitement was in store in San Francisco. At 4:00 A.M. on October 12, Blanche Burke, who had been ill, woke up and saw the shadow of a man passing the window and making his way into the adjoining suite, in which the Ziegfelds slept. Thinking it was a nightmare, she went back to sleep.

The next morning the Ziegfelds awoke and discovered that Billie's chamois jewel bag was missing. It had contained an $8,000 ring, a diamond guard ring, and a diamond wristwatch. But a $10,00 necklace in a secret compartment of an otherwise empty jewel box was intact.

Billie took the news hysterically, asking Ziegfeld if it was "another stunt." He shook his head. A few moments

later William Pinkerton, of the Pinkerton Bureau, asked
the same question. Pinkerton had not forgotten the Anna
Held train robbery any more than Billie had.

"On my honor, this is real," Ziegfeld told Pinkerton. He
took Billie and her mother back to Hastings, leaving Pinkerton a $1,000 fee to begin taking charge of the case. On
November 5, Pinkerton cabled Ziegfeld that everything
except the setting of the $8,000 ring had been recovered—
from a cat burglar known as Peter Isgren, a specialist in
jewel thefts.

In the fall of 1915 the *Chicago Tribune*, in need of a
circulation stunt, had decided to plunge into motion picture production, running one episode per week of a serial,
Gloria's Romance. The show was to be shot in 20 chapters
in Florida. It was written by Mr. and Mrs. Rupert Hughes
and would be produced by George Kleine. Max Annenberg, the *Tribune's* circulation manager, waylaid Ziegfeld
in Times Square, and they strolled up Broadway to the
Ansonia. After Annenberg outlined the idea, Ziegfeld said,
"Is there a starring role for Billie?" There was: the role
of a madcap, giddy young heiress who is driving to Palm
Beach, Florida, when her car crashes into the ocean. She
has to make her way back through alligator-infested
swamps. She is captured enroute by Seminoles.

"Wait," Ziegfeld stopped him. "Is there any chance for
glamour?" Annenberg reassured him that there was: in
later episodes Billie would be seen in a society ball, would
appear in stunning clothes in a courtroom scene, and
would wear priceless jewels to cheer her up on a sickbed.

"Money?" Ziegfeld snapped through his cigar.

"Plenty."

Ziegfeld cocked one eyebrow. "Yes?"

"Seventy-five thousand."

"Double it or no deal."

"But that would be more than any actress has ever been paid."

Ziegfeld frowned. "And Billie is the best actress who ever lived."

"How much will you take?"

Ziegfeld stubbed out his cigar. "One hundred and thirty thousand."

"I'll talk to the boss."

Two weeks later the deal was set.

Ziegfeld laid down some staggering terms: real mahogany on the sets, which were to be submitted to him and Urban for approval; at least 20 costume changes; a present of a powder blue Rolls Royce with Billie's initials in gold on each door; a collection of jewels from Cartier; permission to live at home and work short hours when the unit was shooting on Long Island; and a lavish home in Palm Beach, which she could continue to use after the film was finished shooting. Annenberg agreed to everything.

When Ziegfeld came to the set to visit Billie, he burst out laughing: the demands of orthochromatic film, which could not photograph red, were maddening: Billie's face was pale green, with purple lips, and she had to wear special eye makeup in case her blue eyes photographed white. She giggled so much during the scene in which she was carried on a couch after an illness that finally the director ordered the lights turned off and the set closed for the rest of the day. Billie was still giggling when the Rolls Royce got back to Burkely Crest.

Ziegfeld—who discovered a taste for Palm Beach while on location in Florida—kept an eye on Billie as she appeared in the 20 chapters, including "Lost in the Everglades," "Caught by the Seminoles," "Hidden Fires," "The Mask of Mystery," "The Floating Trap," "The Bitter Truth," and "The Midnight Terror."

The serial was released in New York on May 18, 1916, and, thanks to Ziegfeld's assiduous promotion, it was shown at the Globe—the first serial to make it onto Broadway. Billie tried to help by fainting spectacularly in an orchestra seat during the première of Ince's *Civilization* that June.

Despite the advance ballyhoo. the serial proved to be far too gentle for a public already bored even by the thrills of a Pearl White. It flopped. Its failure in no way dampened Billie's spirits. Besides, more important things were ahead: that summer she discovered that she was pregnant.

Ziegfeld was overwhelmed when he heard the news. He immediately increased the staff at Burkely Crest in preparation for the new arrival. Meanwhile he became involved in the presentation of the 1916 *Follies*.

He had a staff ranging from an overseer and five chauffeurs (to drive five Rolls Royces, all of different colors), to chefs, waitresses, housemaids, and gardeners. A gymnasium was added, at a cost of $20,000, and indoor and outdoor swimming pools, both designed by Joseph Urban, were installed. Four dogs—Tutti, Frutti (poodles), Gollywog (Pekingese), and Bill (Boston Bull)—Ziegfeld's favorite monkey, Chiquita, 2,000 pigeons, and 500 chickens were lavishly housed in kennels and coops. Ziegfeld also redecorated the Ansonia suite and added scores of photographs of Billie.

The 1916 *Follies* had a Shakespearean motif: Bert Williams was a witty Othello, Bernard Granville was Romeo, and Ina Claire played Juliet. Sam B. Hardy made a resplendent Henry VIII. Urban's version of the great sphinx appeared glowing against a background of *eau de nil*, while beautiful girls appeared in costumes of many periods, from 1907 to 1916. Bernard Granville played Marc Antony.

Carl Randall imitated Nijinski brilliantly, and Ina Claire

was superb in an imitation of a chirruping Billie Burke
(she went to see her to study her voice); Geraldine Farrar
and Jane Cowl were excellent, and W. C. Fields appeared
as Teddy Roosevelt. Urban even showed a naval battle
in the North Sea and brilliantly decorated a dance by Ann
Pennington.

Aside from the redecorating of Burkely Crest and his
concern for Billie, who was resting at the Ansonia and
awaiting the baby's arrival, Ziegfeld was busy that fall of
1916 with *The Century Girl*, composed by Victor Herbert
and Irving Berlin. The show was produced in association
with Charles Dillingham and presented at the Century
Theater on November 6. More coordinated than the
Follies, it was in essence an extension of them, with
Urban's designs at their most inspired. A brilliant cast
represented the great women of many ages, including
May Leslie as Boadicea, Simone d'Herlys as Helen of
Troy, Hazel Lewis as Joan of Arc, Lilyan Tashman as the
Empress Josephine, and—emerging from a trapdoor as all
these proud beauties descended a great curving staircase—
Hazel Dawn, ravishing as the twentieth-century girl.

The staircase scene, reproduced in countless film musicals dealing with Ziegfeld's life, was the most lavish of
his career to date and brought the opening night audience
to its feet. As usual, in one scene Ziegfeld showed his
two composers, Victor Herbert (played by Arthur Cun-
ningham) and Irving Berlin (played by John Slavin) having a comic discussion. Urban's settings ranged from the
celestial staircase itself, with its setting of purple and pink
clouds, to Grand Central Station, a glade full of exotic
flowers and cool green leaves, and a perfect reproduction
of Tenniel's drawings in an *Alice in Wonderland* scene.

In the third act Urban dazzled the audience with an
underwater sequence, in which a diver in a suit and hel-

met conducted a chaste romance with a shoal of mermaids. The lilting score, the witty lines, and the incredible spectacle made *The Century Girl* an unforgettable experience for the audience.

On October 24, Billie was in labor at the Ansonia. The birth was easy, and on the following day Ziegfeld, a perfect picture of an anxious father, was admitted in a disheveled condition to the sacred precincts. Billie looked healthy and divinely happy, her fair hair outlined against the embroidered pillow. Although it was not the boy he had hoped for, Ziegfeld was enchanted by the moppet held up for his inspection: Florenz Patricia.

The child had clear cut features. Her eyes were blue, deep, and thoughtful, and she boasted a mass of curly red hair. She looked exactly like Ziegfeld himself, and he swore that he could detect his own vocal intonation in her voice. He was beside himself, and he called a bedroom press conference as soon as it was possible, cooing over the crib of pink and white as Billie, in a heap of lilac-scented pillows, spoke of every single thing the child had done in her 15 days of life.

Three weeks later Billie was well enough to attend a performance of *The Century Girl* and a fashion show at Lady Duff-Gordon's home. Early in 1917 Ziegfeld approved her signing a contract with Famous Players-Lasky, widely announced as "her new adventure in Shadowland," for a production called *The Mysterious Miss Terry*, from a story by Gellett Burgess.

8
Marilyn

In the spring of 1917, in the midst of rehearsals for the *Follies* in Atlantic City, Olive Thomas met a handsome young man from Hollywood, who had just appeared as Pip in a version of *Great Expectations*. He was Jack Pickford, brother of Mary Pickford—a high-strung, motor-mad boy of 20, with a tiny, stringy body and a slightly equine, hypersensitive face. They met on a Sunday night at a beach club dance, and the rapport was instantaneous. Pickford assured Olive that she would have a brilliant career in motion pictures, and he suggested that she break off her liaison with Ziegfeld and abandon the stage. The idea went to her head. After the slow grind of the *Follies*, Hollywood appealed to her enormously. Besides, she was tiring of Ziegfeld: his refusal to divorce Billie Burke, his constant dating of Anna Daly, her girlfriend from Pittsburgh.

When she told Ziegfeld that she was going to give up her relationship with him and with the *Follies*, he was speechless. He sank into a chair. He told her she was insane to marry Pickford, that a motion picture career would ruin her talent. She simply picked up her sealskin coat and left for her hotel. She never appeared in the *Follies* again. Soon after that she signed with the producer Myron Selznick to appear in a series of films at $2,500 a week. After eight months of constant drinking, dancing, and filmmaking, Jack Pickford and Olive Thomas were married in May, 1917.

In the spring of 1917 Ziegfeld recovered from the shock of Olive Thomas's abandonment of him with his usual speed. He was extremely busy, with a child to consider, and he spent much time consoling a distraught Lillian Russell (Diamond Jim Brady died in April). The running of Burkely Crest and the building of a pool designed by Joseph Urban also took up his time.

At the same time he was involved in preparing *Miss 1917*, the successor to *The Century Girl*, at the Century Theater. P.G. Wodehouse and Guy Bolton as co-authors were given the costume and set designs and told to weave the book and lyrics around them. As they revealed it in their book, *Bring On The Girls*, no sooner had Ziegfeld handed them the designs than they were replaced. The team then would have to write entirely new material. The one moment of comic relief in otherwise troublesome rehearsals occurred when an Italian tenor stood on the stage at rehearsal and sang "Ridi Pagliacco": the revolving stage began to move, and he vanished in the wings, reemerging in as good voice as before.

Vivienne Segal was the vivacious ingenue of the show. In the first-act finale she sang a series of numbers called "The Land Where The Good Songs Go." Bessie McCoy Davis made her comeback as the "Yama-Yama" girl in the preceding number. It was extremely difficult for Vivienne to follow her. Jerome Kern wanted her to follow Bessie

McCoy in his "They Didn't Believe Me," but she felt that it was far too light to follow Bessie McCoy. Charles Dillingham took her aside and advised her to sing Victor Herbert's "Kiss Me Again," which was almost invariably a show-stopper. He told her to plunge right into the song without warning. When she began to rehearse, Victor Herbert was sitting on one aisle and Jerome Kern on the other. George Gershwin, the rehearsal pianist, started to play "Kiss Me Again." Jerome Kern clapped his hands together and told him to stop. He shouted, "You're going to sing 'They Didn't Believe Me.'"

She said, "No, I'm going to sing 'Kiss Me Again.'"

Kern and Herbert almost came to blows. Finally Ziegfeld said, "Oh, let her sing what she wants to sing!"

She did so, to tremendous applause. Jerome Kern never forgave her.

During 1917 Ziegfeld poured a cornucopia of gifts on Patricia: jewelry, fabulous clothes, flowers, animals, birds, and a vast collection of toys. In later years he added a playhouse, an exact copy of Martha Washington's Mount Vernon home. He bought her a baby elephant and a diamond tiara.

He lavished extraordinary love and devotion on Billie herself. He was spurred on still further when Olive Thomas married Jack Pickford, in May. It was as though he was trying to expunge the memory of their affair and make up for his guilty feelings.

The 1917 *Follies*, designed to celebrate the advent of Florenz Patricia, was a masterpiece. Urban created a Chinese lacquer setting, which dissolved in showers of colored water, followed by three sets of crossed red and gold ladders. Sixty girls in Chinese costumes climbed up and down in unison while the ladder rungs glowed in the dark. In one scene the girls were dressed as flowers, springing up seemingly from the earth. An opalescent backdrop was laced with what seemed to be thousands of pearls (actually they were horse pills dipped in silver paint). At the end of the flower scene two young Venuses emerged, floating in shimmering soap bubbles. A fleet of American warships appeared with guns firing and signals flashing, sailing toward the audience.

The 1917 *Follies* introduced Eddie Cantor, a gifted blackface comedian. In one scene he played an effeminate porter's son, just out of college, shocked by the illiteracy of his father, played by Bert Williams. Will Rogers twirled his lariat, W.C. Fields gave comically disastrous displays of tennis, croquet, and billiards, and the lovely Dolores walked across the stage—for $600 a week—in "Episode of the Chiffon."

On a trip to Los Angeles earlier that year Ziegfeld had seen Eddie Cantor in *Canary Cottage*, with Charles Ruggles and Trixie Friganza. Cantor played a chauffeur in blackface, his 15 entrances and exits laced with delicious off-color humor. Ziegfeld and Billie broke up with laughter when, as the immense Trixie Friganza trundled off stage, Cantor gagged and said, "My God! A milk wagon!"

Ziegfeld decided to give him a one night tryout in New York and went backstage to tell him so. Five minutes later Cantor was telling anyone who would listen that Ziegfeld had signed him to a five-year contract.

Cantor's opening night at the New Amsterdam was a smash hit. He also appeared in one scene of the 1917 *Frolics* as a card-trick expert. He handed the cards to Diamond Jim Brady, Charles Dillingham, and William Randolph Hearst in the audience. At the end of the act he said he would identify what cards they were holding. He sang a series of meaningless songs and started to leave the stage. "Hey! What do we do with the cards?" Dillingham yelled. "Play with them, dummy," Cantor shouted back. He brought the house down.

In the fall Billie, who had been wanting to return to the stage, told Ziegfeld that she was interested in a play by Claire Kummer, *The Rescuing Angel*. Ziegfeld begged her not to do it; he was adamant that it was worthless. She insisted, and she signed with Arthur Hopkins for a season of 30 weeks at a weekly salary of $1,500 and 37.5 percent of the profits. She was to earn not less than $45,000.

The play opened—and flopped. Ziegfeld encouraged her to sue for $34,500. Hopkins claimed that he had offered to put her on the road but that she had refused. When the newspapers printed the story, in January, 1918, Ziegfeld sent a form letter to every editor in the country, denying that Hopkins had made any such offer. He said that Billie had realized that the play was hopeless while she was at the out-of-town tryouts but that Hopkins refused to make any changes. Ziegfeld's last sentence was typically ruthless: "*The Rescuing Angel* production was placed in the storehouse with Mr. Hopkins's *The Deluge, The Happy Ending*, and Marie Doro's play, which lasted only a week or two, with all the rest of his failures." Hopkins finally settled the case out of court, and Billie presented the money to the Red Cross.

During the winter of 1917–1918 Ziegfeld was in love again. Ironically, Billie Burke had sparked off this new affair herself. She had seen the Shubert production *Show of Wonders* and had been enormously impressed with a blonde, exquisitely graceful 19-year-old dancer, whom the Shuberts had discovered in London for their *Passing Show* revues. She was the epitome of youthful grace, freshness, and loveliness. The girl's name was Marilyn Miller (then spelled `Marilynn`). Returning to the Ansonia after the show, Billie told Ziegfeld that he ought to hire the girl, but he wasn't interested. He had promised the Shuberts, whom he hated, that he wouldn't poach from them.

But he ran into Marilyn at parties, and gradually he became fascinated. She had a sunny, fun-loving, but ruthless charm, a glitter that made every man in a room turn around when she walked in. For years she had been a member of the famous family act, the Five Columbians Troupe, on the vaudeville circuits. She had a well-known passion for chorus boys, having given up numerous chances of marriage to wealthy middle-aged men in favor of a handsome face.

Ziegfeld's passion for Marilyn Miller was not reciprocated. She accepted his attentions and enjoyed the bouquets, brooches, and champagne suppers. She probably spent nights with him, but she never felt any physical attraction for him. She was skillful enough to wrest from him the ultimate accolade: a major role in the 1918 *Follies*.

She was an overwhelming success with the first-night audience, despite a tinny voice and negligible acting talent. She stepped down an Urban staircase in a minstrel costume, displaying legs that, in Billie Burke's words, "have never been matched for slim, provocative beauty." Ziegfeld added enormously to the scene by having Fanny Brice sit in an aisle seat as part of the audience and stand up to make a series of comments—all hilarious—on Marilyn's every movement. Despite the clowning of Eddie Cantor and the flawless dancing of Ann Pennington, Marilyn Miller was undoubtedly the sensation of the show. She even succeeded at the 1918 midnight *Frolics* in competing successfully with Lillian Lorraine's sensational comeback as Tipperary Mary—a scrubwoman in a gingham gown, carrying a galvanized iron pail. When Erlanger said that Lillian would be so drunk she would not be able to stand up during the number, Ziegfeld simply had her play it without getting up off the floor.

Ziegfeld's joy in his daughter, in Marilyn Miller's emergence as a great star, and in Lillian Lorraine's comeback (he was still deeply fond of her) was severely tempered during 1918 by the shocking news that Anna Held had been suddenly stricken with a rare fatal disease.

Anna, who had been living chiefly in Paris since their "divorce," had finally abandoned the city and come to America in 1917 to tour for the Shuberts in *Follow Me*. In January, 1918, she fell ill from some undiagnosed ailment while on tour, and her daughter, Liane Carrera, took over her role. She returned to New York and checked into the state suite at the Savoy in which Ziegfeld had first presented her at the *Parlor Match* press conference. Doctors told her she had a spongy condition of the bone tissue known as myeloma, of which only 204 cases had previously been reported since its discovery, in 1889. The nation's sobsisters immediately said that she had been dieting, had had ribs cut out, or had used various other extreme methods to keep her waist down to 18 inches at 45 years of age, but there was no truth in these stories. Ziegfeld visited her privately and was shocked by her condition. She was pale; she weighed only 70 lbs, and she clung feebly to his hand before turning her head to the wall and asking him to go away.

In late May, Ziegfeld left town with Marilyn for the Atlantic City tryouts of the *Follies*. There he heard that Anna had rallied. Lillian Russell went to see her and told Ziegfeld that she believed that Anna "might live." To cheer Anna Ziegfeld arranged a performance for her of *Maid of Honor*, a new playlet about Joan of Arc, to be given privately in the ballroom of the Savoy. A squad of stagehands and scenery experts, acting on secret orders, moved into the ballroom and created, on a specially built stage, a superb arrangement of *fleur de lys* curtains and screens supervised by Urban.

Anna was brought in on a wheeled reclining chair as the great chandeliers were turned on and off, and a small group of musicians played "La Marseillaise." Then, with the curtains firmly drawn against the public, with only a doctor and a nurse as other members of the audience, Anna saw Josephine Victor, Guy Sazièses, and Walter Reynolds enact highlights of Joan of Arc's saintly career. After the burning at the stake, suggested by flickering red lights, Anna shook each member of the cast's hand. As they stepped back to their positions on the stage, she said, "Now I can die bravely, like my compatriot!" She asked for a large bouquet of roses to be sent to Miss Victor.

She was comparatively comfortable during early summer, but in August the severe heat affected her drastically. She was delirious as a result of pneumonia and could not recognize even her own daughter. She told Dr. Donald McCaskey: "It is the last curtain. I have lived, and I will hold out to the last. It is the spirit of Joan of Arc and the spirit of my parentage—the indomitable French."

According to Liane Carrera, Anna begged to see Ziegfeld, but he could not be found. Actually the doctors had asked him not to come to the bedside because it might unsettle the patient and make her last hours too painful.

Ina Claire recalls talking to Ziegfeld during those last dreadful weeks. "Why does that poor, good woman have to suffer so?" he asked, with tears in his eyes.

Anna died at 5:22 P.M. on August 13, 1918. She was 45 years old. Beatrice, her devoted maid, and Lillian Russell's sister, Susanne, were at her bedside. Ziegfeld made sure that she had a magnificent funeral, at the Campbell Funeral Church, followed by a superb High Mass at St. Patrick's Cathedral. He personally supervised the exquisite bouquet of orchids, roses, and lilies of the valley placed on the steel coffin, with the simple card, "From Flo." He did not attend the funeral. He had a horror of them, a fear of death.

Floral offerings came from Lillian Russell, Gertrude Hoffman, Lee Shubert, and Charles Hanlon. Liane, trying to console the sobbing Beatrice, occupied the family pew. The pallbearers were Gene Buck, Gus Edwards, Charles Evan Evans, and John P. Slocum. One thousand five hundred people packed the church, among them almost every theatrical celebrity of that time. As the cortège left the church, a crowd of 5,000 people, jamming the sidewalk along Broadway from 66th to 68th Street, pressed dangerously in, making movement difficult.

On September 14 the spectacular High Mass for Anna was staged in St. Patrick's Cathedral, with the Reverend William B. Martin, assistant rector, as celebrant. A full choir under the directorship of Professor J.C. Ungerer performed many of the most famous of Anna's songs. After the beautiful ceremony the body was interred at Mount Pleasant, in Westchester County.

Ziegfeld, deeply upset by Anna's death, was still more distressed by the accusations of cruelty and neglect made against him by Liane Carrera then and in subsequent years. However, he never made public his visits to Anna or his work to ease her final weeks. Except for an occasional comment to Julian Mitchell he never talked of Anna Held again.

9

"Sally"

THE 1918 *Follies* was the ultimate in patriotism. Kay
Laurell stood on top of a revolving globe as the "Spirit of
the *Follies*," and in one magnificent effect the audience
saw a tableau of war, including little French girls in rags,
a dying soldier attended by Red Cross volunteers, and a
trench over which doughboys charged amid devastating
gunfire which filled the theater. Bare-bosomed Kay Laurell
led the soldiers on to victory.

During the run of the 1918 *Follies*, Ziegfeld was increasingly disturbed by the realization that Marilyn Miller
was falling in love with Frank Carter, the handsome and
gifted dancer-comedian who sang in Irving Berlin's "I'm
Goin' to Pin a Medal on the Girl I Left Behind" in the
show. The *Follies* cast was on Marilyn's side: they all felt
that Ziegfeld was too old for her and that the affair would
always be hopelessly one-sided. Alongside the 51-year-old
Ziegfeld Marilyn looked entirely wrong. Frank Carter was
an ideal choice as a husband.

Ziegfeld was fiercely jealous of Carter. He was still more irritated when, in the spring of 1919, he heard that Eddie Cantor, who was rooming with Frank Carter at the time, had arranged private meetings for the young couple at various restaurants. There was very little Ziegfeld could do about it, however. He simply made Carter's and Cantor's life as difficult as possible in the *Follies*. When the two men came to him with a suggestion for a white-face number, he coldly informed them that the idea was ridiculous. But Gene Buck sided with them, telling Ziegfeld that it was absurd to let his personal feelings about Marilyn upset a brilliant scene. Carter married Marilyn in May, 1919.

Another vexation of 1918–1919 was a major fight with new-formed ticket speculators. Although Ziegfeld was not averse to dipping his hand in the box office when nobody was looking and taking out a few tickets to sell privately at large profits, he resented anyone who indulged in "scalping."

Usually the ticket brokers united for the purchase of numerous tickets to shows for several weeks ahead, charging heavily over the normal price. Ziegfeld announced that in the future he would only sell tickets directly to the public. The speculators struck back by planting people in the New Amsterdam Theater box office lines who turned over the tickets to the speculators.

When a mail order for five seats in the front row arrived from a Philadelphia girls' school, Ziegfeld called the head teacher personally and found out that the school's name was being used as a front by a speculator. It took him several months to break their power. On July 7, 1919, Ziegfeld sent a triumphant (but overly optimistic) cable to the *New York Times*: "SPECULATORS DEFEATED FOLLIES PLAYED TO SEVENTY THOUSAND SIX HUNDRED AND EIGHTY TWO DOLLARS IN TWO

WEEKS AND FIVE DAYS BIGGEST RECEIPTS IN THE HISTORY OF THE NEW AMSTERDAM FOR THAT LENGTH OF TIME EVERY SEAT SOLD AT THE BOX OFFICE PRICES NOT A SEAT PLACED IN HOTEL AGENCIES ZIEGFELD."

When District Attorney Swann talked of an ordinance's being passed to prevent speculation, Ziegfeld wired him: "SINCERELY TRUST YOU WILL SUCCEED IN HAVING PROPOSED ORDINANCE PASSED BUT DOUBT IT I FOUGHT THEM TOOTH AND NAIL ALDERMAN QUINN PROPOSED AN ORDINANCE THAT WOULD HAVE WIPED SPECULATORS OUT ENTIRELY BUT LIKE ALL ORDINANCES AGAINST THESE SPECULATORS IT IS THE LAST YOU HEAR OF THEM AND SPECULATORS GO ON THEIR MERRY WAY IF THEY OBJECT TO ORDINANCE YOU PROPOSE COMPEL THE PASSING OF THE QUINN ORDINANCE THAT PUTS THEM OUT OF BUSINESS THEIR INFLUENCE THEY BRAG OF I HOPE YOU WILL COMPEL IMMEDIATE ACTION THIS TIME."

No final action was taken, and speculation selling was a thorn in Ziegfeld's side 10 years later.

Ziegfeld had not only to cope with the battle against the ticket speculators that summer of 1919, he was also faced with an actors' strike. Only a few weeks after the 1919 *Follies* opened, the members of Equity, disgruntled by their poor wages and hard work, suddenly abandoned every theater in New York. Following the Shuberts' angry action in suing Equity for $500,000, Ziegfeld obtained temporary injunctions against every member of the *Follies* company and every officer in Equity. As the company arrived for the performance on the night of August 11, injunctions were presented to them one by one. Ziegfeld's affidavit covered eight typewritten pages. It stated that

$175,000 would be lost if the *Follies* closed. Justice Richard P. Lydon of the Supreme Court gave permission for performances to continue for the time being.

On August 13 five *Follies* principals—including Eddie Cantor, Ray Dooley, Van and Schenck, and John Steel, who sang "A Pretty Girl Is Like a Melody"—failed to appear at the theater. Ziegfeld had been so confident that everything would be settled by arbitration that he had not gone to the theater that night; when word of the principals' decision reached him at the Ansonia, he drove quickly to the theater in his Rolls. He arrived with his valet just after the theater manager, Malcolm Douglas, went on stage to announce the news. He was answered with a chorus of jeers, cheers, and laughter; the members of the audience eventually formed a line at the box office to get their money back.

When the strike was finally settled, in the summer, Ziegfeld celebrated with a lavish eighth edition of the midnight *Frolics*. The show offered a superb Urban set of two twisted trees against a background of shifting emeralds and amethysts, the chorus shimmering in darkness like fireflies against a black velvet sky. He also launched the first of his short-lived *Tonight at 8:10* Sunday concerts—with Raymond Hitchcock as master of ceremonies and a superb cast, including Marilyn Miller, Eddie Cantor, Irving Berlin, Fanny Brice, W.C. Fields, and Ted Lewis and his jazz band.

Utterly modern and free of the clinging fustian quality of some Ziegfeld productions, *Sunday at 8:10* ushered in a new era. Like the *Follies* and the *Frolics*, it was an immediate and overwhelming success. But by the usual irony that marked Ziegfeld's life, only two days after *Tonight at 8:10* opened—on October 28, 1919—the Prohibition Enforcement Act was passed by Congress over President Wilson's veto. Planned to go into effect on

January 1, 1920, it forbade among other things the selling
of liquor in places of entertainment. The law meant certain death, as Ziegfeld knew at once, to the midnight
Frolics and its world of boozy excitement.

In the midst of the strike and its aftermath, the ticket
war, the tension of getting the *Frolics* prepared, and the
threat of prohibition, Ziegfeld managed somehow to
find time to produce a new play by Somerset Maugham,
Caesar's Wife, for Billie Burke. Set in Egypt, it was the
slight but well-told story of Violet, a young woman married to Sir Arthur Little, a man 20 years her senior. She
is taken to live in Cairo, where he is the British Consul.

As is inevitable in such stories, Violet falls in love with
Sir Arthur's diplomatic secretary, a handsome young man
of her own age. In the end she abandons her lover and
decides to remain with her husband. Ziegfeld's super-
vision of the play was scrupulously tasteful and discreet,
proving him to be inspired not only in directing spectacle
but in managing intimate drama. Billie was a splendid
heroine, and the other parts were quite expertly played;
Norman Trevor made a smooth and accomplished Sir
Arthur. Urban's setting of the Nile Basin was subtly con-
vincing, with a romantic suggestion of palms, dark green
waters, and dusky purple sky.

To such aesthetic pleasures Ziegfeld added the harsher
one of Frank Carter's summary removal from the 1919
Follies before it opened in New York. Marilyn Miller protested bitterly, but Ziegfeld was adamant: Carter would
never work for him again. Quarrels between Ziegfeld and
Marilyn were frequent and squalid. By the spring of 1920
they were barely on speaking terms. In April, when she
was appearing with the touring 1919 *Follies* in Boston,
she threw a diamond bracelet that Ziegfeld had given her
petulantly in his face. Then out of the blue something
happened to resolve their quarrel.

One night Marilyn was preparing to go on stage when she received a telephone call from Maryland. She set the telephone in its cradle and collapsed on her dressing room floor. Her maid called Ziegfeld, who held her in his arms and begged her to tell him what had happened. "Frank's dead!" she told him. Frank Carter—who had been driving a Packard from Wheeling, West Virginia, where he had just completed the run of *See Saw*—had mistaken a bend at Cumberland, Maryland, for a straight stretch of road and had crashed, crushing his chest. Ziegfeld did his best to console Marilyn but told her brutally that she must go on stage that night. She looked at him with an expression of horror at his callousness; then abruptly she stopped crying. Her determination was as fierce as his. "You're right," she said. "I've never missed a performance, and I'm not going to miss one now."

She gave strict instructions that nobody was to speak to her, not even Ziegfeld, before she went on stage. As soon as she heard the opening bars, Ziegfeld squeezed her hand, director Ned Wayburn winked at her, and she crouched down like a runner. She sprinted into the wings and suddenly straightened up and strolled elegantly into an Urban blue spotlight to deliver "Sweet Sixteen." After that song and another specialty, Irving Berlin's "Mandy," she broke down, weeping uncontrollably. A moment later she stepped back on stage as glitteringly doll-like and technically flawless as before.

Ziegfeld stayed with her as long as possible before trial runs for the 1920 *Follies* began in Atlantic City. He excused her from the cast and sent her on an expensive European tour to recover. In the meantime, he had been planning an elaborate new vehicle for her talents: *Sally*.

He had begun to devise the musical during February at Palm Beach, Florida. Palm Beach was a newly booming resort, which millionaires Paris Singer and A. J. Drexel Biddle had helped to develop as a society playground during World War I. With the closing of Biarritz and Monte Carlo, Palm Beach became a magnet for the very rich; the palm trees, pale blue lagoons, lovely beaches, and perfect climate made it an ideal escapist paradise. Rum and whiskey runners insured a constant flow of liquor into the local speakeasies, and there was a superbly appointed gambling club, Bradley's, excellent golf links, and the best deep sea fishing available in America.

Ziegfeld—who first went there in the fall of 1915 to see Billie making *Gloria's Romance*—fell in love with it at once, not so much because it looked like an Urban set but because it offered him a chance to crash into high society. With Billie and four-year-old Patricia he arrived at the height of the season and began entertaining splendidly. He stayed at the Breakers Hotel before renting a house and began working with Jerome Kern on a basic plot for *Sally* in between catching sailfish and losing $10,000 or so at Bradley's.

Guy Bolton and P.G. Wodehouse arrived by train in the early spring, and Ziegfeld chartered the millionaire Leopold Replogle's yacht, *The Wench*, for a leisurely cruise through the Everglades. Peering down at the moss-colored alligators and the drifting weeds of the swamp, the collaborators had pleasant company: Olive Thomas returned briefly to the Ziegfeld harem for the trip; other leading players and chorus girls lay picturesquely around the decks in the sun; and after particularly heavy drinking nights a millionaire or two was liable to roll out of the scuppers.

Ziegfeld returned to Burkely Crest with plans set: Jerome Kern and Guy Bolton would work in New York and P. G. Wodehouse, in London. *Sally* would concern an orphan Cinderella who poses as a high-born girl, meets Prince Charming on Long Island, and becomes a singing and dancing star of the *Follies*.

In New York in the spring of 1920 Ziegfeld was shocked to discover that neither Erlanger nor Charles Dillingham was interested in *Sally*. They questioned the value of a Cinderella story in an increasingly sophisticated age. Ziegfeld stormed at them, screaming with hysterical rage that they were out of their minds. In the silence that followed Erlanger began jotting down figures. Finally he said: "It will cost a quarter of a million."

"I will find the money myself," Ziegfeld said. He immediately plunged every liquid cent he had into the production. It was a colossal gamble, which could have ruined him if it had fallen through. But he was determined to go ahead.

During the summer Ziegfeld was also faced with an unpleasant row with Eddie Cantor. Ever since the strike, relations between the two men had been extremely strained. Cantor finally left the *Follies*. Later, Ziegfeld claimed, Cantor committed an act of plagiarism.

Cantor and George LeMaire had jointly presented a comic sketch by Ziegfeld and Rennold Wolf called *The Osteopath's Office* in the 1919 *Follies*. Ziegfeld claimed that Cantor and LeMaire had rewritten the number and represented it as *The Dentist's Office* in LeMaire's new Shubert show, *Broadway Brevities*. Ziegfeld won the suit, and the act was dropped from the Shubert show.

On September 10, 1920, Ziegfeld received tragic news that Olive Thomas, of whom he was still deeply fond and whose presence on *The Wench* had been a pleasure to everyone who sailed on that voyage, had died suddenly in Paris at the age of 22. The news was an immeasurable shock to him. His deep paternal instinct was as powerful as his physical passion, and he felt that he had lost not only an adorable and enchanting mistress but a daughter. The circumstances of her death were lurid enough for the most jaded gossip columnist.

She had patched up her relationship with Jack Pickford and sailed to Paris that fall for what she told the press was "a second honeymoon." Actually it was more like an armed truce. Pickford by then had begun to experiment with drugs, supplied to him by a man who, together with Owen Moore, traveled with the couple. (Owen Moore was Mary Pickford's recently divorced husband.) There was vague talk of a movie to be directed by Owen Moore in England and starring Olive and Jack and of a stage production in Paris.

Checking into the Ritz, the couple quarreled almost constantly, their arguments alternating with parties in Montmartre. One morning the Sûreté arrived at the Ritz: Olive Thomas had been poisoned. Pickford's version was that she had been suffering from insomnia and had accidentally swallowed "some poison pills." Actually he was referring to an empty bottle of mercury bichloride, a crystal substance insoluble in water, a common prescribed treatment for syphilis.

Ziegfeld and his friends were far from happy with the "official" reports of Olive Thomas's death. The police were not completely satisfied with the verdict of accidental death, and they kept the file open for some years afterward. They questioned a number of people, including several who had taken part in a champagne and cocaine party and Captain Spalding, a former army man who was serving a six-month sentence for drug peddling. They were also gravely suspicious of the fact that the doctor who attended Olive Thomas at the end had examined her for a life insurance policy, made out in Jack Pickford's favor just before the couple left for Paris.

The public and private pressure on the Sûreté was so

extreme that the officials in charge of the case were compelled to approve the embalming of the body before the official autopsy disclosing the contents of the stomach could be issued. When the autopsy was finally made out, it showed that there were no traces of mercury in her system at all. Moreover, Jack Pickford's statement that "Ollie had gone for sleeping pills" made no sense at all. Had she done so, the cupboard, which lit up as the door opened, would easily have disclosed the pills. The case was closed with a clumsy disregard for any degree of proper investigation, and Pickford and Owen Moore were allowed to leave for London virtually unquestioned.

On September 18 Olive's body left on the SS *Mauretania* for New York, despite the statements of several passengers that they would cancel due to a fear of a "jinx" on the ship. Jack Pickford began to jump overboard halfway across but was pulled back by a fellow passenger. Four days later, when the body was in the mid-Atlantic, Anna Daly, Olive's closest friend, swallowed Veronal and died in Bellevue Hospital, in New York.

She left a note: "He doesn't love me anymore and I can't stand it and Olive is dead." Several people said that the girl's note referred to Ziegfeld, but the press discreetly described the man as "a New Yorker, now in Chicago." Ziegfeld had been seeing Anna Daly regularly for several months and had given her gifts, among them a diamond-studded cigarette case.

In New York on September 29 Ziegfeld helped arrange Olive Thomas's funeral, at St. Thomas Church, but according to his custom he refused to attend, asking Gene Buck to help carry the coffin in his place. Eugene O'Brien, Owen Moore, Thomas Meighan, Harrison Fisher, Myron Selznick, and Alan Crosland were the other pallbearers, and among the ushers was Irving Berlin. Mary Pickford's was the most spectacular bouquet, made of roses, orchids, and lilies. The 60 Club's superb wreath was inscribed with the words "Our Little Ollie," and as the body was carried out to the strains of "I Need Thee Every Hour," a huge crowd bore down on the mourners. Despite the efforts of the ushers, the crush was almost overwhelming, and several women leaving the church fainted and were carried down under the feet of the crowd. Eight cars carried the family and friends to Woodlawn, where the body was placed in a white marble vault.

Hearing of this was a horrible ordeal for Ziegfeld. With his loathing of ugliness and the reminders of mortality, he was disgusted by the whole business of death and its aftermath. The misery of the experience inspired him all the more to make *Sally* a hymn to life and beauty. He told Urban that he would give him absolute *carte blanche* to make *Sally* the loveliest musical ever, and he may indeed have achieved that aim. Its rags-to-riches Cinderella story of an orphan waif who crashes high society was beautifully worked out.

While Wodehouse in London and Bolton and Kern in New York continued to work on *Sally*, Ziegfeld and Erlanger decided to dislodge Marc Klaw from their long-standing partnership. In Europe Klaw had talked of settling on the Riviera, and he had said various things critical of the others to reporters in Paris. Before he returned, on September 10, Ziegfeld and Erlanger ruthlessly removed him from the business, eliminated his share in the *Follies* and *Frolics*, and stopped all payments to him in breach of contract. The resulting case dragged on for years.

Sally opened at the New Amsterdam Theater on December 21, 1920. It was an immediate smash hit. On one particular night the ovation was so overwhelming that it was impossible for Marilyn Miller to leave the stage.

Finally she ran down a ramp to the aisle and out of the theater. The audience followed her en masse and formed a crocodile around the block, returning to their seats afterward to cheer her again and again.

Shortly after the show opened, an amusing incident took place. Leon Errol played the Grand Duke of Checkogovonia in the play. Several members of the Lambs Club, whose members were largely theatrical people, told Leon Errol that the king of the Balkan state of which he was a Grand Duke would shortly be visiting America. Errol told them this was absurd: the kingdom was mythical. But they were quite unshaken; the king would arrive on a Saturday night, they said.

Club members dressed a Polish bootblack in hired theatrical clothes to play a fake national anthem when the king came in with his courtiers. Ziegfeld was in on the joke. As the procession entered the Royal Box, the orchestra struck up the fake anthem—composed by Dave Stamper—and Leon Errol spent the performance with one eye fixed in agony on the box.

According to eye-witness accounts, *Sally* was the most enchantingly light and airy of Broadway productions, with Marilyn Miller an exquisite heroine and the transitions from orphanage to Long Island house parties magically fluid and graceful in Urban sets and Ziegfeld lighting.

Although Marilyn's voice was not good, her version of "Look for the Silver Lining" was an enchantment because she sang it very simply, wearing a cheap dress. At first Ziegfeld did not want to introduce her in the opening scene looking like a ragamuffin, but Gene Buck pointed out that the transition to the lovely clothes of the second half would be all the more effective if her early attire was as drab as possible.

Not even Ziegfeld could fault her appearance in a wedding dress in "The Little Church Around The Corner" finale. The reviewers were ecstatic. Ziegfeld, who had had his doubts, was so completely overcome with joy that he even took Patricia, whom he usually kept away from the theater, to see *Sally*. Patricia was delighted (at the age of four she seems to have been remarkably precocious), but a trip backstage rapidly disillusioned her. When father and daughter visited Marilyn in her dressing room, the temperamental star berated Ziegfeld with foul abuse, complaining bitterly that her costume in the last act was too heavy. After this charmless exhibition in front of a child— it.was a matter that could easily have been discussed at any other time—relations between Ziegfeld and Marilyn cooled to the freezing point.

During the next few months Marilyn proved impossible. She accused Ziegfeld of constantly trying to seduce her, of conducting indiscreet affairs with chorus girls, and of behaving infamously in the girls' dressing rooms. The gossip she stirred up upset Ziegfeld dreadfully, as did the reawakening of public interest in his affair with Lillian Lorraine.

In January, 1921, Lillian fell on an icy New York sidewalk and severely injured her spine. For a time it seemed that she might never walk again. Lillian told him when he visited her in the hospital that she was bankrupt and that there were several suits out against her for unpaid restaurant, clothing, and hotel bills. He asked where her husband was; she said that Gresheimer was still serving a term in the Tombs Prison. Ziegfeld paid her bills but told her that she must not come near him again. There was already too much talk of their relationship's being resumed. She wept miserably in his arms.

The worst part of this wretched business was that Ziegfeld still loved Lillian. To the end of his life he kept a pair of exquisite nude paintings of her in his desk drawer. He would constantly take them out to look at them, and his eyes would fill with tears. If only she had not drunk, had not married badly, had not . . . He would mutter a few grim words on the subject to friends and close the drawer.

While *Sally* still packed the New Amsterdam, the 1921 *Follies* appeared at the slightly smaller Globe. Produced at a cost of $250,000, it was the most dazzling show of the series to date. Into the three crowded hours of the show Ziegfeld poured an extraordinary cornucopia of talent. New features included sumptuous new scenes designed by the great James Reynolds—a twelfth-century Persian episode and a recreation of the Royal Gardens of Versailles. Ben Ali Haggin created two tableaux, which glittered with brilliant colors. But the finest feature of the production was Fanny Brice singing the unforgettable "My Man."

French star Mistinguett had been engaged to sing Maurice Yvain's plaintive song of doomed love, but Ziegfeld disliked her and sent her back to Paris after one audition; he saw immediately that the song would be ideal for Fanny Brice. It was perfect because Fanny, whom he adored, needed to develop a new image, and her tragic affair with Nicky Arnstein was currently making national headlines. He told her to memorize "My Man" for rehearsal. He was horrified when she walked on stage dressed up like a female impersonator in a grotesque red wig and shawl. Ziegfeld ran up to the stage, ripped off the wig, and flung it in the wings. He pulled her shawl off and tore her dress from neck to hem. Then he knelt on the stage, smeared his hands with dust, and covered her arms, legs, and costume with the dirt. Fanny started to cry.

"*Now* sing it!" he cried triumphantly, and with a genuine sob in the voice she delivered the heartbreaking lyrics to perfection. Ziegfeld applauded her. When she sang "My Man" on opening night, the audience was in tears. Ziegfeld always felt it was the supreme moment of his career—that ragged, dust-smeared figure on the stage and the audience too overcome with emotion to applaud.

Another exciting event of 1921 took place in March at Palm Beach. Ziegfeld had borrowed Leonard Replogle's speedboat *Sea Rover* for a day's fishing and was peacefully casting his line off the coast when a huge devil fish snapped at the bait, and he was dragged out to sea. Luckily, Captain Bent Hiscock, a Florida waterway guide, was in another boat and was able to follow Ziegfeld out. Two other boats followed and did their best to shoot and harpoon the beast, without success. The struggle continued for 17 miles, until night fell. Exhausted, Ziegfeld finally had to let the beast go.

Back in New York in May, he announced grimly that the midnight *Frolics* would finally have to close because of Prohibition. He had become infuriated by the presence of officials in the audience and backstage. He told the *New York Times* that he was maddened by the fact that police stood by the tables and watched the customers drinking. Several customers had been arrested for carrying drinks into the theater. He announced that he would transfer the entire show to London in association with Gilbert Miller.

He cabled the *Times*: "THE CLOSING OF THE MID-NIGHT FROLICS ROOF IS SYMBOLIC OF THE FACT THAT THE MOST PRIZED POSSESSION OF AMERICAN LIBERTY IS DEAD PATRIOTISM IS AT A LOW EBB WHEN AMERICANS RETURNING FROM ABROAD LOOK AT THE STATUE OF LIBERTY AND LAUGH OUT LOUD I AM QUITTING FOR A PRINCIPLE AND THAT PRINCIPLE IS MORE FAR REACHING THAN MOST PEOPLE KNOW."

In 1921 Ziegfeld had a battle with Equity, which

reached a peak in December. While the 1921 *Follies* was
playing at the Colonial Theater in Chicago, he dismissed
Elizabeth Chatterton, a chorus girl who he felt was not
performing as well as she should. The Chicago officials of
Equity announced that unless she was reinstated, the
show would not go on. When the Equity man announced
this fact on stage during a rehearsal, W. C. Fields, Raymond Hitchcock, and Fanny Brice cheered.

Ziegfeld summoned reporters to the Colonial's roof, and
as he watched Leon Errol teaching the road aspirants to
the midnight *Frolics* their paces, he said: "If George M.
Cohan can't make a go of it because of the Equity grip,
I'm sure I can't. He found he could not, and he quit producing. Nobody is going to tell me how to run a show. I
put $200,000 into a production and then the Equity tells
me how to run it. Not me! I've been paying about $50,000
a year to some actresses and actors. There are seven in
the Chicago company who get $1,000 a week, and the ac-
tors have just no complaint against me. I don't want to
fight them or their union. That's why I am quitting. When
producing is made a continual wrangle, then I want to get
out."

He said he would move to London, after presenting a
Follies which would be based on the subject of the folly
of a producer trying to create under Equity conditions.
He did not keep his promise, and he was forced finally to
bow to Equity's accelerated demands.

In the summer, after the *Follies* was launched, Ziegfeld
was tired. He felt an overwhelming need to escape from
everything, even from the smart and ruthless Palm Beach
set. With characteristic boldness, he set out in July with
his family and servants, headed by the ubiquitous Sidney,
his valet, for northern Canada. Captain Gray, the Ziegfelds' guide at Palm Beach, found them an ideal vacation
site near Riley's Brook, in New Brunswick. They left on

August 10 in a private car recently refurnished by Ziegfeld. Riley's Brook was a miserable experience: it rained
constantly; there was only one rough cabin, which even
Billie Burke could not render comfortable. The entire
group breathed a sigh of relief when they finally left.

The following year Ziegfeld decided to go further: he
bought an island in the Laurentians, called it Billie Burke
Island, and named the camp he built on it Camp Patricia.
The log house, the adjoining guest lodge and kitchen
quarters, and Billie Burke's cottage made up a sizable
settlement, linked to the mainland by Cris-Craft. A chef
from Dinty Moore—Ziegfeld's favorite restaurant in New
York—was in charge of the corned beef and cabbage, and
there were six servants, eight guides, and a constant flow
of guests. Later, the entire ménage shifted to a house on
the shores of Lake Edward, north of Quebec, where Ziegfeld could shoot game birds and (despite Billie's objec-
tions) deer.

In April, 1922, Ziegfeld was in Boston, where *Sally* was
on tour after its run at the New Amsterdam. He was trying to patch up his relationship with Marilyn after a series
of rows with Billie. Marilyn locked him out of her dressing room, insulted him in public, and did her utmost to
dissuade him from any possible reentry into her life.

After the 1922 *Follies* were underway, Ziegfeld left for
a stay in Paris and London, where he again began ill-fated
plans to shift the *Follies* to a British base. While he was
abroad, Marilyn Miller started a new series of accusations
against him, and he read in a New York paper that Billie
had been in tears, talking of a divorce. Although this was
quite untrue, he panicked. He sent Billie a telegram at her
summer retreat with Patricia in York Harbor, Maine:
"BILLIE DARLING I AM NEARLY INSANE FOR
GODS SAKE CABLE ME WHAT IT IS ALL ABOUT
I AM NOT AFRAID OF THE TRUTH AND I SWEAR

TO GOD THERE IS NOTHING TO WHICH YOU CAN TAKE EXCEPTION WAIT UNTIL I AM PROVEN GUILTY YOU AND PATRICIA ARE ALL THAT MEAN ANYTHING TO ME BE FAIR DEAREST WILL SAIL ON THE NEXT BOAT."

Interviewed at York Harbor by the *New York Times*, Billie was in tears. She admitted that she had cabled Ziegfeld demanding an explanation of Marilyn's statement that she was "oblivious" of her husband's love life. The miserable business dragged on until Ziegfeld got back from Europe.

Meanwhile, in midsummer Marilyn Miller attended a lavish house party at the Great Neck, Long Island, home of Hollywood director Alan Dwan; there she met and danced with Jack Pickford, and they talked of their mutual bereavements. Within a few days they had fallen in love: both tough, prankish, irresponsible, fun-loving, and fiercely ambitious, they had a great deal in common. On his return to New York, Ziegfeld heard ·that Jack Pickford had taken yet another of his mistresses off his hands.

He was beside himself, but he had to admit that Marilyn had by then become a thorn in his side, and he told Billie so. She refused to believe him, and when he gave her a diamond bracelet as a peace offering, she flung it to the corner of the room. She relented only when Jack Pickford married Marilyn Miller at Pickfair, the Hollywood home of Mary Pickford and Douglas Fairbanks, in late July.

10
Goldie

A<small>T</small> the end of 1922 Ziegfeld was a tired man. To the public he seemed a remote and enviable figure, surrounded by dazzling luminaries as a star is surrounded by its attendant planets, married to a lovely and generous stage star, the father of a pretty six-year-old child. He had a mansion on the Hudson and a fortune, largely earned by *Sally*, approaching $2 million.

Yet he was deeply troubled: Lillian's agonizingly slow recovery from near-paralysis was a burden; Billie Burke's jealous tantrums infuriated him; Marilyn Miller was telling everyone that he was making her life impossible even after her marriage; and in the New York courts there was a severe struggle with Marc Klaw, who was battling for restitution of sums Erlanger and Ziegfeld had failed to pay him.

During that winter Ziegfeld's nagging worries brought him to the edge of total melancholia. His eccentricities increased: he began carrying a small red cornelian elephant with its trunk up for luck, and if anyone brought him an elephant with its trunk down, he would scream with terror, cower against a wall, and order it smashed to pieces. Elephants marched across the bizarre clutter of his desk in his ninth floor office at the New Amsterdam, each with its trunk held triumphantly high. These creatures—he had adopted the elephant-collecting habit after his first visit to Ringling Brothers circus with Anna Held—were his protection against misfortune, but he still lived in a cloud of anxiety only partly concealed by his reckless spending.

Bert Williams's sudden death, from pneumonia, in 1922 and the death of Ziegfeld's father in 1923 deeply depressed him.

Another major problem was his crumbling, decrepit office and his squabbling staff. For all his passion for beauty and perfection, he had failed to create a beautiful or efficient environment in which to work. Instead he toiled in summer heat and winter cold without proper ventilation in a stuffy, shabby, ugly cluster of little rooms with bilious green walls. The office's atmosphere was a shock to everyone who visited it.

Ziegfeld's own office at the time was poorly furnished, overlooking 42nd Street; right outside his windows was the huge New Amsterdam sign with enormous metal bars, which blocked out light and air and flashed intermittently at night, making his room look as though it were illuminated by lightning. At the other end of the dimly lit hall that led from his door Sam Kingston, the indispensable general manager, had his tiny room, with his roll-topped desk.

Ziegfeld's aging secretary, Emily England, sat in the room adjoining Kingston's; she had worked with Flo since the spring of 1912, and she was growing old and slow in her responses. Facing the alley behind 42nd Street was the Ziegfeld office switchboard, jammed into a cubicle. It was run by Alice Poole, the famous "telephone girl," a gaunt, thin woman who listened in on every conversation.

Dissatisfaction was extreme among this tiny staff, and Ziegfeld scarcely helped matters by arriving at odd hours of the afternoon after spending the mornings in bed at Hastings talking to Emily, dictating cables, and generally raising the roof. It was impossible for Emily to keep his desk tidy. It was piled high with every kind of paper that could be imagined, some of them crushed into tiny balls. Often he would scream for a missing contract, and when he went out, the staff would find it written on a scrap of notepaper almost unrecognizably mangled and buried under a litter of stockings, color schemes, and ubiquitous elephants.

If Ziegfeld saw someone he liked in a show, he often would simply tear out a leaf from a pocket notebook, have the person sign it backstage, and declare it a contract. The speed at which he lived left no time for care in making agreements.

The problems of running his office proved insuperable by the outset of 1923. Luckily Ziegfeld found an escape valve in a new addition to the staff: Matilda Golden; a bright, black-haired smart girl with immense charm who was known as "the last virgin on Broadway." He christened her Goldie. She had been working for press agent Will A. Page at Fox Film Corporation, and she followed Page into Ziegfeld's employ on her twenty-first birthday, on February 25. At first Ziegfeld was barely conscious of her presence, but soon he began to realize that she was an invaluable standby. Goldie eventually assumed immense importance in his life, acting as conscience, custodian, and keeper of secrets of the Ziegfeld empire.

On the day she arrived at the office everything was in

chaos. Members of Ziegfeld's staff were screaming at one another like the inhabitants of an insane asylum. Aside from Emily England (Ziegfeld's secretary) there was Nellie Hurley and Kathryn Dix, Billie Burke's secretary. Various composers would wander in and out in a crazy fashion. Ziegfeld himself would arrive late in the afternoons, looming in a huge beaver-lined coat and a $50 gray Stetson hat with a narrow brim and a slit in the middle of the crown. Everyone was terrified when he walked in—everyone except Goldie.

Anyone seeing him in his office would have forgotten the smoothly elegant public image at once; they would have seen and heard him screaming "Jesus, what kind of a goddamn place am I running around here?" Aside from Goldie, the only member of the office staff who was able to handle him was Sally, a large chimpanzee that was constantly stationed at Goldie's desk, pounding away at the typewriter.

It was Goldie's job to help Ziegfeld in a complex pattern of lies. She covered for him when he failed to show up for appointments—an eccentricity he developed in the 1920s—and helped him block the first trickle of process servers, which later increased to a deluge. One of Goldie's rare indiscretions occurred when a reporter asked her why Ziegfeld rarely came into the office. "Mr. Ziegfeld does his best work in bed," she said.

Goldie played an innocent role in Victor Herbert's death, in 1926. She had told him that Ziegfeld was out (Ziegfeld was making love to a girl in his office, and he did not want to see Herbert because he owed him royalties). When Herbert discovered that Ziegfeld was really in—he caught a glimpse of him as the girl left—he went purple. He flew out the door and had a fatal stroke a few minutes later.

No sooner would Goldie get home to the Bronx, at some

unearthly hour of the night, than Ziegfeld would call her. He would phone her from Hastings with a whole new set of instructions or with requests for correct spellings of words in 50-page telegrams.

During the difficult years of the early 1920s Ziegfeld's friends stood loyal: Gene Buck, suave and accomplished as always, Julian Mitchell, who had reluctantly returned to the fold, Ned Wayburn, Joseph Urban, Fanny Brice, and his bosom companion, Will Rogers. At home he continued to lavish gifts that he could not afford on Patricia. He remained a devoted if still wandering husband to Billie. He hated the decade as much as he had loved the previous one—a sure sign that he was quite firmly middle-aged.

He continued to work as ferociously as ever, trying to stem his engulfing boredom and despair with 18-hour shifts as he badgered and bullied the designers, scene painters, and the writers, all of whom were expected to produce at a moment's notice. He constantly scrapped whole scenes and sets of costumes without warning—capriciously and foolishly rather than with the inspiration of the past. He kept strands of colored ribbon in his pocket, which he played with. Often he would fish one out and redo an entire show in that color. The always erratic, compulsive, almost crazed side of his genius emerged, to the consternation of his employees. His overworked press agents—among them O.O. McIntyre and Will A. Page—tried by dint of a constant flow of beatific articles supposedly penned by Ziegfeld to give the impression that he was as smooth, calm, and kind-hearted as ever.

During that period the stunts grew more frequent and more bizarre. They were desperate flings at sustaining a notoriety in a time when the competition from his imitators, among them Earl Carroll and his former employee,

George White, was particularly threatening, and when Abe Erlanger was growing increasingly testy about Ziegfeld's gambling losses.

One showgirl, Jessie Reed, was married in a blaze of publicity to a fake millionaire. She divorced him, likewise publicly, and married an obscure Chicago-born advertising clerk. Both marriages were organized by Will A. Page. A cow-milking stunt between Ann Pennington and Mae Daw was arranged by Page: the contest took place at the home of the boxer James J. Corbett, and a swarm of photographers and reporters recorded every detail of the encounter.

The shimmying Gilda Gray was launched when Ziegfeld arranged for a "plant" to toss a $100,000 necklace into her lap from a stage box; the man—a humble employee— was supposed to be a Texas oil tycoon.

In 1922 showgirl Ruth Urban was telling the press that she would "sooner have dinner with a pig than with some men I know." Will Page arranged immediately for a pig dinner at the Casino in Central Park. A carefully selected group of authors, actors, and "society" people took their places at the table; the seat beside Ruth Urban was vacant. As a band started to play, a white pig dressed in violet silk ribbons walked in and was tied to the high chair. It tucked in to corned beef and cabbage while the other guests feasted on champagne and terrapin. "*Actress Prefers Pig to Fiancé*" was a typical headline. It was Will Page who put across Ann Pennington as a big star. Although she was only a fair dancer and singer, he managed to make her famous for her "dimpled knees."

Perhaps the most elaborate stunt engineered for the *Follies* was the *Follies* boat race on Central Park Lake, with Park Commissioner Francis H. Gallatin as umpire. Huge police squads kept back the crowds. Although few of the girls had the slightest idea of how to row, they all tackled the oars with great energy. One girl, Pearl Eaton—Mary Eaton's sister—made a serious mistake and crashed into another boat, capsizing and throwing Pearl and her companions into the water. A brave young policeman dived in and helped to rescue the pretty girls.

Other splendid stories emerged from Jean Stewart's constant companion (a baby lamb on a golden leash) and the magnificent "surf jazz" *Follies* party at Rockaway, in which the girls played saxophones as they danced in the water under the full moon, and shadowy couples embraced under cover of the rocks. At the Sound View Golf Club Shirley Vernon played a golf tournament dressed only in a rain barrel, thus starting a craze for "strip golf," in which the players removed a garment every time they lost a hole.

More lurid than these minor events—and less to Ziegfeld's liking—was the immense publicity attached to the quarrels of two *Follies* stars—blackface comedian Frank Tinney and showgirl Imogene Wilson. Tinney, a difficult, bad-tempered man, had first fallen in love with Imogene Wilson when he gave her a lift home in a taxi in a thunderstorm. He did not return to his wife and son that night, and he neglected to mention their existence to Imogene. When she asked him about it, he made a widely quoted remark: "I have a mortgage and an appendix as well as a wife. Why bring these things up and spoil a pleasant time?"

Imogene Wilson made the headlines again when she burst into Tinney's Long Island home and demanded that he leave his wife. In a showdown at his West 72nd Street apartment, Tinney told Imogene that he was through with her. She ran to a cupboard, swallowed what she said was poison, and called the police. When the policemen arrived, they found that she displayed no symptoms of poisoning. Tinney told the press that he had anticipated her action and had replaced the poison pills with harmless ones.

When a reporter arrived to ask her the true story behind the suicide attempt, Tinney threw him to the ground and kicked the girl, who complained to Magistrate Thomas F. McAndrews that Tinney had tried to kill her. He was arrested and imprisoned for assault and battery. Ziegfeld's doctor, Dr. Jerome Wagner, testified that Imogene looked as though she had been "struck by an automobile." Ziegfeld, half-revolted by the publicity but realizing that the bookings were unprecedented as a result, announced that despite everything, "Miss Wilson would be engaged for the 1924 *Follies.*"

The case opened in New York on May 30, 1924. Imogene Wilson was unable to appear in court on the first day. On the second day she made a magnificently dramatic entrance, accompanied by her sister and her maid. Chalky-white, heavily rouged, and gaudily dressed in a blue suit, cloche hat, and pink stockings, she was carried in by two attendants in a chair. She could barely be heard as she described Tinney's assaults on her. The audience created such a hubbub that Judge Goddard ordered the court cleared and asked "What is this, a circus?"

Tinney claimed that the entire story of the assault was fictitious, and finally a Supreme Court decision upheld his case. Still the garish story—given one front-page spread after another—continued as Imogene Wilson chased Tinney onto the *Bremen* in New York Harbor and continued a furious quarrel in front of reporters until she was ordered down the gangplank at sailing time. That display was enough for Ziegfeld, who fired her from the *Follies* at once.

In another stunt Ziegfeld telegraphed Postmaster General Harry S. New on October 1, 1925, offering to finance an entire issue of one million postage stamps if they would carry Billie's photograph. When the *New York Times* asked him what on earth he was up to, he said on the telephone: "The offer is made in perfectly good faith. The idea came to me from the recent announcement of the Italian government that it would sell advertising privileges on government postage stamps to raise special revenue. The Italians have estimated that by this means the Treasury should profit to the extent of between $10 million and $15 million annually, and I do not see that it would be beneath the dignity of the United States government to follow the example of Rome. I offer the government 60 percent of gross receipts on the same terms as requested by the Italian Government." The offer was, of course, ignored.

One episode that was not devised as a stunt was the extraordinary event of the Montana cowgirl. In 1923 a big fight was held between Dempsey and Gibbons in Shelby, Montana. A number of famous newspaper reporters were sent to cover it, including Percy Hammond and Heywood Broun. They combined forces to play a special practical joke on Ziegfeld. They cabled him that they had found a raving beauty called Patricia Salmon, who was the toast of Montana, and that he must immediately sign her for the *Follies*. Ziegfeld was beside himself with excitement, and cabled to them: "SEND COWGIRL AT ONCE."

She was imported to New York in his private car, and a suite was booked for her at the Ritz-Carlton. When she arrived Ziegfeld nearly passed out. She was short, fat, and plain, and she had the shadow of a moustache on her upper lip. In 30 seconds Ziegfeld realized he had been the victim of a joke. In 60 he decided not to lose face. Immediately he went ahead and had the girl made up, dressed, slimmed down, and exploited to the hilt as "Montana cowgirl joins the *Follies*." He never let the astonished girl know that he was on to her joke, and he even staged a whole Montana Cowgirl number around her in the *Follies*, with a lavish set by Urban.

During those awkward years Ziegfeld tried to proceed with his career as a producer of straight plays starring Billie. The first of these was *Intimate Strangers*, by Booth Tarkington, in which Billie appeared with the Lunts; *Rose Briar*, also by Tarkington, which was unsuccessful; and *Annie Dear* (filmed by Billie as *Good Gracious, Annabelle*), which exasperated Ziegfeld, since the author, Claire Kummer, deliberately circumvented any of his changes by special terms of her contract.

Ziegfeld never really had his heart in any of these productions, and in 1924, after *Annie Dear* closed, he was glad to loan Billie out to other producers: Kenneth Mac-Gowan and Sidney Ross presented her in *The Marquise*, with A. E. Mathews; Earle Crooker and Lowell Brenano presented her in *Family Affairs*, a flop that lasted only seven performances; and finally Ziegfeld's bitter enemy, Lee Shubert, presented her in *The Truth Game*, with Ivor Novello as co-star and author.

In the early 1920s Ziegfeld had a complicated relationship with his comedians. He resented their interruption of the rapid flow and dazzle of a performance with their static acts, but behind the scenes he was fonder of them than they realized. He was capable of sending Fanny Brice an angry telegram when she left a show to have a baby, but at the same time he would advance her $240,000 (lying that it was all he had) when she needed money to help her gangster friend, Nicky Arnstein.

He found W.C. Fields murderously unfunny and even fined him for lost tennis balls in a tennis act. He hated using the chorus girls as props for Fields's acts. Most of all, he loathed and feared Fields's dwarf, Shorty. With his horror of freakishness and deformity and his superstition that dwarfs brought bad luck, he screamed with rage when Shorty came anywhere near his office.

On one occasion Fields played a scene with Fanny Brice and Ray Dooley: a family is out in a Ford, and the father is proud of its perfect glittering polish. A man comes along and strikes a match on it to light a cigarette, and a blind man strikes it with his stick. Ziegfeld hated the act, and Fields had to hire a rehearsal hall and prepare it in secret. With the collusion of the stage manager it was slipped in during the first tryout at Atlantic City. The audience laughed hysterically, but Ziegfeld was furious. "Slows up the show," he said.

Another scene he hated had Fields trying to sleep on a back porch swing while milkmen came up the stairs with clattering bottles, babies dropped things on his head, and icemen shouted in the alley. Ziegfeld was furious. On opening night the audience was helpless with laughter. "They don't mean it," Ziegfeld said.

One comedian he especially liked was Eddie Cantor. It was therefore with great pleasure that he heard of plans to sell him on the idea of a new Cantor musical, set in Palm Beach. The idea of this show, *Kid Boots*, had originated early in 1923 when the writer William Anthony McGuire, a flamboyant, hard-drinking personality, and his wife Lou met with Joe McCarthy and Harry Tierney, the creators of the musical *Irene*.

The meeting was at Pelham, near New York. As the group enjoyed martinis one Sunday afternoon, Eddie Cantor drove over dressed in a bizarre golfing outfit with checked knickerbockers and a garishly ugly golf cap. McGuire laughed loudly and said to Cantor that a very funny musical show could be written around the outfit. They developed it as a group, in a series of conferences clouded with cigar smoke, with the help of Cantor and

lyricist Otto Harbach. Ziegfeld was immediately enthusiastic. It was only after three weeks of laborious, heavily
overemphatic pages of dialogue had come onto his desk
that Ziegfeld suddenly lost interest. He called Eddie in to
say that he had decided to call the whole thing off. Cantor was horrified and immediately flung himself into an
extraordinary routine in which he took every part in the
show. Ziegfeld laughed loudly at this exhibition and decided, against his better judgment, to take the gamble.

The show was divided into two acts. Cantor played
Boots, a caddy-master and official bootlegger of a Palm
Beach golf club, who also dealt in crooked golf balls. The
story had him tricked at his own game, and his friend, the
local champion, secures a loaded ball and loses the season's biggest match. On the side Boots is shown acting
as Cupid in a relationship between the lovely Polly
(played by beautiful Mary Eaton) and Tom (Harry
Fender). Jobyna Howland appeared as the club's hilarious
PT director, Dr. Josephine Fitch, who in one very funny
scene pummels the unfortunate Boots into jelly.

Cantor and Ziegfeld felt that the score lacked one really
superb song and introduced "Dinah," by Akst, Young, and
Lewis, which Cantor delivered with great élan in the last
act. Harry Akst had played it to Cantor in his hotel suite,
and the comedian fell in love with it at once.

The first night in Pittsburgh went off with a tremendous
bang, and the audience loved the show. Ziegfeld was over-
joyed. He shook hands with saturnine British director
Edward Royce and Eddie Cantor, and they dropped a
ring of roses on the stage as soon as the curtain fell. Late
that night, carried away by exuberance, Ziegfeld played
out a complete drunken scene himself to show comedian
Harland Dixon how it should be done. Then, after telling
the rest of the company not to do so on pain of dismissal, he
himself cabled every newspaper in New York to tell them

of the show's success. At midnight he and Eddie Cantor went to supper in a Chinese restaurant. "From now on," Ziegfeld told him, "I'm not Mr. Ziegfeld. I'm Flo or Ziggy."

The New Year's Eve opening, at the Earl Carroll Theater in New York—at $16.50 a ticket—was another triumph. Ziegfeld had scrapped and replaced the whole of the first act finale's sets and costumes and had recast minor roles, all to tremendous effect. But he wasn't happy. As the crowds poured backstage to congratulate Cantor and Mary Eaton, Ziegfeld turned to Lou McGuire and said, "Isn't it funny, Lou? I haven't had a telegram from Patricia tonight." Then he turned, with tears in his eyes, and said to Eddie Cantor, "Happy New Year." He gave him a bottle of vintage hock and a note, left on the makeup shelf: "Drink a toast to me and the show."

During the run of *Kid Boots* Ziegfeld became dissatisfied with the financial arrangements imposed on him by Earl Carroll for the use of the theater. Without warning one day he moved the entire show to the Selwyn Theater, leaving Carroll astonished, without a tenant, and in severe financial difficulties.

Later, while *Kid Boots* was on tour in Chicago after its New York run, Ziegfeld sent Cantor a 12-page telegram full of suggestions for last-minute changes in the performance. Exasperated by the whole thing, Cantor wired back one word: "YES."

Ziegfeld sent another telegram: "WHAT DO YOU MEAN YES DO YOU MEAN YES YOU WILL TAKE OUT THE SONG OR YES YOU WILL PUT IN THE LINES OR YES YOU WILL FIX THAT SCENE OR YES YOU HAVE TALKED TO THOSE ACTORS."

Cantor replied "NO."

Ziegfeld absolutely forbade Cantor to play at benefits, believing that such work would drain him completely.

One night Ziegfeld heard that Cantor would appear in a benefit at a ballroom. Cantor denied it. When Cantor appeared on the stage, he saw Ziegfeld and Billie Burke sitting in the front row. He leaned over the footlights and said, "This isn't me you see up here!" Ziegfeld laughed hysterically.

11

Into the Twenties

In March, 1924, Ziegfeld presented Sigmund Romberg's lavish *Louie the XIV*, designed as a vehicle for the Australian Leon Errol. Since the *Follies* was still running at the New Amsterdam, the production was staged at William Randolph Hearst's Cosmopolitan Theater, recently abandoned as a movie house following the collapse of Hearst's plans to launch Marion Davies as a popular star through a series of Cosmopolitan pictures. The Cosmopolitan Theater was situated near Central Park, away from the thriving theater district, and Hearst gave Erlanger, Dillingham, and Ziegfeld remarkably good business terms for the lease.

On top of the theater was an unusual feature: a sumptuously furnished apartment with several bedrooms and a giant living room furnished with heavy Spanish chairs, chests of drawers, tables, and lamps. Ziegfeld installed Goldie in the apartment during the run of *Louie the XIV* so that she could be on call 24 hours a day. He ordered

163

from Joseph Urban and Urban's daughter, Gretl, the most extraordinary sets built in the theater up to that time, including a banquet room. The banquet table ran the whole length of the stage and was covered with real gold cloth and a real gold service, which Ziegfeld had imported from Paris in 1922 and had used at Burkely Crest. It cost $50,000. The guests ate real food prepared by a chef in the wings.

Ziegfeld forbade Romberg to use any brass in the score. (This was another dislike that had grown to overwhelming proportions with the passage of years. Even in shows that demanded brass, he would stand at the orchestra pit screaming, "Take that brass down!")

Ethel Shutta—still active in New York theater—performed in the show. She also appeared simultaneously in the *Follies of 1924*. She would leave the stage at the Cosmopolitan Theater with her makeup still on, and with Goldie at her side she would race in a police car arranged by the mayor. Sirens at full blast, they would go screaming along the streets to the New Amsterdam. She would play her number, change her clothes, and go screaming back.

Louie the XIV was a flop—it played 79 performances—and on tour it suffered a severe interruption, which finally resulted in its closure. Leon Errol fell from a parallel bar and smashed both his ankles. Since his most famous routine was "rubberlegs," he covered for several performances. But finally he had to leave for Europe and a series of treatments.

Through those years the lawsuits went on and on. In August, 1924, Bert Green, a cartoonist whom Ziegfeld had commissioned to create some animated film effects in a *Follies* scene, sued him for nonpayment (Ziegfeld had turned the basic drawings down). For a week Green's representative tried to serve the process without success.

Finally his lawyer, W. Wright Moxley, devised a scheme by which they could reach Ziegfeld.

The men bought six bottles of whiskey, emptied them out, and filled them with water. They sent an associate, George Thompson, with them to Ziegfeld's office on a Thursday afternoon. Thompson said to Tommy Caldwell, an attendant, "I've got something for Mr. Ziegfeld." When Emily England came out, he said, "It's a gift from the captain of a Cunard White Star ship. I'm not to give it to anyone but Mr. Ziegfeld in person." Emily reappeared and said Ziegfeld would see him. Thompson placed the box on the floor and handed Ziegfeld an envelope. "It's a note from the captain," he said.

"What captain, what ship?" Ziegfeld snapped irritably.

"The note tells all about it," Thompson said, backing to the door.

Ziegfeld opened the letter and read the writ. Thompson fled past the secretary and out of the building while Ziegfeld stood aghast with the writ in his hand.

Other cases were legion. A soprano named Olive Cornell sued and won $7,280 because Ziegfeld had dismissed her without warning from the *Follies*. Gallagher and Shean, famous comedians, sued for being arbitrarily contracted so that they could not appear for any other management; the case was settled by Ziegfeld out of court. Mischa Elman, a violinist, kept Ziegfeld in court for eight years on a charge of having canceled a contract for an operetta without warning. Again Ziegfeld was forced to settle out of court.

To pay for these lawsuits Ziegfeld prepared a new musical, J.P. McEvoy's *The Comic Supplement*, as a vehicle for W.C. Fields, in 1924. Much as he disliked Fields, he was forced to admit to Gene Buck's contention that the man was a money spinner. Fields had been in Hollywood, and Ziegfeld invited him back.

Ziegfeld disliked J.P. McEvoy, who had masses of black hair and a huge moustache and never washed. Ziegfeld called him the Buffalo, but he respected his talent. He had seen McEvoy's *The Potters* and had called him around to ask him, quietly and apologetically, if he would write a show for him based on simple comedy, a comedy of the people. McEvoy said that he had just finished *The Comic Supplement*, a daring satirical commentary on America, with all the characters dressed in brutal yellows and reds and greens and representing the world of the Sunday paper funnies. After listening to him Ziegfeld said: "All right, I'll take it. How much do you want?"

McEvoy took a deep breath and said: "Three thousand dollars."

Ziegfeld said all right and pressed a button. He told his secretary, "Make out a check for $3,000 to Mr. McEvoy. Charge it to *The Comic Supplement*." And they were in business.

Once the show was completed, Ziegfeld was fascinated by it, and he brought Julian Mitchell in to stage it. W.C. Fields did extensive work on the book and was engaged to play several parts, co-starring with brilliant comic Ray Dooley, who introduced the Baby Snooks idea that Fanny Brice adopted later on.

One Fields sketch was especially inspired. It was set at the back of an apartment house on a fire escape; Fields was struggling down the fire escape carrying a huge chunk of ice, which began to melt as he did so. The girls were dressed in costumes by John Held, Jr., all bizarre and representing some of the famous funnies female characters.

The show's most inventive number showed a young working girl coming home from work, followed by chorus girls, stenographers, and waitresses. They climbed a real stairway and were shown in tiers of windows in shadow play, an immense and complex pattern of silhouettes illustrating in abstract how they filled the evening. It was an astonishing and daring concept, of which Ziegfeld, designer Norman Bel Geddes, and Mitchell were justly proud. It equaled the very best work of Max Reinhardt. But McEvoy's French wife was shocked by Julian Mitchell's frank staging, which showed the girls removing their girdles and scratching. At a rehearsal in Newark she jumped up to her feet and screamed, "I will not have them do that in my husband's show!" The scratching was dropped.

The production was much too *avant-garde* for the Newark audiences, and it lasted only three weeks. Ziegfeld had grown impatient with it as soon as he sensed the audience's disinterest, and he abandoned his superb concept without a tremor. He did not even open it in New York. Moreover, he was so vexed by the running battle between Marc Klaw and Abe Erlanger about the right of Erlanger to use the exclusive title of *The Follies* that he decided to abandon the *Follies* that year as well.

First, though, he decided to go to Europe for a vacation. On July 25, 1925, with Billie and Patricia, a large entourage, and a mountain of wardrobe trunks, he set said on the *Majestic*. The crossing was uneventful, and the family checked into the Ritz in Paris. They went to Deauville for Patricia's health, visited the *Folies Bergères*, aid sailed for England. In London they also put up at the Ritz. When Ziegfeld announced that he wanted to see British recruits for the *Follies*, 5,000 girls jammed Piccadilly. He sent out several lieutenants to announce that they would not be auditioned at the hotel, but that if they came to New York, they would be given a chance. Two girls bribed maids to lend them their uniforms, and they carried trays into Ziegfeld's suite. Suddenly the "maids" broke into a song-and-dance routine. He and Billie were so amused by this degree of enterprise that they brought the girls to America. However, they were forced to send them back when Equity forbade their employment.

Just before returning on the steamship *Leviathan*, on August 29, the family went out to see Eugene Sandow, who was living in a cottage near London. Old grudges were forgotten as Ziegfeld and the ailing strong man talked about the lion incident, the railroad carriage wheel stunt, and the long tours with their show. Not long after he returned to America, Ziegfeld was saddened to learn that Sandow had died—of a stroke after trying to lift an automobile out of a muddy ditch.

Ziegfeld felt greatly refreshed by the trip. He had been feeling tired and ill and increasingly isolated from Billie; the voyage had almost been a second honeymoon, and he avoided all other women in those happy weeks. Once he was back, he started to make enthusiastic plans for a new show, called *The Palm Beach Girl*. His weariness and irritation had disappeared. The show was to be staged first in Palm Beach and then in New York.

The Palm Beach Girl was designed as Palm Beach's first major fling at theater.

Paris Singer, A. J. Drexel Biddle, and Ziegfeld combined forces to create a new Palm Beach playhouse—the Montmartre. The theater was situated at Lake Worth, just north of the Everglades Club, and it offered a restaurant and a dance band. Formerly an assembly hall, it was brilliantly redecorated, by Urban, with a new sliding roof that opened up to show the dark sky and the stars.

Given a *carte blanche* budget by his millionaire friends, Ziegfeld was carried away by the heady excitement of the occasion. Instead of his usual roster of famous stars, he featured some exciting newcomers: Edmonde Guy, a French star, whom he fired early on because the audience could not understand her; Norah Blaney and Gwen

Farrar; and Louise Brown, who he believed had a future but who disappointed him. One of the few major new names was Claire Luce; she appeared in a glittering glass ball covered in mirrors, which opened to release her like a chicken from an egg. On one occasion, however, it failed to open, and she was almost stifled in her oval cage.

Opening night in Palm Beach was an enormous success. Tickets sold for $200 each. The millionaires, led by Rep Replogle, Ed Hutton, and the other backers, arrived at the head of a dazzling social set, and each number was applauded ecstatically, regardless of its quality.

Once again Ziegfeld was constantly casting, recasting, taking out numbers, and adding others. During the 1924 *Follies* he had introduced a girl called Peggy Fears, whom he showed as a sleeping prince surrounded by wooden soldiers as she dreams of them marching at her command. The music was written by Victor Herbert, and the number was an immense triumph. He admired Peggy deeply (she reminded him of Lillian Lorraine) and decided to star her in the New York production of *The Palm Beach Girl*, supported by the belief in her of W.C. Fields, Ray Dooley, Fanny Brice, and Will Rogers.

Ziegfeld and Billie took Peggy back to Hastings on weekends to make her feel at ease, and they became very close personal friends, lecturing her about beaux and late hours as though they were her parents. Ziegfeld sometimes would put his hand on her face, look into her eyes, which were just like Lillian's, and say, "Don't drink as she did. Don't go with bad men; don't dissipate."

Then he would sigh and say, "Lillian wouldn't listen to me." He was still, Peggy Fears believed, in love with Lillian, who by then had become a hopeless alcoholic. Rudolf Friml worked out some new songs for Peggy, and Ziegfeld would sit with her for hours listening to Friml play. Just as Peggy was about to go to Palm Beach for the opening, she suddenly changed her mind and went to Hollywood for a screen test. She began to work at Warner Brothers in *The Girl From Nowhere,* for Ernst Lubitsch, Edmund Lowe, and Lilyan Tashman.

Ziegfeld was furious. He sent dozens of telegrams, began a legal suit, and otherwise threatened her, without success. Finally he cabled her: "I'M GOING TO TAKE THE SHOW BACK TO NEW YORK IT WILL BE A HIT IT'S A SHAME TO WASTE YOUR VOICE IN SILENT PICTURES."

She loathed Hollywood by this time, getting up at 6:00 A.M. and sitting around the set. One day Lilyan Tashman said to her: "If the boss wanted me back, I wouldn't be here 10 minutes."

Ziegfeld sent her a telegram offering her the last chance to have her part. She had been exasperated by 16 takes of a shot of her closing a door, and something snapped. She walked off the picture. She took a train to New York. Warner Brothers sued her, but they lost the case because she was able to prove that the film had run beyond the time to which she had been signed.

She went into rehearsals immediately for *The Palm Beach Girl,* retitled *No Foolin'* for New York. She sang the title song (which she thought dreadful) to Clarence Nordstrom with great style, and sang "Florida" and "The Moon and You" with Irving Fisher. She remembers the Urban setting vividly: "Out of the ocean came these marvelous girls. They looked as though they were dripping wet, in one-piece backless coveralls and enormous white headdresses of feathers all the way to the ground, so that they looked like the foam on the ocean coming in."

Julian Mitchell directed the number brilliantly; Jack Harkrider's costumes were stunning; and among the chorus girls were two legendary names: Paulette Goddard and Louise Brooks. Later the entire chorus appeared in their superb costumes at the Beaux Arts Ball. Ziegfeld had become obsessed with Harkrider, allowing almost no one else to design his costumes.

One night during the show Lillian Lorraine burst into Peggy Fears's dressing room with a full bottle in one hand and a half-full bottle in the other. "Come on," she said. "Have a drink." Peggy replied, "I can't drink. I'm going on stage in a moment." Suddenly Fanny Brice, who was looking after Lillian, appeared. Lillian began screaming, "I want to see what you look like! They say you look like me!" She slumped into Fanny Brice's arms.

On February 27, 1925, Billie had a narrow escape from death in an automobile crash. She had long been haunted by automobile problems: a few years earlier her successive chauffeurs had been fired for drunken driving, and she had twice been sued for mishaps in which her car ran over young children. On both occasions her drivers were found to be at fault.

On a February morning at 4:30 Billie was returning from the Everglades Club Masked Ball, and Ziegfeld was following in his own Rolls. Billie's limousine was traveling west on Burton Avenue and was just about to turn into County Road when a touring car speeding at 40 mph down Burton Avenue crashed into her and overturned her car. Two friends, Gurnee Munn and James Hyde (who had been driving), were flung out and managed to drag Billie loose.

Another friend, Gertrude Manigault, also returning home from the ball, saw the accident and drove after the two boys who had jumped from the touring car and run off. She overtook one and dragged him into her car; then she called the police. The second speeder was pulled down from the shelter of a coconut palm, where he was perched. The youths were accused of reckless driving, but one of the boys escaped during the interrogation. Twenty-four hours later the boy was located on Sunset Avenue and returned to police custody. Billie returned home and collapsed in Ziegfeld's arms.

During the New York run of *No Foolin'* Julian Mitchell had a stroke during a rehearsal and died. His death was a grievous blow to Ziegfeld.

The collapse of his next show, *Betsy*, was a terrific disappointment. A horrible disaster, it ran only 39 performances, opening on December 28, 1926. He was talked into producing the show. He hated it and was glad when it closed. The book was written by Irving Caesar and David Freedman, the lyrics by Lorenz Hart, and the music by Richard Rodgers. It was kind to draw a veil over that unhappy event.

During that fall and winter there were some distractions from the limping *No Foolin'* and the horrible *Betsy*. Ziegfeld began a ferocious campaign to form an Alliance to Reform the Stage, inspired by his distress at the increasing ugliness, crudity, and vulgarity of the Earl Carroll shows. It was inspired also by a great hunger for publicity.

Ziegfeld appointed Sumner, of the Society of the Suppression of Vice, as chairman of a play jury. His duty was to keep the *Follies* "as sweet and pure as he has discovered his audiences to be," in the words of the *New York Times*. Aided by his publicists, Ziegfeld began a "back from nudity to artistry" campaign, described by skeptics as "the commercialization of virtue."

Ziegfeld kept issuing bulletins that made headlines. He announced that the women of 1926 were too thin, that they must fatten up and stop wearing cosmetics. "I will admit more robust candidates to my choruses," he told the *Times*. The best stunt of all came during the run of *No Foolin'*. Forty blondes in the chorus voted to strike because Ziegfeld had told the press that he preferred a chorus of brunettes, with an occasional blonde as a foil. Ziegfeld received the grievance committee—headed by Paulette Goddard—and Paulette replied to Ziegfeld's charges in front of 50 members of the press.

"I'll see if I can't put some blondes in when I do a Latin American show," he responded. "Of course, all Latins are supposed to be brunettes."

"My answer to that," Miss Goddard declared, "is that audiences don't care much about anthropology and would not complain about a few blonde Latins."

The publicity proved enormously helpful, as did the publicity surrounding the building of a new theater for Ziegfeld in 1926, the true fulfillment of a marvelous dream.

For years Ziegfeld had dreamed of having his own theater, far from the tensions and squabbles of the New Amsterdam and the endless interferences of Abe Erlanger. His friendship with William Randolph Hearst, which had begun when he rented Hearst's yacht and leased the Cosmopolitan Theater, had recently blossomed, and the two men found a great deal in common. Hearst owned some real estate on 54th Street and Sixth Avenue, and he had decided to join Arthur Brisbane in building a theater there, in defiance of the off-Broadway jinx.

He arranged for Ziegfeld to supervise its construction. Ziegfeld immediately decided to make it the loveliest theater New York had ever seen. That he achieved his aim was confirmd by everyone who set foot in it.

Hearst gave Urban the task of creating the theater, a reversal to Urban's earlier role as an architect. The auditorium was egg-shaped and decorated with panels representing legendary figures of the Middle Ages, set against pitch-black walls with a border of chrome yellow at the foot. Knights and their ladies, clowns, archers, jousters, wildly romantic castles, and Urban blue skies made up a superb panoply, which framed the audience on three sides. Seats were upholstered in gold; and the foyer, on the second story, was decorated in white and gold. There was a terrace on which the customers could stroll on balmy evenings. Electrically lighted signs were forbidden on the front of the house, which was curved like a bow and illuminated by hundreds of concealed bulbs. The facade gave off a rich glow reminiscent of tropical moonlight. The theater was Urban's and Ziegfeld's masterpiece.

On December 9, 1926, the cornerstone was laid. Will Rogers was master of ceremonies, and Vincent Lopez and his band played against an icy wind. The ceremony began with a stirring version of the national anthem, which was cheered by the immense mid-afternoon crowd. Among the 1,500 celebrities present were Joseph Urban, Elizabeth Hines, Lois Wilson, Ned Wayburn, Marilyn Miller, Gene Buck, and former Ambassador James W. Gerard.

Will Rogers delivered a speech, in which he said, "Mr. Ziegfeld chose this corner because of the absence of saloons. Since the saloons have disappeared, there have been many more theaters, and this accounts for the fact that the entertainment is not as good as it was."

After the speech Billie Burke and Patricia placed in a large iron box a collection of mementos: programs of Sandow at the Trocadero, photographs of Ziegfeld's mother, Billie, and Patricia, a program for *Sally* and of the first *Follies* in 1907, and a picture of Charles Frohman. A brick from an ancient Greek theater was also inserted into the cornerstone, which was cemented by Patricia. After the little ceremony the guests trooped into the Hotel Warwick for a lavish reception. The entire proceedings were broadcast by WGBS Radio.

To introduce the theater, which was to open on February 27, Ziegfeld planned the dazzling *Rio Rita*, based on the book by Guy Bolton and Fred Thompson. The lyrics were written by Joe McCarthy and the music, by Harry Tierney. The show's story offered plenty of opportunity for both Urban and Harkrider to display their talents. The hero, Jim (played by J. Harold Murray), is a Texas Ranger who is hunting for a bandit along the Rio Grande. In Mexico he falls in love with Rio Rita (Ethylind Terry), who is also loved by General Esteban (Vincent Serrano). The general tells Rita that Jim's only concern is to capture the bandit, believed to be her brother. At the end it is revealed that the bandit is not related to her at all, and the climax is very romantic as the lovers ride off together into the sunset, leaving General Esteban desolate.

Urban's Mexican sets, based on extensive study, were extraordinary in their elegance, and Harkrider's costumes made the stage glow with a constant fiesta of dazzling color. Murray and Terry made a wonderful pair of lovers, handsome and in superb voice throughout. The spectacular first night crowd would, Ziegfeld's press agent Bernard Sobel announced, pay $27.50 a ticket. Fashionable society, headed by Otto Kahn, William Randolph Hearst, and the Astors, turned out in full force for the occasion.

The reviews were ecstatic: Brooks Atkinson in the *New York Times* wrote: "In decorative showmanship, Mr. Ziegfeld is the master of style . . . for sheer extravagance of beauty, animated and rhythmic, *Rio Rita* has no rival among contemporaries." He wrote with enthusiasm of the dances: "[The girls went] spinning across the stage, stamping their chic feet in unison or singing in chorus on any number of hot-blooded themes. In the most lustrous costumes—silver sombreros, blood-red shirts, fluffy ballet stuffs, embroidered velvet waistcoats—they whirled in squads, one on the heels of another, until the stage was as furious with design as the wall decorations."

Urban's designs created a breathtaking sense of space and distance: his blue sky over cactus patches and stretches of desert and his bull ring and sunlight-filled hallways were a constant feast for the eye.

Rio Rita was an immediate smash. On July 22 the happy cast of *Rio Rita* presented Ziegfeld with a bronze plaque, financed by the contribution of every member of the company for 20 successive weeks and beautifully executed by Oscar Davidson. It bore his profile in bas relief and was incribed with the names of the 140 donors.

Ziegfeld was not allowed to enjoy the triumph of *Rio Rita* undisturbed, however. He had a losing streak at Bradley's, in Palm Beach, and on returning he was stricken with a severe attack of bronchitis. He was exhausted with constant work as well as his gigantic losses at the tables, and he began to undergo sun-ray treatments at Burkely Crest. One day, tired and irritable, he flung himself on the table without the necessary dark glasses. A few moments later he screamed with pain; the light was burning him, and for a few moments he felt as though he had gone blind. The pain was unbearable. Although his sight was not dangerously affected, the blisters forced him to wear smoke-colored spectacles during the daytime. After the grand opening of *Rio Rita* he became more seriously ill, coughing blood and tossing in the grip of a severe fever. He lay in a suite at the Warwick—opposite the theater offices—in a state of complete misery, and his doctors told him that he had to postpone all work indefinitely.

He spent much of his "complete rest" renewing his battle against nudity on the stage. One typical telegram to New York District Attorney Benton read: "ACCEPT MY CONGRATULATIONS ON THE STAND YOU ARE TAKING. I HOPE YOU WILL INVESTIGATE THE REVUES NOW PLAYING IN NEW YORK. NOT ONE OF THEM WOULD BE TOLERATED IN BOSTON

AND PHILADELPHIA. THE BARING OF THE BREASTS OF THE YOUTH OF AMERICA TO DRAW A FEW EXTRA DOLLARS AND ABSOLUTE NUDE FIGURES DANCING AROUND THE STAGE SHOULD BE STOPPED BOTH IN THE REVIEW AND THE NIGHTCLUBS. . . ."

And this from the man who had introduced bare breasts to the American stage!

The run of *Rio Rita* was tarnished by a distasteful court battle between Ziegfeld and its English director, Edward Royce. The hearing was held before Supreme Court Justice A.H.F. Seeger in the fall of 1927. According to Royce's counsel, Irving M. Neuberger, Royce was offered $1,000 a week for five weeks and one percent of the gross receipts, which at the time of the hearing were at least $100,000. Royce charged that Ziegfeld was broke and unable to pay his bills, that he had immense gambling debts accumulated in New York and Palm Beach, and that he was "meddlesome," his knowledge of the stage restricted to "women and costumes." Ziegfeld's reply was stinging: Royce was a has-been and a heavy drinker; he had called for rehearsals at which he had failed to appear; and he had been quarrelsome and intolerable to work with. Denying that he was in financial difficulties, Ziegfeld announced that he owned 87.5 percent of the stock of the *Rio Rita* Company, 65 percent of the Ziegfeld Theater, one third interest in the lease of the New Amsterdam, and 62.5 percent of the *Ziegfeld Follies*. The case dragged on for years; finally it was settled out of court in Royce's favor.

In 1927, Ziegfeld's attorney pointed out to him that he had little or·no investments in the stock market. He had always been uncertain and somewhat unsure of buying shares, but in the last weeks of the run of *Rio Rita* he suddenly began investing large sums, until by August he had over $2 million in stocks, including heavy investments in Chrysler Corporation, Eaton Axle, and Mexican Seaboard Oil. Ziegfeld bought the shares through his friend Edward Hutton's (Barbara's uncle) stockbroking company.

In the summer of 1927, Ziegfeld gave a return Twenty-First Anniversary Edition of the *Follies* at the New Amsterdam. For the first time in years the *Follies* had genuine pace, style and brilliance; it cost $289,035.35 to produce the show. Irving Berlin, who worked around the clock, wrote the entire score, putting in numbers from produced or rejected shows, and Eddie Cantor returned as the star. One number illustrated once again that Ziegfeld was the natural father of Busby Berkeley: 19 pretty girls were shown playing 19 white pianos and in an *avant-garde* band. In the show's most extraordinary scene Claire Luce rode a live ostrich with a rhinestone collar across the stage. Not only was the ostrich fond of depositing its droppings on the stage, but it moulted before the opening night performance. Jack Harkrider had to stick it all over with ostrich feathers formerly intended for some of the girls. Another entertaining number was Berlin's "Shaking the Blues Away," superbly sung by Ruth Etting, symbolic of a new age of optimism in America.

Splendid though the show was, it was to be eclipsed that year by *Show Boat,* Jerome Kern's and Oscar Hammerstein's superb musical production which was destined to become the greatest dazzlement of the late 1920s stage and to re-establish Ziegfeld as the most important figure of the American musical theatre.

12

"Show Boat"

T HOUGH he did not at first realize it, *Show Boat* was the consummation of Ziegfeld's entire career, a brilliant demonstration of his talent and a summary of everything he had dreamed of since the first shows with Anna Held at the turn of the century. It embodied all of his basic tenets at once: that excitement on the stage was achieved by means of speed and constant changes of scenery; that every costume had to blend with every prop; that music and lyrics must flow naturally out of action; and that comedy scenes must never be permitted to bring the flow of a performance to even a momentary halt. Moreover, by his technique of integrating, telescoping, and rearranging scenes, he achieved a fluidity as great as any achieved by motion pictures.

Show Boat exemplified Ziegfeld's ideals of beauty: subdued taste and elegance rather than garish brilliance; the predominant colors gray, blue, and pink; and a heightened evocation of life itself in the realism, sharpness, and intensity of the acted sequences. Unbeknown to his detractors and even perhaps to his friends, every single scene in *Show Boat* harked back to earlier times: a pinch of *Miss Innocence* here, a sprinkle of *The Parisian Model* there, fragments of many of the *Follies* and even of some of the straight plays he had produced for Billie Burke. Moreover, Ziegfeld set the show firmly in environments he understood. With an intense feeling of nostalgia he staged one of the most spectacular scenes at the Chicago World's Fair, a hymn to the White City and its Midway remembered from 30 years before. He affectionately dubbed the Chicago music hall in another scene the Trocadero. Those who denigrated his role in the production in later years quite clearly overlooked these significant interpolations. It was typical, too, of the man who developed Bert Williams that in 1928 he would have a real black chorus on the stage.

However, at first Ziegfeld did not think that *Show Boat* would be a popular attraction; he felt that it would be against the tenor of the Jazz Age. To his very great credit, he realized early on that he was wrong, and he flung all of his genius into making the show a masterpiece, a revolutionary triumph and the finest musical production since *Sally* in the history of the American stage.

Edna Ferber had written the novel *Show Boat* in 1926, obtaining its central theme from the distinguished theatrical producer Winthrop Ames, who had spoken to her of the great age of Mississippi show boats. After Ames's comments she rushed to South Carolina, found a still extant floating palace, but discovered too late that it was laid up for the winter. She went on to New York and mentioned her idea enthusiastically to the members of the Algonquin Club Round Table luncheons. In the spring of 1926 she returned to the South Carolina show boat and traveled aboard it for several days. In the summer she

Gladys Feldman in the *Follies*.

Irene Hopping in *The Girl Who Smiles*.

Olive Thomas, who had a passionate affair with Flo, in the *Follies*. She is said to haunt the New Amsterdam Roof Theater.

Ziegfeld with Eddie Cantor in about 1930. *Goldie Clough Collection.*

Brilliant and prolific composer Irving Berlin collaborated with Ziegfeld on many musicals. *Robert Baral Collection, property of Charles Higham.*

Comedian and singer Fanny Brice (above), one of Ziegfeld's greatest stars and friends, singing "My Man." Her unique offbeat style created an immediate sensation.

Ed Wynn in *Simple Simon*. *Ziegfeld Club Collection*.

Hazel Dawn in the title role of *The Pink Lady*.

The inimitable W. C. Fields appeared in early *Follies* productions. *Robert Baral Collection, property of Charles Higham*.

Dancer Jack Donahue shows Marilyn Miller a few steps, and George Gershwin accompanies. Leaning on the piano are Flo Ziegfeld and Sigmund Romberg.

F. ZIEGFELD JR'S 12 ANNUAL PRODUCTION

ZIEGFELD FOLLIES 1918

PRODUCED AT THE
NEW AMSTERDAM THEATRE, N.Y.

LYRICS BY
GENE BUCK

MUSIC BY
DAVE STAMPER

The *Follies of 1918* included
music by Buck and Stamper,
staging by Ned Wayburn, sets
by Joseph Urban, and glamour
by Flo's showgirls.

Phyliss, Mauricette, Dinarzade, and Dolores, the original models of Lady Duff-Gordon's fashion salon. Their presence in *Miss 1917* ushered in a new showgirl glamour on Broadway. *Robert Baral Collection, property of Charles Higham.*

Irene Castle in *Miss 1917.*

Will Rogers and unidentified *Follies* beauty in the *Follies of 1918*.

Marion Davies in the *Follies of 1915*. She later became the mistress of William Randolph Hearst. *Alfred Cheney Johnston.*

A scene from *No Foolin'*. From left to right the chorus girls are: Audrey Dale, Alice Fitzgerald, Mabel Beade, Barbara La May, Marion Strasmick, Susan Fleming, Marjorie Leet, Ivanelle Ladd, Hilda Olsen, Flo Lane, Elsie Behrens, Paulette Goddard. and Dorothy Mason. *Ivanelle Ladd Collection.*

A Ben Ali Haggin tableau from the *Follies of 1919. Robert Baral Collection, property of Charles Higham.*

Gilda Gray, creator of
"The Shimmy." *Alfred
Cheney Johnston.*

The July, 1922, wedding of Marilyn Miller
and Jack Pickford caused a minor sensation.
The couple is pictured here with the offici-
ating minister, the Reverend Arthur Dodd.

"The Follies Mirror," a Ben Ali Haggin tableau.

ae Dooley (above) was a far cry from
egfeld chorus girl Ann Pennington (right),
t Rae's hilarious antics attracted a great
al of attention in the *Follies*.

Ziegfeld outdid himself on costumes for *No Foolin'*, presented in 1926. Marion Benda is in the center. *Robert Baral Collection, property of Charles Higham.*

The facade of the Ziegfeld Theater, designed by Joseph Urban, which opened on January 27, 1927. *New York Times Collection.*

Betty Compton, 1927 *Follies* star.

The Albertina Rasch Dancers in *Rio Rita,* the extremely successful show that introduced the new Ziegfeld Theater. *Alfred Cheney Johnston.*

A scene from the 1927 production of *Show Boat,* by Jerome Kern and Oscar Hammerstein. The play was the most dazzling musical of the late 1920s. *Hoblitzelle Theatre Arts Library, University of Texas.*

Dennis King, star of the revived production of *Show Boat* in 1932.

Ruth Etting, whose life was later portrayed in the movie *Love Me or Leave Me*, in the 1931 *Follies*.

Ziegfeld's greatest discovery for *Show Boat* was Helen Morgan. The torch singer is pictured sitting on a piano, her trademark.

Follies star George White, the eventual producer of the *Scandals*.

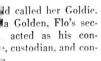

ld called her Goldie.
a Golden, Flo's sec-
acted as his con-
, custodian, and con-
.

Three of Ziegfeld's most popular stars: Fred Astaire, Marilyn Miller, and Adele Astaire. *Hoblitzelle Theatre Arts Library, University of Texas.*

Hot pants circa 1927. Florenz Ziegfeld at a rehearsal of the twenty-first anniversary of the Ziegfeld *Follies. Hoblitzelle Theatre Arts Library, University of Texas.*

Montages of the Ziegfeld Follies and their popular songs by Robert Baral.

The Ziegfeld family at Burkely Crest: Flo, Billie Burke, and their daughter, Florenz Patricia.

Burkely Crest, the family home of Flo and Billie Burke. *Collection of the Public Library of the City of New York.*

Florenz Ziegfeld with his mother, his wife, Billie Burke, and Patricia.

went to Europe and began work on the book at St. Jean-
de-Luz, France.

Doubleday published *Show Boat* to ecstatic reviews.
Jerome Kern read it, fell in love with it, and wrote to
Edna Ferber saying that he wanted to turn it into a musical. She was shocked and immediately ruled out the idea.
Kern spotted critic and columnist Alexander Woollcott in
the lobby of the Globe Theater between the acts of a show
called *Stepping Stones* and asked if Woollcott would introduce him to Miss Ferber. Woollcott screeched across
the lobby to Edna Ferber, who was there as his date:
"Come on over, Edna!" Small and owlish, Kern peered at
her over his spectacles, talked very fast, and finally convinced her—with Woollcott's aid.

Week after week Kern came to her with the music and
played it to her, spiritedly singing Oscar Hammerstein's
marvelous lyrics. Finally he brought her the glorious and
incomparable "Ol' Man River." Edna Ferber wrote in her
memoirs: "The music mounted, mounted, and I give you
my word my hair stood on end, the tears came to my eyes.
I breathed like a heroine in a melodrama. That was music
that would outlast Jerome Kern's day and mine."

The *Show Boat* setting was the Cotton Blossom, a magnificent Mississippi show boat, peopled with some tenderly
drawn characters: the lovely, melancholy Julie Laverne
cast out because of Negro blood, Cap'n Andy and his
shrewish wife, Parthy, their daughter Magnolia, the dashing worthless river gambler Gaylord Ravenal, and the
black stevedore Joe, who addresses the song to "Ol' Man
River."

Kern and Hammerstein begged Ziegfeld to take on the
production. At first he refused point blank; but gradually
he relented. Then they began to worry that he would not
be able to finance it, as *Rio Rita* was reputed to have
bankrupted him (it had not, though he had lost $100,000

at Bradley's during its run). Hammerstein and Kern drove down to Hastings to see Ziegfeld; Sidney, haughty as ever, ushered them into the sumptuous living room.

Hammerstein told the rest of the story to David Ewen for his biography of Jerome Kern: "A maid, dressed in exquisite lace and who herself might have just stepped out of some Ziegfeld production, conducted us to Ziegfeld's private quarters upstairs, through a regal bedroom, and into an immense bathroom in which the producer was being shaved by his personal barber. The shaving over, Ziegfeld put on his silk, brocaded dressing gown and invited us to have a snack with him. The 'snack' consisted of a royal meal of beef and champagne with all the trimmings, attended by a retinue of butlers and waiters. By the time we left Ziegfeld, late in the afternoon, not even Jerry had the brashness to ask if he had any money."

Shortly after the meeting Ziegfeld left for some fishing with Captain Gray at Palm Beach. He was pleased with Kern's score as it came in, but he was disappointed by Hammerstein's sprawling book.

On March 3, 1927, Ziegfeld wired Kern from Palm Beach: "I FEEL HAMMERSTEIN NOT KEEN ON MY DOING SHOW BOAT I AM VERY KEEN ON DOING IT ON ACCOUNT OF YOUR MUSIC BUT HAMMERSTEIN BOOK IN PRESENT SHAPE HAS NOT GOT A CHANCE EXCEPT WITH CRITICS BUT THE PUBLIC NO AND I HAVE STOPPED PRODUCING FOR CRITICS AND EMPTY HOUSES I DON'T WANT BOLTON OR ANYONE ELSE IF HAMMERSTEIN CAN AND WILL DO THE WORK IF NOT THEN FOR ALL CONCERNED WE SHOULD HAVE SOMEONE HELP HOW ABOUT DOROTHY DONNELLY OR ANYONE YOU SUGGEST OR HAMMERSTEIN SUGGESTS I AM TOLD HAMMERSTEIN NEVER DID ANYTHING ALONE HIS PRESENT LAYOUT TOO

SERIOUS NOT ENOUGH COMEDY AFTER MAR-
RIAGE REMEMBER YOUR LOVE INTEREST IS
ELIMINATED NO ONE ON EARTH JERRY KNOWS
MUSICAL COMEDY BETTER THAN YOU AND
YOURSELF TOLD ME YOU WOULD RISK A DOL-
LAR ON IT IF HAMMERSTEIN WILL FIX THE
BOOK I WANT TO DO IT IF HE REFUSES TO
CHANGE IT OR ALLOW ANYONE ELSE TO BE
CALLED IN IF NECESSARY YOU AND HE RETURN
THE ADVANCE AS YOU YOURSELF SUGGESTED
YOU WOULD AND LET SOMEONE ELSE DO IT IF
HAMMERSTEIN IS READY TO WORK WITH ME TO
GET IT RIGHT AND YOU AND HE WILL EXTEND
THE TIME UNTIL OCT FIRST LET'S DO IT TO-
GETHER I REALLY WANT TO IF OH IS REASON-
ABLE ALL WE WANT IS SUCCESS ANSWER."

After months of work Ziegfeld finally obtained a libretto
he liked, though he was always aggravated by the book
and the sprawling character of Edna Ferber's story.

Ziegfeld's greatest discovery for the show was Helen
Morgan, cast to perfection as the tender-hearted Julie. She
was 26 at the time; oddly enough, though he had quite
forgotten it, she had worked for him many years before.
At 18 she had been spotted by one of Ziegfeld's staff behind the counter at Marshall Field's department store in
Chicago. He had cast her in the chorus of *Sally*. When she
had demanded a singing role, he had dismissed her at
once. Later she met Ziegfeld again when she won a beauty
contest; he had also forgotten this second meeting.

Billy Rose gave Helen a chance at his Backstage Club;
when it seemed that she was so small that nobody would
see her, Ring Lardner lifted her on top of a piano. She
was hired by George White for the *Scandals*; she replaced
the leading lady, Helen Hudson, at a moment's notice and
later opened her own nightclub. Ziegfeld saw her fre-

quently at the Helen Morgan Club, singing her tragic songs on a white baby grand piano, and appearing in the revue *Americana*. Finally he made up his mind, called her to his office, and told her that she could play Julie if she wanted to. She broke down and cried and flung her arms around him in gratitude.

Ziegfeld cast the show with Charles Winninger as the warm and open-hearted Cap'n Andy, Edna Mae Oliver as Parthy, Jules Bledsoe as Joe, and Norma Terris as Magnolia. The cast worked like Trojans on day-and-night shifts.

After several exhausting weeks of rehearsal at the New Amsterdam the show opened in Washington for its trial run. The curtain rose at 8:15 and fell at 12:30. Though the production was overlong, the audience was captivated. The next morning Ziegfeld called a rehearsal at 11:00 A.M. and began making cuts. The cast played the matinee, had another rehearsal, and went into the evening performance without dinner.

Though he was exhausted by another attack of bronchitis, Ziegfeld refused to give up. Back in New York, he worked 18 hours before the opening, making further changes, switching scenes, recasting the entire last act. On December 27 *Show Boat* finally opened, at the Ziegfeld theater.

At the last minute Ziegfeld's conviction that the show would be a flop became completely overwhelming. On the first night he sat on the stairs to the balcony with Goldie, noted that there was little applause for the big numbers, and began to cry. When the big Chicago World's Fair scene failed to bring cheers, he sobbed helplessly. "They don't like it," he said. "Goddamn it, I knew they wouldn't."

At the intermission Ziegfeld's friends mingled with the crowd, which seemed to be stunned, almost silent. In the next scenes the audience was no more vociferous in its reactions. Most people filed out at the end as though they were leaving a funeral. Ziegfeld took off with Stanley Sharpe, his manager, to Dinty Moore's restaurant for corned beef and cabbage. Goldie went with a big crowd to a speakeasy round the corner. Then, in the early hours of the morning, someone brought Ziegfeld the papers. The reviews were ecstatic, the finest for any show in years. "Maybe the critics did like it, but the public won't," he said sourly, and his chauffeur, Ernest, drove him home to Hastings.

When he arrived at the theater the following day, thousands of people were lined up around the block, waiting to buy tickets. "Must be a fire!" he said sourly. But two hours later he told Stanley Sharpe, "I guess we made it."

Four nights after *Show Boat* opened, it almost had to close. Very much against Ziegfeld's wishes, Helen Morgan was continuing to sing into the small hours at her club after each performance. On New Year's Eve she was sobbing out a new torch song when one of the club's main doors flew open. Twenty-five armed FBI agents, led by Prohibition Administrator Maurice Campbell, burst in. Without a word the raiders went to work, smashed hundreds of liquor bottles, tore down expensive drapes, and shot the lights out of the chandeliers. Helen Morgan was driven to FBI headquarters in a police van and charged with selling bootleg liquor. Told of the incident, Ziegfeld became almost apoplectic. On a hunch he called Campbell and said: "Did you have a warrant?" Campbell admitted that he did not, and Helen Morgan was allowed to return to *Show Boat*.

After the opening the phones never stopped ringing for house seat tickets. The ticket brokers, selling at $50 each, were constantly chasing Goldie, trying to buy house seats from her. Ziegfeld put a clamp on the tickets, insisting that nothing must leave the office unless he personally gave his approval. The show grossed $50,000 a week and was booked for months ahead. Even Ziegfeld had to admit that it was an overwhelming triumph. Many theatrical producers came back to see Jack Harkrider's costumes, Sammy Lee's dances, and Urban's stunning designs again and again. But they neglected to note that the magic that made the elements all knit flawlessly together was Ziegfeld's and Ziegfeld's alone.

By the summer of 1928 *Show Boat* had already become established as a classic. "Ol' Man River" (which Ziegfeld never liked), "My Bill," "Life Upon the Wicked Stage," and a dozen other great songs permanently entered the musical repertoire, and the show earned its backers well over a million dollars.

In the early stages of the immense and exhausting effort of *Show Boat*, Ziegfeld had gone to Palm Beach for a complete rest. Early in 1927, he received a telegram of Ziegfeldian length—42 pages—from William Anthony McGuire, who was in debt and drinking heavily. It outlined a silly and complicated plot based on the famous visit of Queen Marie of Rumania to America: the story of a Ruritanian Queen, Rosalie of Romanza, who falls in love with a West Point lieutenant; at first her royal position stands between them, but after her father, King Cyril, abdicates, the couple is happily united. Ziegfeld thought little of this confection, but he was pleased with McGuire's shrewdness in naming the show after Mrs. Ziegfeld, Sr. (Rosalie de Gez), and he cabled his mother at 1448 West Adams Street that he was producing a show in her honor.

Never above using his family for his own purposes, he also cabled his sister Louise, married to a wealthy industrialist, in Detroit, and asked her to help to finance the production as a gesture to their parent. She agreed at once. Ziegfeld asked Guy Bolton to collaborate with McGuire because he did not trust McGuire to come up with

finished material; P. G. Wodehouse was engaged also.
Ziegfeld brought Marilyn Miller back to his charmed circle
for the show, co-starring her with Frank Morgan and Jack
Donahue, her lover. To his great relief she had split up
with Jack Pickford after a brief, hectic, and finally disastrous marriage.

Several attempts to acquire European composers for the
score failed, and Ziegfeld decided to engage Sigmund
Romberg. Romberg turned him down flat: he was, he said,
just about to go into rehearsals for *New Moon*. Ziegfeld
was adamant. Finally Romberg scratched his chin thought-
fully and suggested that to ease the workload he should
collaborate with George Gershwin. Ziegfeld snatched up
his famous gold telephone and called Gershwin. When
Gershwin arrived at the office, he said that he was too
busy also—he was preparing to present *Funny Face*.

According to Elliott Arnold, Romberg's biographer,
Ziegfeld looked at the two men and said: "Gentlemen, it
is hopeless to argue with me. Both of you had better agree
now. It will save a world of argument." When the two men
reluctantly bowed to his hurricane force, he added a characteristic afterthought: "And remember, gentlemen, I
have to have the music in three weeks. Not a day later."

Preparations for *Rosalie* were incredibly hectic. Marilyn
was ill with sinus trouble, which had started in 1916 when
during a rehearsal for Shubert's *Show of Wonders* dancer
Theodore Kosloff had accidentally struck her and splin-
tered her nose. McGuire was constantly drinking and rewriting scenes up to and after the first night. Romberg
and Gershwin had to squeeze rehearsals in between work
on their other shows, and everyone in Ziegfeld's office
started to experience the first symptoms of a nervous
breakdown.

As if all this work were not enough, Ziegfeld was also
involved with a new Rudolph Friml work, *The Three*

Musketeers, based on the Dumas novel. His central impulse in all this mass of activity was known only to a tiny handful of his intimates. He wanted to provide a trust fund for Patricia, then a sturdy girl of 12. Two percent of every show he produced was banked in her favor and could not be touched. He regretted this decision later, but even when he was desperate for money, his business managers would not let him touch the fund.

Another permanent transaction never changed, by his own order: a monthly allowance to Lillian Lorraine, who by 1928 was living in Atlantic City. Her calls were always received on his private telephone in a small room at the back of his offices at the Ziegfeld Theater. When Goldie answered, a sad faraway voice would say, "Mary Brennan speaking," and Ziegfeld would speak to her. Invariably he would listen to long stories of her intense worries and constant pain from her injured back, and when she had hung up, he would slump sadly in his chair. Finally, for reasons unknown, he said to Goldie: "If she calls again, say I'm out." He never spoke to her again.

Fortunately, Billie Burke never learned of these transactions. She had grown increasingly jealous over the years. The marriage had become more and more one of convenience, though Ziegfeld returned home night after night to Burkely Crest and spent most of the day doing business by telephone in his massive walnut bed. Every spare moment he could find was devoted to Patricia, and it is doubtful whether any spark was left by then of his sexual attraction to Billie. His brief affairs with showgirls continued as fiercely as ever, but no woman occupied a really important place in his heart.

Though he attempted to revive it, the relationship with Marilyn Miller was completely burned out by this time. During the run he had Bernard Sobel prepare a lavishly mounted book of her clippings, and he sent it to her in her

gold-leafed Urban dressing room. She did not even thank
him for it. In his memoirs Sobel described a pathetic scene
in which Ziegfeld stood outside the star's dressing room
saying, "Will my Princess Rosalie deign to see me?" And
she yelled "No!" at him through the door. To everyone
else, of course, she sustained her pose of glittering en-
chantress. She captured the audience from the very first
night of *Rosalie* when she overcame a momentary mishap.

In one scene several flunkies came down a flight of stairs
toward Rosalie, who was carrying a cat on a pillow. Gene
McVey tripped, and the cat flew into the wings. Marilyn
laughed so loud that the audience laughed with her, and
she simply sat and talked to them at the footlights until
the cat was found.

Ziegfeld may have been aggravated by Marilyn's bad
temper and gracelessness, but he marveled at her courage.
Often she would fall down in the wings as a result of
blinding sinus headaches, and she was out of the show
three times. She consoled herself for the constant physical
distress with her affair with Jack Donahue, and later, in
1928, with film star Ben Lyon.

The Three Musketeers was an immense problem. While
Rosalie went into the New Amsterdam, in January, 1928,
The Three Musketeers went into the Lyric only two
months later, on March 13. At least on *Rosalie* Guy Bolton
could stabilize and control William Anthony McGuire, but
on *Musketeers* McGuire was writing alone, and his behavior exasperated Ziegfeld beyond endurance. McGuire
was constantly being picked up in back alleys, he never
had a script ready on time, and when the show first went
into rehearsal, he had only the first half of the first act
completed. He used to rush into the office, give Goldie
some wet kisses on the back of her neck, and throw some
pages onto Ziegfeld's desk.

One day Goldie picked up a knife and said, "Leave me

alone!" in a tone of mock drama. He kissed her hand, loosened the knife, and it fell to the floor. He yelled, "Jesus Christ, there's my scene for the bedroom!" McGuire dashed off to the nearest bar and began writing. The next day he was back in the office with some more pages. "I've used your scene!" he told Goldie. He had included a new episode in which D'Artagnan came through the window of Milady de Winter, who was hiding some important diamonds in her bosom. She had a knife on the table, and as he came in, she picked up the knife to stab him; he kissed her hand, and she dropped the knife.

The show was late into rehearsals when McGuire finally began work on the third act. By that time everyone was ready to murder him. He managed to stall at the last minute by having Fred Niblo's 1921 film version of *The Three Musketeers* with Douglas Fairbanks projected for Ziegfeld and the cast. Since it lasted over two hours, it gave him time to slip away to an upstairs office and produce the required number of pages, with the aid of an ample supply of liquor. Just as the last title appeared on the screen, he thrust the pages into the astonished Ziegfeld's hand.

Even on opening night McGuire was writing and rewriting, and many of the actors simply read their lines off cards in their hands. Dennis King—superb as D'Artagnan—was infuriated by these problems and kept blowing up at Ziegfeld and McGuire offstage. Rudolph Friml was even more temperamental, constantly playing practical jokes.

One day there was a conference at the office at which Friml, Harkrider, Urban, and McGuire were present. The cigar smoke made breathing practically impossible. Ziegfeld rang for Goldie. When she walked in, Friml crouched down, rushed at her like a lion, seized her, and pretended to rape her. Ziegfeld was furious. He yelled, "Rudy, you leave that little girl alone. Don't you ever do anything like that again!" The whole office broke up with laughter.

A continual running feud built up between Dennis King and his co-star, Vivienne Segal, who played Constance Bonacieux Winter. Their temperaments were totally at odds, and King resented the amount of attention that Segal won away from him with her magnificent Harkrider costumes and tremendous personality. One love scene required them to sing an aria while holding each other in a tight and passionate embrace. Usually King managed to persuade Ziegfeld, who disliked the love scenes anyway, to cut the whole of this duet out of the action. But one evening Otto Kahn arrived to see the show, and he had a well-known penchant for stage romance. As one of the backers he had to have his way. King began the scene normally enough, but when Vivienne Segal's turn came to sing, he pinched her so tight in the ribs that she wobbled badly on the high notes. She waited for a movement in which she had to turn from him in a classic pose with the back of her hand pressed against her forehead. As she moved, she struck him firmly in the solar plexus with her elbow, winding him just as he reached his highest note in the scale. He never forgave her.

At night after the show Ziegfeld, Reginald Owen (who played Cardinal Richelieu), and other friends would go to Dinty Moore for a special soup, prepared by Dinty in the early hours of the morning. With three hits on his hands, Ziegfeld enjoyed his happiest times for years. At first he hadn't been sure that the shows would take off, but when he sent McGuire (who repaired to Palm Beach after the first weeks of the run), a cable ("SHOWS DO-ING BADLY"), and McGuire replied ("CONGRATULA-TIONS IN THE DARKEST HOUR OF YOUR SUC-

CESS"), Ziegfeld knew that he had overcome the terrible hurdles of the three productions. He was actually seen to laugh at Dinty Moore's.

In celebration of all these Ziegfeld triumphs, Billie gave Flo a lavish Palm Beach birthday party on March 15, 1928: his sixty-first. At Louwana Villa, rented for the season, a huge crowd of friends turned up, including Leonard Replogle, Ogden Reid, Edward Hutton, Joseph Urban, John Ringling, Ben Ali Haggin, and Rudolph Friml. Morton Downey's band, assisted by Friml and violinist Benar Barzelay, played and sang excerpts from Ziegfeld's greatest shows. Dinner was served at three large tables, which were blanketed with Ziegfeld's beloved American Beauty roses and white and purple orchids. The patio was illuminated with floodlights arranged by Urban himself and with strings of multicolored lights among the trees.

13
Into Dark Waters

Recharged with new energy that summer, Ziegfeld was preoccupied with a new show by William Anthony McGuire: *Whoopee,* based on Owen Davis's Broadway play *The Nervous Wreck.* Gus Kahn wrote the lyrics, and Walter Donaldson wrote the music. The show was designed as a vehicle for Eddie Cantor, whose on-again, off-again relationship with Ziegfeld had finally blossomed into a deep and lasting friendship. *Whoopee* was ideal for Cantor: it was the story of the hypochondriac Henry Williams, who goes to California to recover from an imaginary illness and on the way arrives in a Wild West settlement.

Ruby Keeler was signed to play opposite Cantor, but her husband, Al Jolson, insisted that she should go to Hollywood to be with him. Ruth Etting took over the role: immensely talented, she sang the beautiful "Love Me or Leave Me" with incomparable bravura and daring shifts of rhythm. Eddie Cantor sang "Makin' Whoopee" and stopped the show. Ziegfeld loved *Whoopee* because it gave him a chance for a fantastic Indian reservation number, with the girls in a dazzling array of feathers, riding their horses across the stage.

One girl was particularly anxious to obtain a role in *Whoopee*. As a rule, the efforts of various hopefuls were confined to stopping Ziegfeld in the street and raising a skirt or breaking into tears and begging Alice, the telephone girl, to admit them to the Ziegfeld outer office, which could be reached only with a special pass. Usually that was as far as girls got. Ziegfeld would arrive, sweep past them, and tell Goldie to get rid of them.

This particular girl was unusually enterprising, however. For months she begged Ziegfeld to see her. Finally she succeeded in gaining entry to his office. She arrived in a mink coat that was so long it literally swept the floor. As she came in, she said to Goldie, "I know if Mr. Ziegfeld sees me the right way, he'll put me in the show." No sooner had she entered Ziegfeld's office when she threw off the mink coat and stood there completely naked. Ziegfeld was furious. He rang the buzzer frantically for Goldie and screamed, "She's crazy!" He used her in the chorus of *Whoopee* anyway.

McGuire was as slow as usual in writing the book of *Whoopee*. After three weeks of work he had failed to come up with an outline. Even after three months the book was nowhere near completion. The work was still being finished when the show—with Gladys Glad also in the cast— went into production in Pittsburgh.

Just before the Pittsburgh opening Cantor came down with laryngitis and was unable to speak. Ziegfeld asked Urban the name of the major throat specialist in Pittsburgh. He learned that the doctor was recovering from a near-fatal car accident. Ziegfeld arrived at the man's house, stormed past his wife into the sick man's room, told him the situation, threw a $1,000 check on a table, and with the aid of two theater attendants dragged the man to a waiting ambulance borrowed from a local hospital. The flustered group, with the doctor on a stretcher, arrived at Cantor's hotel in the early hours of opening night. While Cantor sat on the floor, the doctor painted his throat and gave him a series of pills and injections. At the last moment Cantor's voice came back.

Ruth Etting's husband, professional bodyguard Moe Snyder, known as "The Gimp," would appear at rehearsals and poke guns in people's ribs, jokingly saying, "Put your hands up!" and scaring them half to death. He had an unnerving habit of cornering Ziegfeld in the alley behind the theater and demanding that certain improvements be made in Ruth Etting's presentation. Ziegfeld, who had already insured perfection, quite rightly told him that he could not do any more, whereupon The Gimp would stalk away, muttering angrily to himself.

On opening night in Pittsburgh an odd mishap occurred. After a splendid chorus a cow appeared on the stage to emphasize that the scene was set in the West. The cow ambled on, led by one of the chorus girls, and suddenly it deposited an enormous cowpat on the stage. Eddie Cantor, who was standing in the wings, grabbed a broom and a shovel from an attendant and danced out on the stage. The audience screamed with delight. Ziegfeld tapped Goldie on the shoulder, saying, "Make a note. Keep that in."

On opening night in New York—a huge sensation—the cow behaved perfectly. Ziegfeld was furious.

Four hits in a row, an office staff happily distressed, terrapin, caviar, and pheasant, crêpes suzettes, and marvelous weeks at Palm Beach with "Rep" Replogle, Ed Hutton, and Gene Buck: 1928 was an exciting year for

Ziegfeld. He bloomed like a prize-winning orchid. It was
his best period since 1920, and he knew it. But he did not
see that the new medium of talking movies to which he
had blithely sold the rights for show after show was already casting a shadow across his career, that "his" kind
of show, his kind of world, was doomed.

He had already seen the vanishing of another world,
of New York before World War I, of Rector's, long since
closed, of the overpowering luxury of the great hotels,
the glorious high noon of burlesque, the time of guiltless
expenditure, of Lillian Russell, Diamond Jim Brady, and
Anna Held. Almost all of his friends and colleagues from
that early time were dead. Harry B. Smith still lived on,
though Flo had not seen him for years; Lillian Lorraine
was in exile at Atlantic City; Irving Berlin was still around,
young and full of electric vitality. But many others had
gone for good. Friends occasionally would see Ziegfeld's
face darken as he came across a reminder of the golden
past of the first years of the century: a postcard from
Brussels written by Anna in her scratchy, slanting hand or
a memorandum from Charles Evan Evans about *A Parlor
Match*.

More often, though, in those days of 1928 he was found
to be smiling more frequently than before, and after several rifts he was close to Billie again, loaning her out
cheerfully for theatrical productions, glad to see her back
at work again after the years of raising Patricia. Patricia
was growing up well—not spoiled and frail like so many
children of the rich but plainspoken, amusing, and remarkably uncomplicated. She inherited her mother's
charm and her father's quiet asperity. She remained Flo's
pride and joy, and his gifts of jewelry, animals, and clothes
went on and on.

The year 1929 opened without powerful fanfare. The
Follies were being held in abeyance, too difficult to mount

because of the enormous work involved in the other
musicals and still affected by the interminable litigation
between Klaw and Erlanger. William Anthony McGuire,
still drinking, still subject to unpredictable vanishings,
still as unreliable and charmingly reckless as ever, was
busy on a new production: *Show Girl*. The show was designed as a vehicle for Ruby Keeler. Though Ziegfeld
never attempted to sleep with her, he was fascinated by
Ruby Keeler: her naive charm and her openness captivated him.

Show Girl opened at the Ziegfeld theater on July 2,
1929. It was based on a novel by J. P. McEvoy with a score
by George Gershwin. Basically the story of the rise to
fame of a showgirl, Dixie Dugan, the whole scenario was
designed as a hymn to Ziegfeld himself. The second act
curtain actually rose on a scene of the Ziegfeld Theater,
echoing Ziegfeld's earlier use of the New Amsterdam in
Sally and in some of the *Follies* productions. There were
fine moments of comedy—Jimmy Durante made his most
important early stage appearance; and Eddie Foy, Jr.,
was witty as a greeting card salesman whose cigarette case
blew up every time he opened it and whose gifts contained alarming devices (his routines twice brought the
audience to its feet). The highlight of the entire production was Gershwin's *An American in Paris* ballet, danced
superbly by Harriet Hoctor against a glittering background of the Eiffel Tower and the city skyline. To this
one scene Ziegfeld, passionately fond of Gershwin's music,
gave almost superhuman effort, creating a glittering chiar-
oscuro of color and movement.

Ruby Keeler was extremely nervous during rehearsal,
and Ziegfeld—who worshipped her more every day—and
director Bobby Connolly found it very difficult to get a
good performance out of her. At the dress rehearsal she
reached the top of the superb staircase that had been de-

signed especially for her, and she froze. She stood motion-
less in her tuxedo and high hat, clearly at a loss about
what to do next. Bobby Connolly yelled, "Come on, Ruby!"
Al Jolson, who was out front, jumped up. He sang her
song back at her—Gershwin's "Liza"—and she suddenly
snapped into life, remembered the lyrics, and danced
beautifully down the stairs. Ziegfeld immediately said to
Jolson, "Al, do that on opening night." For several nights,
until Ruby was settled in, Jolson continued to help Ruby
perform the number, creating a sensation with every
audience.

One much-published story was entirely true. In Ruby
Keeler's honor Ziegfeld completely redecorated the star
dressing-room at the Ziegfeld Theater in white organdy,
the walls covered in ruffles. Her dressing table was also
in organdy, the entire décor exquisitely designed by Urban. On opening day Ziegfeld called Goldie from Hastings
and told her to take a taxi to Cartier's to pick up a package. She obeyed the instructions and picked up the
"package"—actually a huge box. When she came back, she
called him and said, "I'm back, and I've got the box. What
do I do now?" He said: "Well, open it!"

She did so. It was a magnificent toilet set of brushes,
mirrors, perfume bottles, and makeup boxes, 21 pieces of
solid gold inlaid with crystal and mother-of-pearl. He
told her to write on it "To the greatest star I've ever had"
in a facsimile of his handwriting and instructed her to hide
in a cupboard in Ruby Keeler's dressing room to report on
Ruby's reaction when she saw the set.

Goldie said: "Mr. Ziegfeld, where am I going to hide?"
He said: "You figure it out!" She was lucky: the dressing
room was so full of flowers that she was able to hide just
behind the door without being seen in the mirror.

When Ruby arrived, late, nervous, red-eyed, and in
the midst of a quarrel with Jolson, Goldie had been hiding

behind the flowers for over an hour. Ruby sat down at the dressing table and began to use the toilet set, too distraught to notice that it was new. Jolson ran in after her and saw the card. He exclaimed, "Look, look at what Flo gave you, look at this!" But she went right on making up her face without comment. Goldie slipped out unobserved. Goldie told Ziegfeld that Ruby hadn't noticed the set until Al Jolson saw it. Ziegfeld was bitterly disappointed, and when he tried to give Ruby Keeler several pairs of $125 silk stockings imported from Paris, Ruby's mother intercepted the gift at the dressing room door.

Show Girl opened on July 2, 1929. Unfortunately the show had only a brief run. That fall Ziegfeld's disappointment was not abated by the painful business of supervising a musical film based on the success story of a typical Ziegfeld girl. The film, *Glorifying the American Girl*, had been planned by Ziegfeld as the first all-talkie following the smash hit of *The Jazz Singer*, but Paramount bosses Jesse L. Lasky and Walter Wanger hovered over the project for 18 months, uncertain that it would work. The film was shot at the Astoria Studios in Long Island, starring Mary Eaton as a music-counter girl who is discovered at an open air staff concert and goes to Broadway and success in the *Follies*. An imitation of the Ziegfeld Theater lobby was mocked up, and Ziegfeld (who always hated being on camera), Otto Kahn, Irving Berlin, Adolph Zukor, Mayor Jimmy Walker, and Charles Dillingham appeared pretending to be attending a first night. They made up meaningless phrases, which were not recorded but replaced by Norman Brokenshire's voice-over commentary identifying them one by one. Mary Eaton was charming, and among the supporting acts were Eddie Cantor, for some reason playing an act from a Shubert show, and Helen Morgan, moaning a torch song on top of her famous white piano. The climax, in two-strip Technicolor—one of the few physical evidences we have of a Ziegfeld production—was a riot of dancing girls, feathers, and sequins. The music was written by Irving Berlin.

That year Ziegfeld began a series of elaborate motion picture deals. *Sally* was resold to Warner Brothers as a screen vehicle for Marilyn Miller (a silent version with Colleen Moore had been made), *Rosalie* to International Pictures (which never shot it), and *Kid Boots* and *Whoopee* to Sam Goldwyn on a co-production deal under the aegis of the Z-G Corporation, financed to the tune of $125,000 each by the two men.

In the fall of 1929 Ziegfeld, in association with Archie Selwyn, imported Noel Coward and *Bitter Sweet*, his hit British show. Opening in London, it was the story of the Marchioness of Shayne, who in 1929 recollects her past: in 1875 she had fallen in love with her music teacher, Carl Linden, and gone to Vienna, where five years later she became known as Sari, an entertainer in a Viennese cafe. Carl has a quarrel over Sari with Captain August, and Carl is shot dead. Later Sari becomes a prima donna and marries Lord Shayne. The whole production is framed within her memories. This sugary romantic musical was not Ziegfeld's kind of thing, and he was annoyed because the young Coward brightly refused to change his production or to introduce a single Ziegfeld girl to the show. Ziegfeld summoned the polished Englishman to lunch and told him peremptorily that in view of his recalcitrance he would do nothing to promote the play at all.

Coward wrote in *Present Indicative*, his memoirs: "I received this dispiriting announcement apathetically, by far too exhausted to care whether he gave the seats away with a packet of chewing gum."

Ziegfeld told Gene Buck that he found Coward tired and effete; in his turn, Coward told friends that he was irritated beyond measure by Ziegfeld's arrogant and high-handed way of conducting business. The two eventually made an armed truce, and after some nerve-wracking rehearsals, in which a leading tenor gave them much trouble, the show opened in Boston. The tenor, Alexandro Rosati, had finally to be replaced because he could not be understood by the audience. Gerald Nodin took over the role.

Evelyn Laye, an English star, was an enchanting Sari. She sang with immense style, and the Coward songs, "I'll See You Again" and "Zigeuner" among them, were enchanting. Ziegfeld was quite won over to the show by the enthusiasm of the Boston audiences, and the opening in New York was a sensation, with $25 tickets sold on the floor by speculators. Delighted, Ziegfeld allowed Coward to call him Flo and gave over his office to Coward, Evelyn Laye, and their friends Gladys Calthrop and Jack Wilson for champagne and caviar between sets. When he came back at the final curtain, beaming through clouds of cigar smoke, they were barely able to stand.

During the Boston run of *Bitter Sweet* the market suddenly broke. On October 29, 1929, the day of the Wall Street crash, Ziegfeld and his entire office staff, including business managers Stanley Sharpe and Dan Curry, were in the courts countersuing over a trivial matter. (The Strauss Sign Company had sued for non-payment of a $1,600 bill for an electric sign specially devised for *Show Girl*. Ziegfeld had rejected the sign and was countersuing on the grounds that it had been poorly designed and worthless. With characteristic insistence, he wanted every man who worked for him to testify on the witness stand.)

The office was empty that day (the switchboard operator was ill). Goldie, of course, sat at Ziegfeld's side during the entire hearing.

Because of this petty matter Ziegfeld was virtually wiped out. His brokers, led by Ed Hutton, continually called the office to beg him to cut his losses, but there was no reply at the switchboard. Frantic attempts to reach him all over town ended in failure. By the time he came out of court, every headline on every newsstand told him that he was ruined. Ziegfeld had had $2 million in stocks, for which he had put up about $50,000 on margin. This money was gone. If he had gotten out a week earlier, he would have saved everything.

When the news came that he had lost every cent he owned, Ziegfeld seemed like a man in a dream, walking about New York in a dazed condition, his face drained of color. Charles Dillingham, also ruined but more philosophical, is said to have remarked on hearing that Ziegfeld was wiped out, "Well, at least that finally makes us even." Ziegfeld came home from New York that night and sank onto the side of his immense walnut bed. Billie asked him what was wrong. He broke into helpless tears and told her that he was through. The next day he did not go to New York but wandered stunned, a ghost at large in the lovely garden of Burkely Crest.

14

The Final Curtain

COWARD'S *Bitter Sweet* lasted until February, 1930. On February 18 Ziegfeld pulled himself together with amazing determination to open *Simple Simon*, possibly his most bizarre musical production to date. With a book by its star, Ed Wynn, and Guy Bolton and music by Richard Rodgers and Lorenz Hart, it was the story of Simon, a Coney Island newspaper shopowner who dreams of fairy tale kingdoms to escape his drab environment.

Bluebeard, Cinderella, Prince Charming, and Old King Cole appeared against fantastic Edmond Dulac-like sets by Urban. The show was too long, and Ziegfeld cut song after song during the out-of-town tryouts, including the attractive but insipid "Dancing on the Ceiling" and "He Was Too Good For Me." He added more numbers on tour, but nothing could awaken widespread interest in the show. Once again Ziegfeld had neglected to secure a first-rate book, and all of his stunning visual effects went for nothing. He was so aggravated with the show that he

203

refused to pay Rodgers and Hart any royalties—or even a fee.

On April 12, Ziegfeld set out for Hollywood to fulfill the terms of his contract with Samuel Goldwyn, which provided an equal partnership in a production of *Whoopee* to be shot in Hollywood and Palm Springs, with Eddie Cantor again as its star. With Billie and Patricia he stopped briefly in New Orleans to deliver some remarks about the exciting possibilities of the motion picture medium, although in fact he despised and feared it.

Once in Hollywood, where William Randolph Hearst loaned him Marion Davies' beach house, Ziegfeld was thoroughly depressed, telling Eddie Cantor that Urban could run the whole setting up in a week. The mountains, ocean, blue sky, and romantic morning fogs bored him unutterably, and he longed for the crude hustle and bustle of Broadway.

As for the shooting of the film itself, that was even less bearable. The sets that represented the Wild West were lit with batteries of powerful arcs used to represent the intense heat of the Arizona sun, and shooting could only continue for just a few minutes at a time. The temperature was close to 110 degrees, and due to a fear of interruption from outside noises on those early days of talkies, the doors of the sound stages were slammed shut. Working in immense boxes that could not move, the camera operators frequently passed out from the suffocating heat and lack of ventilation. Ziegfeld watched his brilliant effects ruined one after another, in conditions similar to those of the Belgian Congo. The only area in which Goldwyn permitted him any influence was in the dance direction. A young man, Busby Berkeley, a discovery of Eddie Cantor, was in charge of the choreography, and he copied many of Ziegfeld's concepts. But the film was a travesty of the stage show, and Ziegfeld loathed it even more than he hated most movies.

Back from Hollywood, Ziegfeld lied to the *New York Sun* (September 8, 1930): "Pictures? I liked them. I liked Hollywood, but the talking picture people have got to realize they're now in the legitimate. They've got to produce 500 hits a year. Who in hell is going to find them? You can't lock an author in a room and say, 'Stay there and write me a hit.' One thing Hollywood has to learn is how to cast a production as Broadway casts a show. Nobody out there knows a damn thing about casting. The smartest man I found on the coast is Irving Thalberg. . . . Nearly everybody out on the coast used to work for me.* There were two stars, though, that I turned down flat. Norma Shearer once asked me for a job, and I said no because she couldn't dance. I threw Nancy Carroll out because she was too fat. . . ."

In New York that fall Ziegfeld decided that he would cast Marilyn Miller together with Fred and Adele Astaire—who were then the rage—in a new musical show. He had received the brief outline of an idea from Noel Coward and had begun to develop it with the aid of novelist Louis Bromfield, who used to drape his long legs over Goldie's desk and spin out his ideas right there in Flo's office. Later William Anthony McGuire, drinking as heavily as ever, came along to add some new—and lame—situations to the basic plot. Ziegfeld cabled the Astaires in London, and they accepted the invitation to work for him without hesitation. They had always been disappointed not to have been in the *Follies.* Vincent Youmans was engaged to write the score.

---

* Among them Billie Dove, Mae Murray, Louise Brooks, Virginia Bruce, Mary Eaton, Marion Davies, and Imogene Wilson, who was masquerading as plain Mary Nolan.

The show was originally called *Tom, Dick and Harry,* but Ziegfeld changed the title to *Smiles.* It was the story of a French orphan adopted by four American doughboys. She comes to America and becomes a Salvation Army girl. Important scenes included the streets of the Lower East Side, a lawn party with Chinese lanterns at Southampton, and Paris, with showgirls dressed in beautiful, shimmering beaded gowns by John Harkrider. Fred and Adele Astaire appeared as society swells.

There was a major row during the rehearsals for the show: McGuire disliked the Astaires and kept accusing them of being late for rehearsals. They accused McGuire of making love to chorus girls in the balcony. Finally Ziegfeld became so exasperated by McGuire's slowness and absenteeism that he fired him from the show and engaged a battery of writers (including Ring Lardner) to fix up his material. As a result of all this rewriting, the show was two weeks late opening in New York, and Ziegfeld refused to pay the cast for the extra time. (Later, when Adele's marriage to Irish nobleman Lord Charles Cavendish was delayed by two weeks, Ziegfeld cabled her: "HOPE YOU GOT PAID THIS TIME.")

Marilyn Miller and Adele Astaire were constantly playing pranks during the preparation for *Smiles.* One morning at 3:00, after hours of costume rehearsals, Ziegfeld sent Goldie to the switchboard to call Jimmy Stroock of Brooks Costumes to make some changes.

"He went home," she said. "You know what time it is."

Ziegfeld snapped: "Get him down here right away."

"It's 3:00 A.M."

"I didn't ask you what time it was, get him down here!"

In order to get to the office where Stroock's unlisted number was Goldie had to take a special elevator, but she could not find a key. The only way she could get up there was via a fire escape to the rehearsal hall, which led to the switchboard room. In pitch darkness she crawled on her knees up the outside metal stairs and across the rehearsal hall, unable to see; finally she managed to grope her way to the switchboard light and turn it on. Just as she did so, a hand went up her skirt and pinched her so hard that she screamed. She whirled around, and there were Marilyn Miller and Adele Astaire lying on the floor laughing hysterically at her distress.

Smiles opened at the Ziegfeld Theater on November 18, 1930, to one of the smartest audiences in the history of Broadway. One or two scenes were good—the Astaires mixing a complicated and very funny cocktail at the Southampton mansion, Astaire dancing a solo, "Do The New York," against a brilliant Urban backdrop of Manhattan, and the lovely duet of "Time on My Hands," but much of the production was dull and depressing. It collapsed quickly.

As the show limped on, Ziegfeld quarreled continuously with Vincent Youmans and with the young musical director, Paul Lannin. When Ziegfeld threatened to remove Lannin, Youmans in his turn threatened to "withdraw the music" of the entire show. Ziegfeld was forced to take the matter to the Superior Court; Youmans was restrained from proceeding by special injunction.

The quarrels continued, their annoyance aggravated for Ziegfeld by an excruciating attack of sciatica, which had him completely bedridden at Hastings. He began making plans with Hammerstein and Kern for a new musical starring Evelyn Laye; then he impatiently canceled them. He also announced a new stage vehicle for Eddie Cantor, although Cantor was under exclusive contract to Goldwyn in Hollywood.

For years Ziegfeld had notoriously feigned illness—to gain sympathy, to escape creditors, or to avoid appearing in court on the innumerable lawsuits that threatened him.

This late fall of 1930, however, he was not faking. The sciatica was genuine. He experienced blinding headaches; he felt his age painfully; and his memory was not as perfect as it had been. The failure of *Smiles* was a profound shock. Many of the cables and letters dictated from his bed made little sense, and he became more rambling and repetitive as the months went on.

During the run of *Smiles*, Ziegfeld had an unsettling experience. For about a year a black woman had been sending him a series of immense cabin trunks from North Carolina, crammed with moldy dresses and ancient letters. On a particular afternoon she arrived armed with a revolver and somehow managed to get past the Ziegfeld office barriers, sweeping into Goldie's office with an umbrella held high. She was enormous and seemed hell-bent on breaking into Ziegfeld's office. Flourishing the gun, she announced her name and yelled out, "I want to see my boy Flo, my baby! He's my son, and Charles Dillingham is his father!"

Goldie ran to the telephone, called the upstairs switchboard, and told Alice to get the police and warn Ziegfeld not to come out of his office. Luckily two crack detectives were on the premises, and they hauled the hysterical woman away.

To make matters worse, Marilyn Miller was ill several times during production with a combination of sicknesses. She had to leave the cast for a week for a complicated and delicate operation on her sinuses. Ziegfeld cut the show, added new songs, and tried obstinately to snatch the show out of total disaster, but nothing he or anyone else did could save it.

After the flop of *Show Girl*, *Simple Simon*, and *Smiles*, all three kept artificially running long after audiences had dwindled to the vanishing point, Ziegfeld was forced to supplement the payroll from his own severely diminished funds. Early in 1931 he was on the edge of total bankruptcy, refusing to pay royalties to any composer or lyricist, constantly in court battling various legal suits. In a desperate fling at restoring the glories of the past Ziegfeld revived the *Follies* with the aid of the Erlanger interests (Abe Erlanger had died in 1930).

Urban created 14 sets; Bobby Connolly did the dance direction; and the music was written by three new composers: J. P. Murray, Mack Gordon, and Harry Revel. Harry Richman played the master of ceremonies, Helen Morgan sang Noel Coward's "Half-Caste Woman," and Ruth Etting sang "Shine On, Harvest Moon." In another echo of the earlier *Follies*, the chorus girls wore guard uniforms and marched up and down in front of a replica of Buckingham Palace. It was a tired repetition of the glorious past, and from the moment the *Follies of 1931* opened on July 21, audiences were indifferent to the format, which already belonged to another age.

In a crude attempt to defy the motion picture medium Ziegfeld printed an advertisement: "One hundred and fifty girls in the flesh, not in the can," but that merely made him look old-fashioned. The *Follies* failed.

Just before the 1931 *Follies* began, Ziegfeld went with Gene Buck to see F.W. Murnau's and Robert Flaherty's famous film, *Tabu*, set in Tahiti. The film starred a lovely girl called Reri, the epitome of dusky South Pacific beauty. The next day Ziegfeld dictated a cable to Goldie from Burkely Crest. It was addressed to a contact in Papeete and read: "SEND ME THE TABU GIRL WITH THE BIG BREASTS."

"WHICH ONE," came the reply.

"THE STAR YOU FOOL," Ziegfeld replied.

Several weeks of negotiations later, Reri arrived with her sister and an uncle. Unfortunately she could barely sing or dance, and she startled the residents of a New

York apartment building by calling down to passersby: "Fifty cents to come to my room!" After a few uncomfortable weeks in a South Seas scene in the *Follies* Reri was shipped home.

Ziegfeld became still more eccentric during 1931. He began sitting up all night writing letters to the members of his cast, authors, composers, and stage managers in pencil on the blue or red-bordered Ziegfeld stationery. He always complained about something in the shows (many of the notes seemed actually to be addressed to himself). His handwriting was so difficult to read that most of the time it could not be understood. As soon as these letters were finished, he would immediately start dictating a second letter, which contained exactly the same material as the first. Then a telegram would follow with the identical complaints.

He hated to answer mail. It had to be placed on his desk unopened, and often he would leave it there for months on end, allowing nobody to take the envelopes away.

He wore the same pair of shoes until there were holes in the soles, yet he developed a fanaticism for detail so extreme that if he saw one single spot on a girl's clothes—and he could see her from the balcony with his crack rifleman's eye—he would scream with rage. He developed an intense dislike of straight line chorus formations on the stage.

At the same time he became more and more trivial about paying bills. On one occasion the wife of a coal merchant at Hastings arrived at his office to collect $16 payment on a bill. Carrying a two-year-old baby, she appeared in the outer office and demanded the money. Goldie went into Ziegfeld's office to ask for the payment.

"No! Get rid of her!" he snapped.

"But it's only . . ."

"Who the hell are you working for?" he demanded. "Me or the coal man?"

By a slight fiddling of the books Goldie paid the bill, and Ziegfeld never knew about it.

Ziegfeld was presented that year with many watches, encrusted with precious stones, but he never carried one; if a clock appeared in his office, it would be relegated to the back room by morning. Clocks were symbolic of his growing fear of death.

He forbade red roses in his office, and although his rooms in his later years were crowded with flowers (his favorites were the sweet-smelling tuberoses), red blooms were never permitted. If Goldie slipped in a red tulip in the middle of a bowl, he would walk across the room as soon as he arrived, pick it up gingerly, and drop it, gazing meaningfully at her, into the nearest wastebasket.

Late in 1931 Ziegfeld's daily life was a constant struggle to obtain funds so that he could continue in business. The Erlanger group gave him some more money, and his sister Louise sent some from Detroit, but in his heart he knew that he had made too many miscalculations, the worst of them being his indulgence of William Anthony McGuire. With the disaster of *Smiles* still a painful memory and the new *Follies* limping depressingly along to half-empty houses, he somehow summoned up enough energy to start again with a new show in 1932, *Hot-Cha*, designed as a vehicle for the film star Lupe Velez, whom he had seen and admired in many films.

Hot-Cha, written by Lew Brown and Ray Henderson, was an attempt to recapture the success of *Rio Rita*, set in a Mexico City nightclub and in the bullrings of that metropolis. Unfortunately, it was a sadly confused and jumbled affair.

The show was financed by Waxey Gordon and Dutch Schultz, gangsters who had long since wanted to get into show business. Various members of the mob hung around during the production and tried to interfere, which infuriated Ziegfeld. There was nothing he could do because, with his record of flops, underground money was virtually all he could obtain.

As Lupe Velez's co-star, Ziegfeld chose the gifted Bert Lahr, whom he had admired for some time in George White productions. He telephoned Lahr on the set of *Flying High* at Metro-Goldwyn-Mayer and offered him $2,250 a week. Lahr accepted: the golden lure of appearing in a Ziegfeld show was still potent. Ziegfeld found Lahr amusing, but like most comedians, he was tense and insecure away from the stage. The two men had an uneasy, only half-trusting relationship.

John Lahr, Bert's son, records in his biography of Bert, *Notes on a Cowardly Lion,* that Ziegfeld met Lahr one time at Childs for a coffee and confessed that he was unhappy with the show, asking, "What can we do to fix this up?" Lahr suggested bringing in new writers to improve the lame work done by Lew Brown, Ray Henderson, and Mark Hellinger, but the energetic trio immediately rejected the idea.

Despite his liking for Lahr, Ziegfeld constantly bombarded him with telegrams during the run. After leaving him in a good mood in his dressing room one night he dictated a cable to Goldie: "CAN'T UNDERSTAND WHY YOU LET SHOW DOWN IN SECOND ACT BULLFIGHT SCENE WHICH COST ME FIFTY THOUSAND YOU RUINED COMPLETELY BETTER REHEARSE ALL DAY TOMORROW SO THAT WONDERFUL COMEDY LINES GET ACROSS EVERYTHING MUST BE PERFCT BY THURSDAY NIGHT CALL ENTIRE COMPANY FOR REHEARSAL LET'S GET PROPER PACING LOVE FLO."

Ziegfeld brought the personable young Buddy Rogers,

also from Hollywood, who played the juvenile lead in the show. Rogers had already accepted an invitation to play at the Pennsylvania Hotel with his first band, but the hotel made arrangements for Rogers to "front" the band and play in *Hot-Cha* simultaneously. Juggling his work was an immense challenge for Rogers. He would conduct the band from 7:30 to 8:15 each night; then he would drive in a special car to the theater for the 8:30 curtain, risking life and limb as he wove through the Manhattan traffic. The song "You Could Make My Life a Bed of Roses," liltingly and attractively sung by him in the show, was warmly received by the audience, and he received rapturous applause for his playing of several instruments on the stage.

Just before the opening of *Hot-Cha* three exquisite white jade Chinese elephants, worth $1,500 each, arrived for Ziegfeld. Late on the afternoon of their arrival Ziegfeld rushed into Goldie's office and screamed: "What have you done? Do you want to ruin me?" He was so purple in the face that she thought he was going to have a stroke.

"What's eating you?" she asked. "The elephants have their trunks down!" he screamed. "Take them out of here right away! This instant!" And he strode out of the office.

Goldie put the three elephants on her desk. When he came back, he saw the elephants right away. "How dare you have them there!" he yelled. "Go down into the alley. Take them and smash them against the wall!" She obeyed him reluctantly. He didn't feel satisfied until she had shown him the pathetic shattered pieces in a paper wrapping.

During the out-of-town tryout of *Hot-Cha* in Pittsburgh, Goldie and almost the entire cast fell ill with a currently raging influenza epidemic. Ziegfeld would come into Goldie's room, adjoining his in the William Penn Hotel, at all hours of the day or night and give her dictation even when she was surrounded by nurses and running a severe temperature. The nurses warned him that the disease was contagious, but he brushed their warnings aside.

Finally he began to feel unpleasant symptoms himself. His bones ached, and he had violent stomach disorders, which left him utterly exhausted. He was forced to take to his bed, and he sent Goldie back to New York to take care of the opening night tickets. She left three days before the show closed in Pittsburgh, taking a special ambulance to the train. At the Pennsylvania Station in New York she was transferred to another ambulance, which took her to the Ziegfeld Theater. There she had a special bed made up, and she slept in the office, feebly handling the theater's affairs from a supine position. Three days later Ziegfeld followed her by the same ambulance-train-ambulance route to the Hotel Warwick opposite the theater. By the time he reached his room, he was too weak to care whether *Hot-Cha* opened or not. He was very ill, but he still had enough energy to scrawl lengthy memoranda on Hotel Warwick stationery to all and sundry, especially his hard-pressed unhappy press agent, Bernard Sobel.

He demanded that Sobel produce immense publicity for the show, condemning anyone who might dare to criticize it and insisting that Lupe Velez was a great star and if New Yorkers did not know it, he'd make them know it.

Lupe was very hard to handle, and her behavior was very strange. Just after the curtain fell on the sixth night in New York, she took her $2,500 check for her first week's work, ran across the street to the bank, banged on the door, and demanded that it open immediately. A large crowd gathered to gaze at her in astonishment.

Later she failed to turn up at a matinee performance, and Ziegfeld sent Goldie to fetch her while the curtain was held for an hour. Goldie arrived at Lupe's hotel and heard a commotion in the room. When the door opened, Goldie was astonished to see Lupe's sister giving the star of *Hot-Cha* a high colonic irrigation on the carpet. "I've got a hangover!" Lupe said rather shakily. Goldie dragged her to her feet and slapped her in the face. Then she hauled Lupe down the stairs, threw her in a taxi, and drove her to the theater, where she struggled through the performance in her drunken condition.

Recovering from his illness, Ziegfeld became conscious that, in his early sixties, he was losing his virility. He had always feared this—the reason no doubt for his endless string of affairs (and perhaps for his fear of seeing elephants with their trunks down). Now that his potency began to wane, he sought a series of hormone treatments from his doctors, and his desk drawers were stuffed with rainbow-colored pills. Day after day young girls from his chorus came to his office so that he could test out the effects of his medication. Goldie had orders to keep the office locked until he called for her, although on one occasion a Western Union boy did go in and ran out yelling to the astonished staff, "Jesus, the guy's laying the dame right there on the desk!"

That year Billie and Patricia were on the West Coast while Billie toured for David Belasco in *The Vinegar Tree*, with Warren William. Billie wrote in her memoirs years later that she could imagine Burkely Crest dismal and forlorn, but in fact the opposite was true. In a last fling at life Ziegfeld began a series of weekend orgies there. The girls were shipped down by Rolls-Royce to Hastings, to the great consternation of the house staff. The riotous parties finally proved too much for Sidney, who wrote to

Billie begging her to return. But it was a while before she could come back, committed as she was to the long-term contract to Belasco.

Ziegfeld's ferocious expression of sexuality in those months was not a joyful thing; it was an act of sad challenge to death and decay, to the certain knowledge that the darkness would soon engulf him. He had no belief at all in an afterlife. He believed that the body was all that counted and knew that it was all too perishable.

After a few weeks of wretched houses Ziegfeld quietly buried *Hot-Cha* and half-heartedly began a weekly radio show for Chrysler Motors, with Jane Froman, Jack Pearl, and Art Jarrett introduced by himself in the high, nasal voice, which had not changed since his youth. When Billie, who was listening from California at five o'clock one afternoon, heard him falter during an introductory passage, she sensed that he was seriously ill. When she got to New York, she saw that his neck had shrunk and his face was drawn and pale. One night when she went with him to the Pennsylvania Hotel to see a performance of Buddy Rogers and his band, Ziegfeld collapsed and had to be carried to a suite to rest.

After *Hot-Cha* folded, the process servers grew thicker and thicker outside the theater. In order to avoid them Goldie had to take Ziegfeld down the back fire escape and through the cellars of the Ziegfeld Theater along an alley behind 54th Street, where the Rolls was waiting. Dan Curry often went along to keep a lookout in case a process server crossed their path.

The office quarrels were constant and terrible. The managers were constantly at loggerheads: Dan Curry accused Stanley Sharpe of stealing funds from behind Ziegfeld's back, and Sharpe accused Dan Curry of drinking too much. Finally Ziegfeld dismissed Sharpe from his service, leaving Curry in charge. Everyone started whispering scandals behind one another's backs, and even Alice Poole and Goldie began quarreling.

Billie was exasperated by Ziegfeld's increasing peccadillos; she threw herself into endless rages on the telephone, all of which Alice overheard. Sometimes Alice became so annoyed by what Ziegfeld was saying that she would cut him off in the middle of a sentence. He threatened her with dismissal, but the threat was useless. Alice knew that he could never countenance anybody else at the switchboard. There was tension, too, between Goldie and Kathryn Dix, Billie Burke's secretary.

One extreme annoyance in the spring of 1932 was that Goldie married George Stanton, Eastern Passenger Agent of the New York Central Railroad. Ziegfeld had never really thought of Goldie as a woman with real feelings, although he occasionally chuckled over the old joke that she was "the last virgin on Broadway." He grudgingly had Alice Poole buy her a silver service but refused to see her off to Bermuda on her honeymoon. When she returned, he was extremely terse with her, obviously regarding her marriage as unforgivable. No sooner had she returned than she came down with appendicitis, and she was rushed to the Postgraduate Hospital, in downtown Manhattan, for an operation. Her recovery was slow, and Ziegfeld fretted.

After *Hot-Cha* had folded, *Show Boat* was revived—a shrewd move since all of the costumes and sets could be brought back from Caine's Warehouse—but after a good start at the Casino Theater it began to flop during the hot summer months. Even the magnificent reviews for Paul Robeson in the role of Joe failed to save it. By July it was barely kept going, propped up by financing from tycoon A.C. Blumenthal, who had married *Follies* star Peggy Fears.

Money was so tight during the new *Show Boat* run that the cast—except for the proud Dennis King—was frequently forced to take a salary cut. In the first week alone the Ziegfeld office was short $7,000 on the payroll. Because of Ziegfeld's illness Goldie was put in complete charge, and Blumenthal footed bill after bill with remarkable generosity.

The strain of the Chrysler show and the orgies at Burkely Crest brought on a severe attack of pleurisy in July. Ziegfeld was reluctantly forced to accept doctor's orders: he must go to California to rest. Billie arrived to meet him, finding a forlorn Burkely Crest. On the night before her arrival the last batch of drunken chorus girls had made their boozy way back to New York. Sidney greeted Billie with a garish account of everything that had happened, while Ziegfeld sat slumped in the drawing room, talking incoherently to himself.

During the days before he left Burkely Crest Ziegfeld scarcely knew what was happening. He began giving meaningless instructions to Goldie on the telephone. On July 5 Goldie's husband and Dan Curry finally got him into the Rolls and drove him with Billie to Harmon, New York, where he boarded the Twentieth-Century Limited. He was exhausted, and his face was an unpleasant yellow color. The heat was stifling, and Billie had to pack blocks of ice behind his pillow in the drawing room of the Pullman. The night after the train left for California, Dan Curry died of a heart attack, brought on by the strain of the previous few weeks.

The journey to California was a nightmare. Ziegfeld tossed in his bed, talking deliriously, remembering snatches of past events like a drowned man reliving his life. He talked of Chicago, Sandow, and all of the exciting events that followed the first glamorous years. Billie sat looking at his shrunken face and dull, listless eyes, and tears ran down her cheeks.

Incredibly, Ziegfeld rallied twice on the journey to send

long, rambling telegrams to Dan Curry. The first was
sent from Kansas City:

"WELL THEY CARRIED ME OUT I HATED TO GO
AND LEAVE SO MANY PROBLEMS IN YOUR HANDS
DOCTOR CLAIMS ITS LIFE OR DEATH WITH ME
FIRST PLEASE SEE MARTIN BECK PRICE AGREED
WAS FIFTEEN THOUSAND CASH 8 WEEKS AGO
FOR WHOOPEE PRODUCTION BEFORE LEAVING
I SIGNED THE CONTRACT FOR TWELVE THOU-
SAND FIVE HUNDRED THEY ALSO WANT THE
OTHER 3 PRODUCTIONS SHOW GIRL ROSALIE
AND THREE MUSKETEERS STOP SOMEONE ALSO
WANTS THE PRODUCTION OF FOLLIES FOR ZIEG-
FELD VAUDEVILLE REVIEW FIVE THOUSAND
CASH AND TWO THOUSAND WEEKLY TO BEGIN
IN AUGUST GODDARD [Bobby Connolly's attorney]
MENTIONED THIS PROPOSITION TO YOU AND
BOBBY CONNOLLY BUT THEY HAVE ALL BEEN
DOUBLE CROSSING EACH OTHER SO MUCH THAT
NO ONE KNOWS WHERE THE PARTICULAR PRO-
DUCTION STANDS I SUGGEST THAT YOU IMME-
DIATELY LAY OFF EVERYBODY POSSIBLE WE
ONLY NEED ONE DOOR MAN AND WE DO NOT
NEED ROSS [Stuart Ross, Ziegfeld's bookkeeper] BUT
BFORE YOU LET HIM GO MAKE SURE YOU HAVE
ALL PAPERS INCLUDING THOSE HE WENT THRU
KINGSTONS [Sam Kingston, Ziegfeld's former manager]
DESK FOR STOP HE HAS NEVER HAD A CORRECT
STATEMENT IN HIS LIFE I AM HELPLESS YOU
HAVE AUTHORITY TO SIGN ON THE CORPORA-
TION SUITS BURKAN [Nathan Burkan, attorney] AND
BICKERTON [Joseph Bickerton, attorney] HAS GET
FROM LEVE THE POWER OF ATTORNEY IMME-
DIATELY AND SEND THEM ON BURKAN AND
LEVE [J. Arthur Leve, attorney] MUST PROTECT US

IN THE MEANTIME I DONT KNOW MY EXACT AD-
DRESS WILL PHONE YOU AS SOON AS I KNOW
IT WILL BE IN THE DESERT SOMEWHERE CUT
SHOW BOAT AND CASINO EXPENSES IMMEDI-
ATELY MY SISTER PHONED DENNIS KING FROM
CHICAGO AM SURE YOU CAN HANDLE HIM IF
NOT USE YOUR OWN JUDGMENT ABOUT EVERY-
THING I WOULD PUT IN EXTRA AD WEDNES-
DAY MATINEE DAY PUT IN MARIE LOUISE MARY
RICE AND FAYNE [Agnes Fayne, a chorus girl] RE-
PLACE THE 3 GIRLS THAT ARE LEAVING CON-
VINCE VERONICA [Veronica Blythe, costumes] LARGY
[income tax official] HUBERT [W. R. Hearst's real estate
representative] AND SHOW BOAT COMPANY AND
THE REST ALIVE AND WELL I AM AN ASSET TO
ALL AND THEY HAVE HAD ALL IVE MADE FOR
YEARS NOW THEY MUST GIVE ME THE CHANCE
I AM PUTTING A LOT ON YOUR SHOULDERS DAN
[Curry] THOMAS [Percy Thomas, in charge of Ziegfeld's
storehouse] MUST TAKE HIS OLD SALARY I SIGNED
CONTRACT WITH RKO CALLING FOR A CASH
PAYMENT TO ME FOR TWELVE THOUSAND FIVE
HUNDRED FOR THE PRODUCTION BICKERTON
HAS THE CONTRACT AND I HAVE OBLIGATED
MYSELF FOR THIS MONEY IT IS TWENTY FIVE
HUNDRED LESS THAN THEY AGREED UPON BUT
I CANNOT TAKE A CHANCE OF THEM NOT GOING
THROUGH WITH IT IMMEDIATELY WIRE IT TO
ME AND I WILL WIRE YOU AND BICKERTON ONE
THOUSAND EACH SEE BECK AND CONNOLLY
PERHAPS YOU CAN SELL THEM SHOW GIRL AND
ROSALIE PRODUCTION AND THE RIGHTS FOR
MUSKETEERS FOR TABLOID DONT LET ANYONE
KNOW WHEN I LET YOU KNOW WHERE I AM
MY WIFE SAW HATTIE CARNEGIE [dressmaker]

PLEASE PAY EVANS HER ATTORNEY FIFTY NINE
DOLLARS GOLDIE KNOWS ABOUT IT YOU MUST
GET ALONG THE SAME AS IF I WAS NOT THERE
ANYMORE TILL I GET WELL."

A second telegram was sent from Albuquerque. It was
received a few minutes after Dan Curry died of a heart
attack:

"THIS LAST WIRE YOU WILL GET FROM ME
HOW I KNOW IVE PLACED YOU IN A TOUGH SPOT
BUT I AM HELPLESS GO TO BURKAN IF YOU
NEED HIM HOPE YOU HAVE CONCLUDED
WITH RKO & SEE BOBBY CONNOLLY ABOUT THE
VAUDEVILLE REVIEW NOT ALLOWED TO USE
THE WORD FOLLIES JUST ZIEGFELD REVIEW
USE FOLLIES PRODUCTION FIVE THOUSAND
CASH TWO THOUSAND WEEK IN ADVANCE
WEEKLY FOR USE OF PRODUCTION OF COURSE
THE PEOPLE MUST BE OKAY HE REFUSED TO
GIVE THE NAMES THEY MUST SATISFY YOU IN
EVERY WAY ARTHUR LEVE HAS ALL PAPERS
SHOULD YOU BE COMPELLED TO CONVINCE
ANYBODY I HAVE NO PERSONAL INTEREST IN
CASINO OR SHOW BOAT HOPE THE TIDE WILL
TURN & WE CAN KEEP OPEN THE BROKERS
COULD HELP AS GREATLY AS FACE THE MUSIC
& CAT FIDDLE ARE CLOSING TROUBLE IS DAN
PRESS DEPARTMENT DOES NOT GET ANYTHING
IN PAPERS THE ENTIRE COUNTRY SHOULD BE
COVERED GET THE LOWDOWN ON PAUL ROBE-
SON WELL DAN EVERYTHING IS UP TO YOU PER-
HAPS I MAY BE ABLE TO RECIPROCATE BE SURE
THEY ATTEND TO PAPERS SERVED ON B B AT
HASTINGS SHE WAS AWAY NOTHING TO DO
WITH HER GOLDIE WILL HAVE TO SEE THORLEY
[of the Thorley Flower Shop] EXPLAIN CIRCUM-

STANCES FEEL IF YOU CUT SHOW BOAT SAL-
ARIES & EXPENSES IT WILL RUN THRU WITHOUT
LOSS."

Upon their arrival in California Billie took Ziegfeld to
a house at 2407 La Mesa Drive, Santa Monica, a comfortable sprawling place near the ocean. His room was
crowded with flowers, and every day he made long-
distance calls—at $80 or more at a time. After a few days
at La Mesa Drive he developed pleurisy again and had
to be transferred to Cedars of Lebanon Hospital.

A series of mustard treatments, extremely primitive by
today's standards, was applied. Ziegfeld found them depressingly uncomfortable. He was in agony, sobbing helplessly like a child. His face was livid, and he began making
figures in the air, talking incoherently to his visitors. By
July 21 he began to sink. The next day he told Sidney
that he wanted to get up and walk. His last impression
of life was Sidney supporting him. Around him was the
sweet, exquisite, overpowering smell of tuberoses.

Billie was at RKO making a test with a young actor,
Walter Pidgeon, for *A Bill of Divorcement* when Sidney
called her to tell her that Ziegfeld was slipping away. The
director, George Cukor, told her to go to her husband's
bedside at once. When she arrived at Cedars, she knew
by the look on Sidney's face that it was too late. Ziegfeld
had died at 3:45 that afternoon, July 22, 1932.

On July 24, 1932, a memorial service was broadcast
from WOR Radio in New York. Ziegfeld stars, led by Paul
Robeson singing "Old Man River," commemorated his
death. Billie heard the program in Hollywood. A simple
funeral service was also held at the Pierce Brothers Mortu-
ary in Los Angeles, with only a hundred personal friends
present. After the horror of both Anna Held's and Olive
Thomas's funerals, Billie insisted on absolute discretion
and privacy.

Ziegfeld was placed in the garish mausoleum of Forest Lawn—a horribly tasteless resting place for a man who, above all, loved good taste. Billie herself selected his perfect epitaph, a brief verse from Shakespeare's *Venus and Adonis*:

> *For him being dead, with him is*
>   *Beauty slain;*
> *And Beauty dead, black chaos*
>   *Comes again.*

After Ziegfeld's death the world seemed to collapse for Billie Burke. She struggled on through *A Bill of Divorcement*, greatly supported by George Cukor's immense patience and kindness. Only the small percentage of the show's earnings that had been set aside for Patricia and the determined help of the financier A.C. Blumenthal staved off total catastrophe. In New York Goldie remained in complete charge until representatives of the New York district attorney closed up the offices of the Ziegfeld Theater and seized every single document in the files.

Something of the misery suffered by Billie Burke—bereaved, saddled with debts, struggling to raise her young daughter—is conveyed by this note, sent from the house at La Mesa Drive on January 3, 1933:

"Dear Goldie—I was grateful for your wire. It seemed to bring Ziegfeld back for a little bit—nothing seems to mean anything anymore. How I should love to have a talk with you. He trusted you so implicitly. Everything is in such a muddle now. I am sure some of that could be straightened out. There must be some equity in *Hot-Cha* and *Musketeers* and all the musical shows he didn't sell. You are the only one who knows about all that. I have been wanting to write you for ages, but it's very hard for me to get hold of things. I have been working so hard at trying to make a little money for our keep that I have neglected his affairs. I think I should come East the first chance I get. Would you be good enough to write me and tell me anything you think would be helpful in putting his affairs in some kind of order?

"His papers seem to have been scattered everywhere. Don't you think you should send me all the papers you have and tell me where others are? Did he have any accounts in any bank, do you know? You might go off to Europe just as I get to N. Y.

"What became of all his papers at the office and all his contracts with the different shows he owned? I would like to have the original agreement with the Ziegfeld Theater—oh, how I hated to do that—and our dear old camp. Of course, that could have been saved. That George Rowley always had his eye on that camp. I do think we could fight that, only there is no money to fight anything. I hope I won't have to pay on the income tax. I seem to feel Mr. Blumenthal can work miracles. I am so glad you are with Mrs. Blumenthal. How marvelously she has come to the fore. Mr. Ziegfeld always had such faith in her.

"Jack Pickford's death marshaled out all the ghosts of my past and all I went thru. Oh Goldie—I loved him so. I don't think anyone knows what his going has meant to me. He was so wonderful, with all his faults—so wonderful. Did you see Mr. Buck's horrible article in the New Yorker? I can't just let it go. I am trying to get Mr. [Will] Rogers to write a defense for Mr. Ziegfeld of every quality he possessed and draped around himself. I am miserable about it.

"I started this as a wire, but I am too nervous to struggle with pen and ink. Maybe you can read it and maybe you will find an opportunity to write and help me straighten out his papers.

"Good luck to you and my deepest gratitude for all you did to help him.

Always,
Billie Burke"

Ziegfeld's pathetic estate was divided between Billie and Patricia, with nothing left to anybody else. There were over a million dollars' worth of debts. The Blumenthals took charge of the affairs of the Florenz Ziegfeld Corporation, to which Ziegfeld had ceded all of his personal interests in the *Follies* in 1929. Arrangements were made to pay the creditors from the profits of *Show Boat*.

On April 21, 1933, a final tribute was held on the Ziegfeld Theater stage to announce its reopening as a movie theater. The ceremonies began at 12:30 in the afternoon. They were attended by countless stars and former stars and more than 1,000 of Ziegfeld's admirers.

At the outset Charles Winninger called for a few minutes of silent appreciation of the producer. Eddie Cantor was solemn as he spoke of "a man we all loved and respected." Gene Buck spoke of Ziegfeld's perfect taste and love of beauty. Anna Santell, one of the original Anna Held Girls, spoke of those long-vanished days.

The most unsettling moment in a deeply moving afternoon took place shortly after two o'clock. Eddie Dowling, as master of ceremonies, suddenly called for Lillian Lorraine to stand up. Everyone turned to look at her. Then he said: "Come up here, Lillian, and sing 'By the Light of the Silvery Moon' for us." She came in a wheelchair down the aisle and stopped just in front of the orchestra pit, while Gus Edwards struck up a few bars at the piano. She started to sing, collapsed, and broke into helpless tears. Rita Gould stood up and took her place.

On April 29, 1940, Billie finally auctioned off practically everything at Burkely Crest. The $250,000 house and the

295 objects at the auction, handled by the Concord Galleries, were bought for a total of $42,000. A $20,750 mortgage still existed on the house, taken out in Ziegfeld's last months. Ziegfeld's early talkie projectors, bought for $15,000, went for $225.

Asked what he would do with them, New York dealer Fred Porrett said they would be sold to a theater "out in the sticks." A grand piano brought $155. The beautiful $6,500 Hepplewhite dining room suite went for $475. Producer Lew Brown bought the cages for Ziegfeld's long dead monkeys. Ziegfeld's own ornate walnut bed brought $31, and the gaudy Chinese wall hangings in his bedroom brought $50. They had cost $4,000 each.

Lillian Lorraine died in 1955 after spending years in poverty at a depressing New York hotel; Ruth Waterbury of the New York *Daily News* interviewed her there and asked her if she would have done anything differently if she had her life to live over again. "I don't think I would have bobbed my hair," she replied.

Marilyn Miller had died long before in 1936, of a jaw and sinus infection, which had plagued her for 20 years. Many people still believe that she died because of syphilis. Jack Pickford had died three years earlier, in Paris, of a disease defined as "multiple neuritis," in the same American hospital in which Olive Thomas had died.

Billie Burke died in Hollywood in 1970 after suffering from increasing senility for many years. Patricia Ziegfeld still lives in Los Angeles. Goldie lives only a few miles away, in Santa Monica.

Burkely Crest has long since been pulled down, followed by the Ziegfeld Theater. There remain the Ansonia—with the old Anna Held suite cut into three—and the New Amsterdam Theater, with its superb green marble staircase still intact, though it is now a "grind" movie house. In Paris Anna Held's apartment still stands in the Faubourg St. Honoré, a fashion house said to be haunted by her perfumed ghost.

It is fervently hoped by his family and remaining friends that Ziegfeld's body will one day be taken from the Forest Lawn Mausoleum and reinterred at Valhalla, New York, in a peaceful shady grave alongside the mortal remains of Billie, where he belongs.

Postscript

The Ziegfeld story has an extraordinary footnote. In 1952 Irving ("Izzy") Cohn, a handyman at the New Amsterdam Theater, was putting some new fabrics on seats in the backstage workshop when he suddenly felt a strange presence in the room. When he looked up, he saw a beautiful girl standing in the doorway wearing a white dress with a gold sash on which appeared the name "Olive." He said, "What are you doing here?" She simply smiled, leaning against the door with one hand and holding a blue bottle and a glass in the other. She turned and ran up a flight of stairs. When he followed her, she vanished.

Cohn was badly shaken by the incident but put it out of his mind. Two weeks later he began to have the same strange feeling that someone was watching him. He looked up once more; she had returned. This time she went downstairs toward the stage. He called up to an electrician, Charlie Breest, who was standing on a ladder,

"Where did she go? Did you see that red-headed girl?"

Charlie said, "Are you drunk? What are you talking about?"

Cohn described the girl minutely.

Charlie froze. Cohn had described Olive Thomas—whom Charlie had worked with and adored—to perfection. To the day of his death Charlie believed that Olive had come back from the grave with the bottle and glass to confirm what many of her friends believed—that she had deliberately taken poison in 1920, not accidentally, and that her motive was horror at having discovered that Jack Pickford had given her syphilis.

The most astonishing touch in the story came later. Some weeks after the bizarre incident Charlie came across some old photographs of the *Follies*. He turned white and almost passed out. There in a stage group was Olive. She wore a gold sash across her white dress, and her name was printed on it.

Epilogue

Ziegfeld remained an enigma to most of his contemporaries because of the extreme contrast between his personal and public lives. Actors and actresses adored him because he understood that their egos had to be fed. He left comedians out of his list of friends with the exception of Will Rogers and Fanny Brice; after the early years he never became very close to composers, to whom he obstinately refused to pay royalties and whom he constantly interfered with, often to the detriment of their scores.

His friendships were superficial, predominantly in the wide world of business. We may assume that William Randolph Hearst, Edward Hutton, Leopold Replogle, and Diamond Jim Brady enjoyed his boisterous company and racy chorus girl stories without penetrating below the surface to the man who lay within. Even Anna Held, his mistress, and his wife, Billie Burke, almost certainly did not grasp the essence of his nature. They loved the passionate extrovert, the generous lover, and the man of the world; they were puzzled by the darker strains that occasionally emerged.

Anna Held endured his many infidelities with a degree of understanding stoicism, but Billie fought jealously to possess him completely. But neither perceived his consuming need for women: the need to own womankind itself.

His secretary, Goldie, came close to understanding him, but since she always saw him at his worst, in the narrow confines of his office, even her view of him was necessarily limited.

Now that we have explored his fantastic and glittering career, what conclusions can we draw about this marvel of marvels, this Lorenzo the Magnificent of the stage?

Ziegfeld was characteristic of the great showmen of his age in many classic particulars. From the outset, his consuming ambition was to become the one and only great and golden figure on Broadway. Even in his earliest days in Chicago this one dream drove him. His compulsion to acquire Anna Held was merely the first step in a steadily constructed edifice of dreams. Through her he gained entry to the highest levels of American society. In this he followed in the footsteps of his socially ambitious father—and far surpassed him.

He not only dreamed of creating a world of glamour and luxury far removed from his straight-laced home, but he wanted to fashion unparalleled luxury and beauty in the theater itself. His need for wealth was reflected in his need for theatrical riches. Money was simply a means to an end: an escape from reality, the essential pettiness and monotony of which continually exasperated him.

He was a dreamer, a supplier of fantasies. He was not even in the usual sense a human being but a strange monster who breathed fire into a moribund vaudeville tradition and into the duller and more phlegmatic spirits of his contemporaries. He cared nothing for politics, literature, news, painting, sculpture, classical music, or psychology. Philosophy and religion were closed books to him.

He was utterly devoid of intellect, which is one of the reasons that his character has remained somewhat mysterious. If a man does not read, we may ask what motivates him at all. His driving force was one of demonic sensuality and a passion for vivid artifice. From the very beginning his stage productions were direct expressions of his essentially primitive sexual character. He was at once witch doctor and organizer of tribal dances. The *Follies* were astonishing demonstrations of the mind of a man who sought to release his need for women in displays of adulation for them. Most American men were obsessed with dreams of glamorous sexual fulfillment, and Ziegfeld provided vicarious means of fulfillment.

More and more the *Follies* and the *Frolics* became shows not only by the rich but for the rich. Ziegfeld had a habit of carrying with him bags of gold pieces before America went off the gold standard, and he would hand fistfuls of them to someone who pleased him. He constantly converted paper money into gold wherever possible. It was his Midas-like desire to convert dross into gold that marked his entire career. Everything he detested involved reality and bitter truth; everything he loved involved gorgeous and sumptuous lies.

Ziegfeld seems unreal to us because he was never real, probably not even to himself. He was a kind of ghost in an immense stage machine. In the early part of the century living as a glittering enhancement of a manly being, enjoying unlimited power, money, success, and beautiful women was possible because of the very character of that gilded age. He simply lived a fantasy in a fantastic period.

Before income tax, before the pressure of war, and before the Depression made America seem all too painfully real, he became the embodiment of American hope. Once the twenties, for all their surface gaiety, began to impinge on the reckless American fiesta of pleasure, Ziegfeld's character rapidly deteriorated. He began to be aware that such a thing as time existed, that he might actually join the human condition by growing old and dying.

It would not take an extensive course in Freudian psychology to understand that his intense fear of clocks and his loathing of elephants with their trunks down betokened a horror of the consciousness of time and of the possibility of impotence. His fear of reality emerged in his avoidance of paying the numerous bills that poured onto his desk.

For all the great successes that marked them, his later years were a nightmare for this extraordinary man. Piece by piece the world of shining pretense in which he lived was torn apart. The bills increased, and the agony of life broke through. He could ignore everything except the decline of his body. He tried passionately to pass on his pleasure to his daughter, Patricia, by showering upon her the greatest gifts the wealthy can afford; but it was not quite the same as being able to look forward to the permanent enjoyment of them himself.

As old age caught up with him, his contradictory nature reached its extreme: he became more and more generous in major things, more and more mean in minor things, more lovable to the great and hateful to the small, more gentle when he needed something and more vicious when he was crossed.

The Wall Street crash was the one catastrophe upon which even he could not turn his back. He resembled

America itself in not quite believing that in one short day the dreams of two generations could vanish. From then on he was a kind of gilded corpse, issuing instructions, making love, and conducting stage shows into disaster. Finally the ultimate truth caught up with him, and he died.

We cannot love this man as Anna Held and Billie Burke and Will Rogers loved him because in restrospect he seems all too frighteningly larger than life. We cannot even admire him as a man because he was cruel, exploitive, and mean. Yet we cannot withhold from him the word *great*, and we cannot withhold from him the statement that he was the supreme master of theatrical spectacle.

He gave birth to a galaxy of great American stage and screen stars. He was the first to bring film presentations to theatrical production in America. He revolutionized at every level: in the use of color in costumes and sets, in the blending of music with action, in the reduction of long comedy acts to sketches integrated with a whole work, in destroying the very word vulgarity in relation to the American stage.

His whole life was the theater, and his private life, an acted play. Let applause follow the ringing down of the curtain. In our age there is no room for dreamers of this magnitude. He was a giant, and he remains one. If in the last analysis he seems impossibly remote, it is because we cannot see quite that high.

Index

Bromfield, Louis, 205
Brooks, Louise, 171, 205n.
Brown, Lew, 211, 212, 226
Buck, Gene, 85, 101, 102-103,
    105, 109, 129, 132, 140,
    142, 153, 165, 174, 195,
    209, 224, 225
Buffalo Bill, 8-9
Burke, Billie, ix, 97-100, 101,
    110, 118, 121, 123, 124,
    125, 126, 135, 137, 147-
    148, 149, 153, 158, 162,
    167, 168, 171-172, 174,
    188, 192, 196, 202, 204,
    215, 216, 217, 218, 221,
    222-225, 226, 227, 231,
    232, 235
  birth of daughter, 119
  films, 111-117, 119
  jewelry theft, 114-115
  marries Ziegfeld, 94-96
  Ziegfeld's courtship of,
    92-94
Burke, Blanche, 93, 94, 114

C

Caesar's Wife, 135
Candy, George, 32-33
Cantor, Eddie, 124, 132, 134,
    138, 159-162, 178, 193-
    195, 199, 204, 207, 225
Carrera, Liane, 26-27, 31,
    127, 128, 129
Carrera, Maximo, 26, 29,
    30-31
Carter, Frank, 131-132,
    135-136

Century Girl, The, 118-119
Chicago Fire, 5-6
Chicago Musical College,
    3-8
Chorus girls
  Anna Held Girls, 56, 64,
    77, 82, 225
  choice of for Frolics, 106
  rules for, 107
Chrysler Motors radio show,
    216, 218
Claire, Ina, ix, 80, 101, 110
    117-118, 128
Clocks, fear of, 211, 234
Clough, Goldie, see Goldie
Cody, "Buffalo Bill," 8-9
Cohn, Irving ("Izzy"), ix,
    229-230
Columbian Exposition,
    10-15
Comic Supplement, The,
    165-167
Connolly, Bobby, 197, 198,
    219, 220, 221
Corwin, Mrs. Halsey, 61
Cosmopolitan Theater, 163
Coward, Noel, 200-201, 203,
    205
Cowgirl incident, 157-158
Cowl, Jane, 118
Cukor, George, ix, 222, 223
Curry, Dan, 201, 216, 218,
    219, 221

D

Daly, Anna, 121, 140
Davies, Marion, 163, 205 n.